"Dave Rich is the world expert on modern antisemitism. Even better, he knows what to do about it. Everyone should read this book. And if you don't think you need to, then you need to read it more than anyone."
Sacha Baron Cohen

"Dave Rich is a lodestar for understanding, and therefore challenging, antisemitism."
David Baddiel

"It's maddening how the world keeps finding ways to complicate the fact that antisemitism is racism. One of the most persistent and ancient forms of racism in the history of the planet, in fact. Dave Rich does totally essential work here, proving a patient, elegant and sometimes even entertaining guide to a toxic problem. I'll be buying this book for many people."
Sathnam Sanghera, author of *Empireland: How Imperialism Has Shaped Modern Britain*

"Dave Rich has written a book that should make all of us feel uncomfortable, Jew and non-Jew alike. In a closely argued and impeccably researched volume, he asks the wider world why people have allowed antisemitism to go unchecked and why they have not felt moved to fight against it. And he challenges Jews, telling us that we too need to try to improve things and to find allies in the wider world. This is an impressive piece of work, which makes depressing reading until you realise it is a call to action."
Julia Neuberger

"This book is compelling, frightening and illuminating. There is nobody who knows more about this subject than Dave Rich, and his ability to express himself matches his diligence and knowledge."
Daniel Finkelstein

"Dave Rich offers an important and detailed tour through the history of antisemitism – and an even more important look at the present, where we haven't made it history at all. His book darts between then and now with warmth, patience, humour – and crescendos as an ardent call to action."
Marina Hyde

"Dave Rich makes sense of the nonsensical with his uniquely gentle and pragmatic yet insightful style. Charting ancient irrational libels to their modern internet incarnations today, he issues a measured warning of what has come before and what could come again. Essential reading for anyone wanting to be able to recognise the ever-changing face of anti-Jewish hate, with up to the minute examples and a rallying call for the modern age, adding something new for everyone from the completely uninitiated to the fully up to speed anti-antisemite."
Rachel Riley

"Clear, cogent and compelling, this book tackles an enduring hatred with freshness, wit and verve. But what sets it apart, besides the fact that it's so fluent and readable, is its generosity of spirit. Dave Rich understands that antisemitism is a racism that can sneak up on those who least expect it, and so he comes not to scold but to enlighten. The result is a book full of humanity, even as it lays bare what can feel like an eternal human failing. *Everyday Hate* is essential reading."
Jonathan Freedland

EVERYDAY HATE

HOW ANTISEMITISM IS BUILT INTO OUR WORLD AND HOW YOU CAN CHANGE IT

DAVE RICH

Biteback Publishing

First published in Great Britain in 2023 by
Biteback Publishing Ltd, London
Copyright © Dave Rich 2023

Dave Rich has asserted his right under the Copyright, Designs and Patents Act 1988 to be identified as the author of this work.

All rights reserved. No part of this publication may be reproduced, stored in a retrieval system or transmitted, in any form or by any means, without the publisher's prior permission in writing.

This book is sold subject to the condition that it shall not, by way of trade or otherwise, be lent, resold, hired out or otherwise circulated without the publisher's prior consent in any form of binding or cover other than that in which it is published and without a similar condition, including this condition, being imposed on the subsequent purchaser.

Every reasonable effort has been made to trace copyright holders of material reproduced in this book, but if any have been inadvertently overlooked the publisher would be glad to hear from them.

ISBN 978-1-78590-790-6

10 9 8 7 6 5 4 3 2 1

A CIP catalogue record for this book is available from the British Library.

Set in Minion Pro

Printed and bound in Great Britain by
CPI Group (UK) Ltd, Croydon CR0 4YY

For my parents

CONTENTS

Introduction		xi
Chapter One	Jewcraft	1
Chapter Two	Filthy Rich	15
Chapter Three	Blood and Fire	39
Chapter Four	Cars, Conspiracies and Covid	65
Chapter Five	Aliens and Their Families	105
Chapter Six	Never Again	135
Chapter Seven	Jerusalem	175
Chapter Eight	Things Can't Only Get Better	219
Conclusion		243
Acknowledgements		267
About the Author		271
Notes		273
Index		285

'Anti-Semitism is the rumour about the Jews.'
THEODOR W. ADORNO, *MINIMA MORALIA*

'The past is never dead. It's not even past.'
WILLIAM FAULKNER, *REQUIEM FOR A NUN*

INTRODUCTION

I'm sitting at my desk in the gloom of an early October morning, the rest of the house still to wake and the street quiet outside, and this is a sample of what has happened, in our country, over the previous seven days:

A Jewish boy, travelling to school on the morning bus, is punched in the face by an adult woman who regularly shouts racist abuse at the Jewish children who take that bus to school each day.

Spectators at a schools' football match between a Jewish school and a non-faith school repeatedly shout 'Hitler' at the Jewish players.

A man walks up to a large menorah (a Jewish candelabra) outside a Jewish school, stands to attention and raises his right arm in a Nazi salute.

A woman shouts 'fuck off you Jewish bastard' out of her car window at somebody who hoots their car horn at her in a traffic jam.

A Jewish university student is chased down the road by men shouting, 'We've got a knife, we're going to get you Jew.'

A Jewish man leaves his house, and a passer-by sees him and says, 'Not another yid.'

Large swastikas are drawn onto the pavement outside a Jewish man's house. Elsewhere in the country, swastikas are painted onto the wall in a skatepark. A sticker in a petrol station reads 'Yid Army' – the Jewish-inspired name that Tottenham Hotspur fans have given themselves – with a Star of David alongside. Somebody has written the word 'gas' over the wording.

'Zionist Jews control the UK Home Office, media, banking and the legal system' is tweeted at a Member of Parliament, along with a picture of Auschwitz concentration camp and a cartoon of a scheming, grasping Jewish figure. Someone else tweets that complaints about antisemitism in the Labour Party under Jeremy Corbyn's leadership were 'false antisemitism allegations led by rats who were financed by Israeli embassy'. Under a tweet from the Prime Minister wishing British Jews a happy Jewish New Year, somebody has replied, 'I will not celebrate anything related to Israel and Jews unless they stop killing Palestinians.'[1]

On a social media site favoured by far-right extremists, posts by one of Britain's most influential far-right leaders elicit these chilling responses:

'The evil serpent Jews and those who serve them are the worst of all.'

'Satanic Talmudist demons.'

Fighting back 'happens when dirty kike jew [sic] bankers, immigration lawyers, and abortion doctors start turning up dead with every bone in their body broken and their skin peeled off with a soldering iron.'

INTRODUCTION

'How has it come to this? Revolution is the only solution.'

One post claims there are 'FOUR Jews in charge of the Ukrainian nation'. Replies include: 'This shit cannot continue. Expose Jewish supremacy indoctrination at every occasion. Don't live life under the thumb of Jewish domination' and 'They need their heads lopped off'.[2]

Further afield over a similar period, supporters of Islamic State launch an online campaign against Muslims who they consider to be too moderate or theologically misguided. The campaign uses a hashtag that brands these Muslim rivals as 'Jews'.[3] In Russia the host of a popular TV show, casting around for somebody to blame for Russia's military setbacks in Ukraine, reads out on air a list of the names of Russian Jews who he deems to be insufficiently patriotic. Another veteran journalist publishes an article calling well-known Russian Jews 'foreign agents'.[4] In the United States, nine student groups at the University of California, Berkeley School of Law adopt a bylaw preventing any speakers who have previously expressed support for Israel or Zionism* from speaking at their events. Only one of these student groups is explicitly focused on Palestine: others include groups for women's rights, LGBT rights and other left-wing campaigns.[5] President Raisi of Iran, in a television interview with CBS News, fails to give a straight answer when asked whether he thought the Holocaust happened: 'Look ... Historical events should be investigated by researchers and historians. There are some signs that it happened. If so, they should allow it to be investigated and

---

* The Zionist movement sought the creation of a Jewish national home. Since the establishment of the State of Israel in 1948 it has come to mean support for Israel's ongoing existence as an expression of Jewish national self-determination.

researched.'⁶ Qatar's permanent representative to the United Nations in Geneva loses a bid to be appointed to an important human rights post after it emerges that she had posted a litany of antisemitic and homophobic comments over several years on Twitter. 'The Jews' focused their investments in industry and the media, 'and that is why they dominated, tyrannised and ruled the world,' reads one tweet. Gay rights are 'disgusting rights' and gay people should be cursed, read others. She is a graduate of two different British universities and received an alumni award from the British Council in 2018.[7]

There was nothing unusual about any of this: if anything, it was a relatively quiet week. According to Home Office records there were 1,919 hate crimes targeting Jews in England and Wales from March 2021 to March 2022, and 1,288 the previous year – a jump of 49 per cent. Jews were the targets of 23 per cent of all religious hate crimes in England and Wales during that year, which, given that Jews make up less than half a per cent of the UK population, is a startling statistic.[8] It is likely that the true figures are much higher: according to a 2018 survey, only around one in five cases of antisemitic harassment in Britain are ever reported to anybody.[9] These numbers ought to be shocking. There are only around 300,000 Jews in the UK, so the people responsible for all those antisemitic hate crimes must be trying really hard to find Jews to attack. They are also getting busier, because four years earlier there were 'only' 672 religious hate crimes targeting Jews, according to the same Home Office figures.[10] Things are getting worse.

In case you were wondering, this is not just a problem of extremists. Antisemitism happens in the most mundane of places, and arguments over antisemitism draw in the most unlikely of people.

INTRODUCTION

In the year before I wrote this book, Amnesty International, the BBC, Facebook, anti-vaccine protesters, the Royal Court Theatre, Port Vale Football Club and Ben & Jerry's ice cream all found themselves at the centre of rows about antisemitism. The Labour Party suffered years of pain, from which it is still recovering, because of antisemitism within its membership. Nor is there a lack of interest in the subject. In this same week as all the anti-Jewish hate crimes I've just described, there are no fewer than six different plays and musicals running in London theatres that address antisemitism, the Holocaust or Jews as a topic.

All this, when Jewish people are a tiny community, barely visible in many places. There are only around 15 million Jews in the whole world: fewer than the number of followers that Wayne Rooney has on Instagram. This isn't normal, and it demands explanation.

The good news is that most people in Britain say they bear no ill-will towards Jewish people. The biggest ever poll on British attitudes towards Jews was done in 2017 and it found that only 2.4 per cent of the population are what you might call hardcore antisemites: by which I mean they don't like Jews, they know that they don't like Jews (which is not always the same thing) and they are willing to tell a random opinion pollster who phones them up one evening, in direct terms, that they don't like Jews. This tallies with the findings of lots of other polls in the past twenty years and, on the surface, it makes the British population one of the least antisemitic in the world. Just 2.4 per cent of the British population is a pretty small slice of the pie, although you might notice that it still amounts to around 1.5 million hardcore antisemites in this country. Or to put it another way, five hardcore Jew-haters for every British Jew.[11]

But most people, when asked by an opinion pollster, say they like Jews. I believe them. Most people are decent: they do not want to be bigots and do not want to think of themselves as prejudiced. However, that is not the whole story. That poll then asked those same people whether they agreed with a range of negative stereotypes and attitudes about Jews. These included statements like 'Jews think they are better than other people', 'Jews get rich at the expense of others', 'Jews have too much power in Britain' and so on. They asked eight different questions and then added up how many people agreed with at least one of them. This led to a dramatic revelation: 30 per cent of people believe at least one antisemitic stereotype or viewpoint. Just to confuse things further, this even included people who had said they like Jews and who had agreed with positive statements about them – but who had also agreed with one or more of the antisemitic ones. Antisemitic ideas are widespread, even if antisemitic people aren't.

We urgently need to make sense of all this, but many people stumble at the first hurdle. I give a lot of talks about antisemitism to lots of different audiences around the UK that are mostly made up of people who are not Jewish but who work in education, or equalities, or who handle complaints of discrimination or just people who are interested. It doesn't matter whether they work for a large multinational or a small campaigning organisation, a political party or a football club, public sector or private, the main thing I have learned from educating others is that most people don't know much about antisemitism beyond the vague notion that it is like racism but affects Jewish people. Everyone recognises that shouting 'fuck off you Jewish bastard' falls into the antisemitic basket. But tweets about Zionists controlling the government? Maybe not so much. As for 'Satanic Talmudist demons' – where to begin with that?

Even the word 'antisemitism' can cloud understanding of the anti-Jewish prejudice, hatred and discrimination it is supposed to describe. According to one opinion poll, 40 per cent of people in Britain, and over half of 18–24-year-olds, don't even know what the word 'antisemitism' means.[12] Other polls have found similar results in the United States. I'm not surprised. It's an ugly word, a jumble of harsh syllables and misleading inferences. Jewish people didn't even come up with it: that honour belongs to a German Jew-hater called Wilhelm Marr, who wanted a modern-sounding name for his new political party, the *Antisemiten-Liga* (League of Antisemites). This was a political party formed in 1879 with 'the one aim of saving our German fatherland from complete Judaisation ... liberating Germanism from the oppressive weight of Jewish influence in social, political and ecclesiastical matters'.[13] Marr chose the word 'antisemitism' because Hebrew, the language of Jewish prayer, is one of several Middle Eastern tongues known collectively as Semitic languages. He thought it sounded more scientific and rational than old-fashioned Jew-hatred, but really it was the same old ideas presented in a new way. His choice of term causes confusion because it misleadingly implies that antisemitism means prejudice against people who speak any Semitic language, which would include Arabic, Amharic, Maltese and several minor Middle Eastern dialects. But Marr was clear that his new word only related to Jews, and it was Jews who were the focus of his new party, the League of Antisemites. Marr's political career was a failure, but the word 'antisemitism' caught on and is now universally used to describe anti-Jewish prejudice and discrimination both before and since Marr's time. Like it or not, we're stuck with it.*

A BRIEF HISTORY OF ANTISEMITISM

There is no shame in not knowing about the often obscure and curious patterns of antisemitic thought and action. This is a very modern phenomenon that reaches back through history for its power. Many of the stereotypes, myths and tropes that populate the antisemitic world today began in the Middle Ages, from the late eleventh century into the fourteenth, when Jews came to be seen as a diabolic presence in Christian Europe. This was the period of successive Crusades to relieve the Holy Land from Muslim rule, and the crusading fervour generated a murderous antisemitism within Europe itself. The first great massacres of Jews in medieval times came in the Rhineland in 1096, when bands of crusaders on their way to Jerusalem left a blood-soaked trail through the Jewish communities of central Europe. Thousands were slaughtered. Enmity for Jews, rooted in the belief that they bore eternal guilt for the death of Christ and were disgraced by their stubborn rejection of his message, was already well-established by that point. What was new was the radicalising atmosphere: a mixture of messianic anticipation around the turn of the millennium, anger at the loss of Jerusalem to Islam, the spirit of holy war and an opportunity

---

* If you have come across the word 'antisemitism' in newspapers or books, especially before the last decade or so, you have probably seen it spelt this way: 'anti-Semitism'. You might think a hyphen can't do much damage, but it's much better to spell it without. 'Anti-Semitism' suggests that there is a thing called 'Semitism' that people can be opposed to, in the same way that they might be anti-racist, anti-bullying or wear anti-glare glasses when they are driving. But antisemitism does not address a real existing problem like racism, bullying or low sunlight in winter. It is a self-contained prejudice based on ignorant stereotypes about Jewish people, which, in its most developed form, involves a completely invented, fantasy image of Jews as powerful, greedy manipulators who can be blamed for all sorts of terrible deeds. There is no 'Semitism' for people to be 'anti', so spelling 'anti-Semitism' with a hyphen makes no sense.

INTRODUCTION

for plunder. New stories circulated of Jews supposedly murdering Christian children and poisoning wells. Town by town, country by country, Jews were expelled from much of western Europe, leaving only the folk memory of the Satanic, deplorable Jew, enemy of humanity.

The modern wave of Jew-hatred that proliferated throughout Europe in the nineteenth century and led to genocide in the twentieth was built on these foundations. It did not disappear between these two peaks, constantly generating new modes of language, imagery and expression, increasingly secularised but always deriving from that same image of the evil, conniving Jew. The outsider, Europe's 'Other' onto whom all the ills of the world would be projected. A parallel story was developing in Muslim-majority countries, deriving not from Christian demonology but from Islam's own traditions about Jews. This was less lethal but nonetheless discriminatory in its own way. The two would combine in the twentieth century, as colonisation exported European antisemitism into Muslim-majority lands and the combination of migration and globalised media reflected this cocktail of old and new back into its traditional heartland.

These periods and places are the backdrop for the explanations in this book of why antisemitism looks and sounds the way that it does today, but who remembers this history now? Jews and antisemites, mainly. Much of it has been forgotten and its current manifestations are often missed. This means it is no irredeemable disgrace to be influenced by it yourself. We sometimes treat the holding of antisemitic views as an unconscionable moral failing, an indication that somebody has been gripped by strange and extreme influences; whereas in fact the only thing you need to do to encounter and absorb antisemitic ideas is simply to live in our society. Anti-Jewish stereotypes and myths are woven into our greatest literature, lurking within popular culture and literally built into some of our most famous buildings. The legacy of this long-forgotten history is that antisemitism is now so commonplace that most people don't even see it. The language is often coded and obscure, changing to reflect the modern world as it evolves. This book is full of examples of people and movements expressing and pursuing antisemitic ideas. Some of these were genuinely hateful, but many were just ignorant. This is what we need to change. If, when reading this book, you recognise things within yourself or people you know, don't be too alarmed. It means it's working.

The challenge of rebuilding this knowledge, and constructing a collective societal defence against Jew-hatred, is what this book hopes to meet. It is my attempt to explain what antisemitism looks, sounds and feels like, to show the impact it has on Jewish people and the danger it poses to society as a whole, and provide some ideas about how to reduce its malign influence. This book will explore some of the more potent antisemitic myths, like the blood libel and *The Protocols of the Elders of Zion*, and explain how and where they emerged. It will look at the difference between a prejudice and a conspiracy theory, and how antisemitism is similar to, and different from, other types of racism. You can't understand modern antisemitism without accounting for the impact of both the Holocaust and the creation of the State of Israel, so this book will address both. We'll take a peek at what the future might hold and how to steer it in the right direction. There is some of my family history thrown in and a few funny stories along the way.

Antisemitism has always interested me. I can't tell you when I

INTRODUCTION

first learned that it existed: I absorbed awareness of it, growing up as a young Jew in Manchester, just as all my contemporaries did. My first personal experience of it probably came at school. Some kids thought it funny to throw a penny on the floor and shout 'Jews up!', as if the Jews in the class would fight to get their hands on the money. I remember more clearly when I first did something to stand against it: a candlelit march through central Manchester in 1984 to raise awareness of the plight of Soviet Jews, trapped behind the iron curtain, prevented from practising their faith and culture but banned from leaving the Soviet Union to seek freedom in the West. In my Jewish youth movement Habonim-Dror we learned about the ghetto fighters who fought an impossible struggle against Nazism, reclaiming Jewish honour even while they lost their lives, and about the pioneers who built the State of Israel, the first expression of Jewish sovereignty and self-determination in 2,000 years.

At university I went on marches against the British National Party, all fired up with righteous anti-Fascism. 'Never Again', we cried as we marched through the streets of east London where my grandparents grew up. The first time I told anyone at university that I am Jewish, their reply was, 'You don't look Jewish,' (this always puzzled me: I am Jewish and I look how I look, so by definition I am what at least one Jew looks like) followed by the sneering 'you aren't one of those Zionists, are you?' One of my fellow anti-fascist students who marched alongside me against the far right complained to me that Jews go on about the Holocaust and antisemitism all the time so that we can get away with killing Palestinians. Another told me that Israel is the most dangerous place in the world for Jews, so it would be better for all the Jews in Israel to just leave. The anti-racism officer in my Students' Union decided to ban the Jewish

Society from taking part in anti-racism week, because we were Zionists and therefore racists. One student contemporary of mine was later imprisoned in Pakistan for his alleged role in the kidnap and murder of Daniel Pearl, an American journalist whose last words, as he knelt before the jihadist knife, were 'I am a Jew'.[14]

I discovered as I went along that antisemitism is not straightforward. It is not limited to one type of politics or religion, or one country or culture. Anyone who tells you that anti-Jewish hatred is just a problem of the right, or the left, or Muslims, or that there would be no antisemitism were it not for Israel or Facebook or Trump or Corbyn, is selling you a dud. The truth is very different. When I joined the Community Security Trust, we were simultaneously confronted with neo-Nazis from Combat 18 and Islamists from Hizb ut-Tahrir, both of whom were calling for Jews to be killed. I spent several years as the handler for a mole inside the British National Party, whose accounts of meetings he went to and conversations he heard made me intimately familiar with the antisemitism of the far right, and I wrote a PhD thesis, and subsequently a book, about the antisemitism of the far left. You can't understand antisemitism, much less work out how to tackle it, if you can only face in one direction.

In the almost three decades that I have worked to combat antisemitism in my professional life, and in all the years of study I've devoted to the subject, the one thing I've learned is never to be surprised by what, and who, pops up next. As if to prove my point, as I am writing this introduction, the rapper Kanye West has gone on a spree of anti-Jewish invective, using his re-emergence on Twitter to threaten 'death con 3 on JEWISH PEOPLE' [*sic*]. I'm not completely sure what he meant by 'death con 3', but it doesn't sound like he wants to give us all a hug. This threat got over 30,000 'likes' on

INTRODUCTION

Twitter before it was deleted; he followed it up with a three-hour podcast rant blaming Jews for everything from his own bad press to President Obama's grey hair.[15] The week before Kanye, Ayatollah Khamenei claimed that protests in Iran following the death of a young woman, Mahsa Amini, while in police custody were 'designed by' America and 'the usurping, fake Zionist regime' – a form of words that feeds off older antisemitic conspiracy theories blaming Jews for social and political unrest and the subversion of traditional values.[16] Then it was President Trump complaining that American Jews are not loyal or supportive enough to him.[17] It won't be long before another prominent public figure goes wading into the antisemitic swamp. They may be a person with a history of extremism and racism, or they may just be someone who blunders into this world without realising. Either is possible, as we will see.

More than anything, antisemitism causes real harm. In the past twenty years Jews have been murdered for being Jewish in, amongst other places, Belgium, Denmark, the United States, Morocco, Tunisia, Turkey and India. In France, at least fourteen Jews were murdered between 2003 and 2022 in different attacks. They included Jewish schoolchildren and Holocaust survivors, men and women, young and old, murdered because they were Jewish. During the same two decades, from 2000 to 2019, somewhere between 75,000 and 100,000 Jews emigrated from France – amounting to fully 15 to 20 per cent of the French Jewish community. Over half went to Israel and a lot came to London. Antisemitism was not the only reason they all left, but it was a major driver and it is the factor that will prevent many from ever returning.[18]

In Britain we have, so far, been lucky by comparison, but even here most Jews will sometimes take steps to hide the fact they are Jewish when they are in public. Whether it is removing a religious skullcap, hiding a Star of David necklace or removing a school blazer on the bus home, 60 per cent of British Jews will sometimes take steps to ensure that they can't be identified as Jewish in public, because they are worried about antisemitism. Seventeen per cent of British Jews always or frequently do this.[19] I've done it myself and not thought much of it, but it isn't a sign of a healthy society. If the United Kingdom is a country where some people feel they must hide who they are because they are scared of being attacked for their identity, then the fundamental pillars of our society, the rule of law, equality for all and the liberal democratic values that bind us together, are failing. This isn't just a problem for Jews: it should be a warning for everyone. Antisemitism targets Jews, but it destabilises entire societies.

This antisemitic moment is happening at a time when it feels like democracy itself is coming apart at the seams. 'New polling shows crisis of faith in democracy,' say the Centre for Policy Studies.[20] 'Lack of trust in politics threatens democracy,' according to Carnegie UK.[21] 'Trust in politicians at lowest level on record' report the IPPR, leading to '"significant and disturbing" decline in satisfaction with democracy, and in trust in key democratic institutions'.[22] 'Misinformation is eroding the public's confidence in democracy,' according to the Brookings Institution.[23] 'Only half of Americans have faith in democracy,' say Axios.[24] Think tanks on the left and right, in the United Kingdom and the United States, are reporting the same phenomenon: public trust in politicians and in political institutions is crumbling, and with it the certainty that democracy is the best way to run a country.

Perhaps this is unsurprising: democratic institutions and politicians have hardly covered themselves in glory in recent years. But

INTRODUCTION

a type of politics – or rather, a type of politician – that disregards democratic norms and plays with conspiracist language has become increasingly popular in many countries over the past decade, and whenever an anti-democratic wave surges antisemitism is usually carried along with the tide. President Trump is the most obvious, and high-profile, example of a mainstream politician who delights in displaying his contempt for the conventions of liberal democracy. According to one count, Trump referred to the media as 'fake news' around 2,000 times during the four years of his presidency.[25] He regularly depicted the entire Washington establishment as enemies of the American people, a 'swamp' that needed cleaning out. He built an entire political movement out of a deeply conspiratorial set of beliefs: what began with a racist conspiracy theory about the birthplace of President Obama ended with another, far more dangerous, myth about a supposedly stolen election in 2020, provoking a violent assault on the seat of American democracy.

As he trampled over the conventions of American politics, Trump emboldened others to express their hatreds more forcefully and directly. Attacks on American Jews rose by 86 per cent in the first quarter of 2017, immediately after Trump's election (Trump suggested these might be fake attacks designed 'to make others look bad').[26] Trump himself is not averse to using the occasional antisemitic stereotype when it suits him. During the 2016 presidential campaign Trump tweeted an image of his opponent, Hillary Clinton, next to a Star of David, surrounded by piles of cash and the slogan 'Most Corrupt Candidate Ever!'[27] The implication was that Clinton had been corrupted by Jewish money.*

---

* After people complained, Trump deleted the tweet, then later said he regretted deleting it and should have left it up.

Conspiracy-infused politics is not limited to the right. Launching Labour's 2017 general election campaign, Jeremy Corbyn claimed that 'a cosy cartel' has been allowed 'to rig the system in favour of a few powerful and wealthy individuals and corporations. It is a rigged system set up by the wealth extractors, for the wealth extractors.' The election, he claimed, was simply 'the establishment versus the people'.[28] Trump and Corbyn are very different people and the contents of their respective political views are opposed in many ways, but their overarching understandings of how the world works are strikingly similar: it's all a fix. I am sure that both would deny in all sincerity that their explanations of how politics and the economy operate have anything to do with antisemitism, but whatever they intended is beside the point: there are enough people who will read between the lines and see a hidden Jewish face lurking within. And just as in the United States, the period of Corbyn's leadership of the Labour Party was marked by a crisis of antisemitism, with allegations of disloyalty flung at prominent British Jews and incessant abuse directed at those who spoke up against the rising Jew-hate they witnessed.

This conspiratorial way of explaining the world is an essential component of populist politics and is also central to antisemitism. It encourages the belief that a small, faceless elite hoards all the power and wealth for itself, preventing others from reaching some promised utopia. The identity of this elite differs depending on country and political affiliation. It might be the Washington swamp, the bankers or the Brussels bureaucrats. It might be the globalists, the Rothschilds or the Israel Lobby. This elite might be from north London or they might be rootless cosmopolitans. Some of these are designed to be antisemitic codes and dog whistles, some are

INTRODUCTION

definitely not, but this is beside the point. Sooner or later, whether intended or not, whenever this type of language is deployed the Jews normally get dragged into the picture because antisemitism relies on a similar conspiratorial way of explaining why things happen.

In Europe a form of nationalism that is hostile to those who are placed outside the national community – however that is defined – is having a period of popularity. Hungarian President Viktor Orbán's model of an 'illiberal democracy' is the trailblazer.[29] In France, Marine Le Pen polled by far the highest vote ever for a far-right presidential candidate, with 41 per cent of the vote, in 2022. Sweden and Italy have both elected parties with historic roots in openly fascist politics into government. If you squint a little, you can even look at the vote for Brexit as a diluted manifestation of this same phenomenon. Much of this is not explicitly antisemitic, but the political emotions that drive it – fear and anxiety, a sense that the outside world poses more of a threat than an opportunity – carry foreboding for those who remember how narrow, exclusionary nationalism tends to treat Jews.

This is another reason why antisemitism matters right now. Just as the weakening of liberal democracy poses a danger to Jewish wellbeing, so this also works in reverse, because the more antisemitism takes hold in a society, the more democracy itself is endangered. There is a common metaphor that Jews are the canary in the coalmine, an early warning sign of toxins circulating in the atmosphere. Just like the small birds taken down into mines so that in the event of a leak of lethal gas they would expire quickly and give the miners time to escape, so the alarm calls of Jews who detect antisemitism should be heeded by anyone concerned for the general health of society. I don't like this metaphor, because I don't want to be a dead canary. But the point is valid: antisemitism thrives when democratic norms weaken. Its growth is a symptom of a divided society in which the institutions and processes we expect to protect us are failing. Antisemitism has a fluid quality, filling whatever space is opened to it, permeating the cracks in society and widening them further. I'd like to hope that you will care about antisemitism because you are a good person and you feel that hating Jews is a bad thing in itself. But even if you are motivated solely by self-interest, you ought to act. Countries and movements that become gripped by antisemitism always end up failing: the only question is how much damage they do in the process.

Despite all this, I'm optimistic. If I thought that Britain was an irredeemably antisemitic country, I wouldn't be writing a book about it, I'd be looking for somewhere else to live. Something else I've learned in the years I've spent working in this field is that most people abhor the idea of antisemitism and, when put on the spot, want to help. As antisemitism has grown in recent years, so has the number of people who worry about it as an issue and want to do something to stop it. My hope is that this book will persuade you to join us and provide you with the knowledge and tools you will need. It won't be an easy task, because this is an insidious form of hatred, woven into our world over many centuries. It will take us a long time to change direction, but I'm confident we can succeed. There's no time to lose.

CHAPTER ONE

JEWCRAFT

The world of anti-Jewish thoughts, beliefs and behaviours is so vast and, seemingly, so endless, that it is hard to know where to start. Some might go back to the very beginning, when the Jews were blamed for killing Jesus and the starting gun was fired for so much of the antisemitism that has followed. We could immerse ourselves in medieval Europe, with its blood libels, well-poisonings, mass conversions and expulsions of entire Jewish populations. Perhaps the best entry point is the rise of modern antisemitism in the nineteenth century, when racial science and conspiracy theories gripped the imaginations of millions of people. There was the systematic suppression of Jewish identity in the Soviet Union during the Cold War; or we could dive straight into the Holocaust and the perpetual arguments over Israel.

We will get to all of these, but for now, let's start with one word: Jew. What should we make of the fact that the word 'Jew' is defined, and used, as an insult in the English language? What does this tell us about the sheer ordinariness of antisemitism, the way that hostility to, and suspicion of, Jews is woven into the fabric of our society and our culture, nestling within the very word itself?

The *Oxford English Dictionary* provides a window into centuries of linguistic anti-Jewish prejudice. After the dictionary's initial definition of 'Jew' as 'a member of a people whose traditional religion is Judaism and who trace their origins through the ancient Hebrew people of Israel to Abraham; a follower or adherent of Judaism',* it goes on to list all the pejorative ways in which 'Jew' has been, and still is, used. There is the definition of 'Jew' as someone who is 'regarded stereotypically as scheming or excessively concerned with making or saving money'. There are phrases like 'as rich as a Jew' and the compound terms 'Jew agitator', 'Jew broker', 'Jew merchant', 'Jew boy', 'Jew girl' and so on. There are ones I have never heard of, like a 'Jew cart' ('a cart used to carry stolen goods', apparently) and Jewcraft, which is not a Jewish version of the computer game Minecraft but means 'conduct or behaviour stereotypically regarded as characteristic of Jewish people' – and is, of course, a 'derogatory or offensive' term. Then you get to the business end – if that is not an unfortunate metaphor – with the verbs 'to Jew' or 'to Jew down', meaning to 'try to get the better of a person by charging too much or paying too little; to haggle', and 'to cheat or swindle'. The dictionary is scrupulous in logging which of these are offensive and provides examples of their use by some of our most lauded literary names. T. S. Eliot, Samuel Taylor Coleridge, Emily Dickinson, Lord Byron, Anthony Trollope and many others have all indulged, at one time or another, in antisemitism.

---

* In suggesting that a Jew is defined as a follower of Judaism and a descendant of Abraham, this definition hints at one of the questions we will get to in a later chapter: are Jews a religion or a race, or both, or neither?

This is different from how racist insults normally work. All minorities are the targets of insults and slurs, either directed at them or used more generally to denigrate them. The N-word is now probably the most offensive, and the most unsayable, word in the English language, and the P-word is not far behind. There are plenty such insults for Jews, as famously recounted in the Monty Python film *The Life of Brian*, when the central character defiantly asserts his Jewish identity: 'I'm a Kike! A Yid! A Hebe! A Hook-nose! I'm Kosher, Mum! I'm a Red Sea Pedestrian, and proud of it!'[1] But there is something else going on here, because this is not a case of slurs and insults directed at, or about, Jewish people. Rather, it provides a record of the many different ways in which the word 'Jew' is used as an insult by people who are not Jewish towards other people who are *also not* Jewish. You don't need a Jew in the conversation for the 'Jew' insult to be deployed. Engrained within our own language is the assumption that being thought of as a Jew is something for everyone else to avoid.

This is a difficult discovery for Anglophone Jews to take in. We may all, Jewish and not, speak the same language, but we are not drawing on the same vocabulary, and we do not all mean the same things when we say the word 'Jew'. Our native tongue has taken the word we Jews use to identify ourselves and turned it into a derisory slur, not to be reflected back at us – that would be bad enough – but as a negative reference point for everyone else, an insult for others to play with. A shared language is one of the things that binds a nation, yet there is a corner of the English language that is cordoned off from us, where the word 'Jew' – our word! – is used by others as a warning to mistrust us, to scorn us and avoid us, a common code to sneer at us behind our backs. It is as if, no matter how integrated

British Jews become, this part of the English language will always say, 'This far, and no more.' British Jews are a small minority, and our collective memory contains many stories of our forebears being rejected, shunned and expelled by nation after nation. The desire to avoid this fate is a constant anxiety for diaspora Jewry, whether expressed openly or not, and here is a permanent reminder of the contingency of Jewish identity buried within the meanings and uses of our own name: Jew.

There is another option for Jews, a way to share the full range of the English language: we could just give in, join in the fun and accept the stereotypes ourselves. I don't mean Jews telling jokes about Jews, because that happens all the time. Larry David made an entire comedy series out of it, and *Curb Your Enthusiasm* is loved by almost every Jew I know. What I mean is to fully buy in to the ideas behind the insults, to breathe in the antisemitism that circulates in the society we call our own and absorb it into our understanding of who we are as Jews. Perhaps what the *Oxford English Dictionary* is telling us is that the only way to be fully British is to embrace the part of Britishness that is antisemitic.

It is tempting to dismiss these dictionary definitions as something from the past, a record of historical antisemitism that modern, tolerant, diverse Britain shed long ago, but I think this misses the point. Firstly, as we will see, the 'Jew' insult is still commonly used. There are plenty of people, from school playgrounds to pubs, from offices to sports stadia, who keep this foul linguistic tradition alive. More importantly, language shapes thought, and the English language has treated 'Jew' as an insult for centuries. It is not simply an entry in a dictionary that can be altered or deleted (the official online dictionary of the Association of British Scrabble Players only removed its definition of 'Jew' as a verb meaning 'to haggle, get the better of' in 2019).[2] This prejudice has been intrinsic to the ways in which Western societies relate to, speak and think about Jews: not the only way, not always the dominant way, but always present, and sometimes built into the foundations of society itself.

Antisemitism is often described in medical terms as a form of infection. 'The virus of antisemitism' constantly mutates, the late Chief Rabbi Jonathan Sacks said in a speech to the European Parliament in 2016, and in recent times has reinfected 'the body politic' in Europe.[3] I can see the appeal of this metaphor: it helps to explain why there are variants of anti-Jewish hatred found in different countries or associated with different ideologies and religions. It encourages the idea that, with the right treatment, society can be cured. Except a virus is an alien invader that infects an otherwise healthy body from the outside, and once the virus has been expelled by that person's natural immune system their body returns to full health. The uses of 'Jew' in the English language tell a different story. Antisemitism has always been a part of this body. It isn't an external infection at all: it is part of the flesh and bones of the world we live in. No wonder, then, that antisemitism keeps recurring.

To sidestep any potential offence, the word 'Jews' regularly gets replaced with the softer phrase 'Jewish people'. The difference between the two is neatly demonstrated by the font of all human knowledge: the Google algorithm. According to Google search data from the years 2004–18, 36 per cent of all searches using the word 'Jew' were likely to be antisemitic, compared to no more than 2 per cent of Google searches with the word 'Jewish'. You can test this with a totally unscientific experiment of your own. Search on Google Images for 'Jewish jokes', and you'll get a page of cute jokes about kids at Hebrew school and ironic rabbis. Do the same for 'Jew Jokes' and you get memes about Adolf Hitler and Anne Frank. Whether someone uses the word 'Jew' online rather than 'Jewish' is also an indicator of other prejudices: a person who searches on Google for 'Jew jokes' is more than a hundred times more likely to also search for 'n****r jokes' (I don't recommend you include this in your experiment).[4]

Despite all of this, Jews say 'Jew' to refer to ourselves, and that shouldn't be a problem. It's our word and I'll be using it throughout this book. If that makes you feel uncomfortable, you won't be alone. A few years ago I was advising an anti-racist organisation who were writing a handbook for tackling antisemitism. They asked me to contribute some text about the Jewish community in this country, and I wrote a few paragraphs about British Jews: how many there are in Britain, the diversity of Jewish life, the presence of Jews in the industry this handbook was written for – all standard stuff. They were happy with my contribution apart from one thing, which they queried in a slightly nervous way: was it really OK to write about 'Jews' rather than 'Jewish people', or isn't that offensive?

I had a similar experience with a TV production company making a documentary about a Jewish family, whose (Jewish) boss got in touch because the (non-Jewish) production team were having an internal debate about whether they could say 'Jews' in the script. In both cases it was well-meaning non-Jewish people who raised concerns, presumably because in their experience they have heard the word 'Jew' used in a negative way too often to ignore. Their discomfort was sensitive and thoughtful, and I appreciated their desire to avoid offence, but I was left wondering whether they were right. Perhaps out there in the majority non-Jewish world, 'Jew' can never be a neutral term, the equivalent of 'Christian', 'Hindu', or 'Asian'. When Jews say the word 'Jew' they just mean a Jew, and when other people say (or hear) the word 'Jew' it may be something quite different that comes to mind. Changing our language is a good start when it comes to reducing antisemitism, but it is the thinking behind the language that needs to shift if we are going to bring about fundamental change.

The meaning of the insult 'Jew' is that Jews are tight with money. Not just that they are rich, but that they get rich through underhand means and then keep their money for themselves. The cricketer Azeem Rafiq, who has campaigned tirelessly against racism within his own sport, got in trouble when it was revealed that he had used the word 'Jew' in this way in an old Facebook chat a decade ago. Rafiq and another friend were joking that a third friend was stingy and wouldn't pay their restaurant bill: 'Hahaha he is a jew ... Only jews do tht [*sic*] sort of sh*t ha,' he wrote. Rafiq apologised and subsequently went to significant lengths to learn about the Jewish community and antisemitism. He learned from that experience, and the sincerity of his apology won him a lot of friends in the Jewish community. I spoke to him a few times during that process and he told me that he didn't know any Jews, and that he didn't even have Jews in mind when he wrote 'Jews' in that Facebook comment. That sounds strange until you remember that neither Rafiq or his two friends were Jewish, nor were they talking about actual Jews. When Rafiq wrote 'Jews', he meant the Jews of the *Oxford English Dictionary*: the ones who are always scheming and 'excessively concerned with making or saving money'. Those Jews, the imaginary ones of the English language, not the real Jews I know. Not the people I mean when I say the word 'Jew'.

The media regulator Ofcom had to grapple with a similar issue in 2020, when they were asked to adjudicate on a political talk show broadcast on Samaa TV, a Pakistani channel that was, at the time, broadcast into the UK via Sky. As the debate became more heated, the exchange between two of the Pakistani panellists became surreal:

'We will teach you. You are a Jew.'

'She called me a Jew.'

'I did'.

'No, no, you can't call anyone a Jew.'

Needless to say, none of the people involved were actually Jewish.[5]

These daily insults are just the tip of a gargantuan cultural iceberg, and I can't think of a better person to demonstrate its scale than the twenty-first century's most famous fictional antisemite: Eric Cartman. As all fans of American TV cartoons know, Cartman is one of four pre-teen boys whose puerile adventures are serialised in the long-running Comedy Central show *South Park*. He is obnoxious, sweary, and repeatedly and outrageously antisemitic, mostly towards one of the other boys, Kyle Broflovski, who is Jewish. This is no passing antisemitism. Cartman regularly insults Kyle with 'Jew', 'stupid Jew', 'shut your goddam Jew-mouth', and other Jew-related insults.[6] When Kyle is struggling to concentrate in class, Cartman suggests sending him to 'concentration camp'.[7] When Mel Gibson's movie *Passion of the Christ* comes out, Cartman dresses up as Hitler and leads a crowd of unwitting Gibson fans past the synagogue chanting 'Wir müssen die Juden ausrotten' (A Nazi-era slogan meaning 'We must exterminate the Jews').[8] And in one episode, Cartman homes in on the most common antisemitic stereotype of them all. The boys are running across a collapsing bridge to flee a burning building, and Cartman stands in Kyle's path to prevent him from escaping. 'Hand over the gold!' shouts Cartman, who pulls out a gun and points it at his bemused and panicky Jewish friend. 'All Jews carry gold in a little bag around their neck … Give me your Jew gold now!' Kyle angrily refuses and insists that Cartman is mistaken, but Cartman insists there is no way past him without handing over the bag of gold he believes all Jews wear around their necks. The stand-off is only broken when Kyle reluctantly concedes defeat, reaches inside his coat and hands over a small bag, just as Cartman demanded. But then the twist comes as Cartman thinks he is being tricked, crying: 'Do you think I'm stupid? I know that all Jews carry fake bags of gold around their necks to keep the real bags of gold around their necks safe. Hand over the real Jew gold Kyle!' At that, Kyle reaches inside his coat once more, pulls out a second bag and throws it over the side of the bridge, before running past Cartman to safety.[9]

There are so many antisemitic motifs to unpack from this one scene. The idea that all Jews are rich. The notion that Jews all keep their wealth in an old-fashioned currency like gold, and that they value their gold so much they carry it around their neck, close to their heart. It's literally medieval. The suggestion that Jews are cunning enough to also carry a fake bag of gold so that they can trick the stupid non-Jews who they fear will rob them. And the outcome, in which the cornered Jew uses his cunning to outsmart his tough, armed, non-Jewish adversary.

I'm not an advocate of cancelling offensive comedy. One of *South Park*'s creators, Matt Stone, is Jewish, and Jews can legitimately have a pretty dark sense of humour when it comes to antisemitism. Plus, some of the antisemitic material in *South Park* is clearly intended to look ridiculous. The episode in which Cartman mistakenly assumes that Mel Gibson made *Passion of the Christ* to encourage an anti-Jewish uprising in America is genuinely satirical. But still, *South Park* is wildly popular and successful, and I sometimes wonder whether the satire is just an excuse to be outrageously antisemitic and get away with it. I wonder how many of *South Park*'s young fans around the world first encounter a (fictional) Jew and (semi-satirical) antisemitism via Kyle and Cartman.

The stereotype that Jews acquire their wealth through dodgy means and have an unseemly desire to hang on to it, rather than spend it as normal people do, has flourished in visual form. There is an antisemitic internet meme called the 'Happy Merchant', which is a cartoon caricature of a religious Jew rubbing his hands together, complete with *yarmulke* (religious skullcap), large nose, hunched shoulders and a sneering expression. Think of Fagin in Charles Dickens's *Oliver Twist*, cackling gleefully as another young boy who has fallen under his spell picks a pocket and hands him the cash, and you'll get the idea. If that is the image that was conjured up in your mind then you are on the right track, because Dickens's Fagin is a Jew, written as an antisemitic caricature by one of our most loved and celebrated writers. The Happy Merchant cartoon is meant to look repulsive and sinister, and it draws on centuries of anti-Jewish imagery bearing similar facial features. The internet has dozens of versions: there is the Happy Merchant capitalist counting his money, the Happy Merchant Communist, the Happy Merchant rat, the Happy Merchant who caused Covid, the Happy Merchant who invented the so-called climate change scam, the Happy Merchant Israeli soldier – and all of them hideously, antisemitically, Jewish. The image was probably created by an American far-right cartoonist in the pre-internet age and first appeared online in around 2001, along with racist images of other minorities drawn by the same hand. In 2021 someone even made posters of the Happy Merchant and stuck them onto lamp posts and bollards near a synagogue and Jewish school in north London, not far from where I live, along with other signs blaming Israel for the 9/11 terrorist attacks.

The 'Happy Merchant' antisemitic meme

The stereotype of the rich, stingy Jew, who cares more about money than anything else, is ubiquitous. In 2019, Trump said in a speech to a Jewish audience in Florida,

> A lot of you are in the real estate business, because I know you very well. You're brutal killers, not nice people at all ... But you have to vote for me – you have no choice ... You're not gonna vote for the wealth tax. Yeah, let's take 100 per cent of your wealth away![10]

Trump was wrong: most Jews voted against him in the 2016 and 2020 presidential elections, just as most American Jews vote Democrat in every election. From the other side of the political spectrum, Ken Livingstone, when standing for London Mayor in 2012, allegedly told a group of Jewish Labour supporters that 'he did not expect the Jewish community to vote Labour, as votes for the left are inversely proportional to wealth levels, and suggested that as the Jewish community is rich we simply wouldn't vote for him'.[11]

From politics to football: in 2014 it emerged that the football manager Malky Mackay had said about a Jewish football agent, 'Nothing like a Jew that sees money slipping through his fingers. The Jews don't like losing money. Nobody likes losing money.' Mackay was appointed manager of Wigan Athletic by the then Wigan chairman, Dave Whelan, who defended his decision and Mackay's comments by saying:

> Do you think Jewish people chase money a little bit more than we do? I think they are very shrewd people. I think Jewish people do chase money more than everybody else. I don't think that's offensive at all. It's telling the truth. Jewish people love money, English people love money; we all love money.[12]

Whelan later said that he meant this as a compliment, and maybe in his own mind he did. He is a wealthy and successful businessman in his own right, after all. It's a reminder that stereotypes can work in different ways, and some are so engrained, and have been around for so long, that they become things people simply 'know' without malice or purpose – and then do with what they want. For Whelan, the 'fact' that Jews supposedly have a special love for money is something to admire. He's hardly an outlier: how many people feel reassured, consciously or otherwise, that their accountant is Jewish?

But the friendly stereotyping by some only perpetuates the damaging stereotype itself, and a lot of people don't even notice that they are doing it.

Then there are the incidental comments by ordinary people that make up the patchwork of daily antisemitism across the country. Like the time I was paying for a drink in a café on Brighton seafront and the café owner, who had an old-fashioned cash register, said, 'I'll just open up the old Jewish piano.' Or the time my wife and I were paying the bill in a restaurant in Finchley (an area of London with a large Jewish community) and we asked the waiter whether the staff get to keep tips, or if the restaurant owners take them. 'Oh yes, we get to keep it,' they said. 'Not like the place I used to work where the owners kept all the tips, but they were Jewish and, you know – Jews and money.' Not the smartest thing to say to a random diner in Finchley. I've sometimes thought of starting a Twitter account called 'What people say about Jews when they think no Jews are listening'. People could submit their stories, and both of these would be on the list.

Incidentally, that comment from the waiter left us with an uncomfortable, but not unfamiliar, dilemma. My first reaction was to angrily think, 'There's no way you're getting a tip after saying that.' Then we worried that if we didn't tip, it would just confirm their assumption that Jews are tight with money. On the other hand, if we left a handsome tip as a way of showing that Jews can be generous and forgiving, they might take it as proof that all Jews are rich. So we had to calibrate a tip that would convey just the right amount of goodwill, but not too much. See? You can't win.

It is tempting to treat each case as just an individual instance of ignorance or prejudice, but the association of Jews with money, and especially with onerous or immoral financial practices, is far more systemic than that. I think we can say with certainty that Donald Trump, Ken Livingstone, Malky Mackay and the waiter from Finchley have never been in a room together. They probably don't have much in common apart from their shared belief that Jews have an unusual love of lucre. Despite their utterly different upbringing, education, background and life experience, it is something they, and millions of other people, think they know about Jews. This isn't because they have all read the same antisemitic books or watched the same videos on YouTube. It is because negative attitudes and beliefs about Jews have long been part of their – our – world and helped to shape the societies we live in. The antisemitic myths and stereotypes people believe in today have been around for centuries, perpetuated and recycled in plain sight by the culture that defines us all. And there is no better example of that than England's most celebrated wordsmith: William Shakespeare.

CHAPTER TWO

FILTHY RICH

There isn't much that *South Park* and Shakespeare have in common, but they have both done their bit to inscribe the image of the rich, greedy Jew into the popular imagination. Unlike Kyle outwitting Cartman, in most fictional tales of Jewish greed it is usually the avaricious Jew who gets their comeuppance, rather than their non-Jewish tormentors, and there is no better-known example of this than the fate of Shylock, the Jewish moneylender in Shakespeare's play *The Merchant of Venice*. This renowned play revolves around a loan made by Shylock to a Christian called Bassanio, who secures his debt against the future income of his friend, the merchant Antonio. Shylock, who has a grudge against Antonio, sets a grisly penalty: if Bassanio defaults on the loan, Shylock will be entitled to a pound of Antonio's flesh. When Bassanio can't pay, Shylock has Antonio brought before the court to extract his gruesome payment. However, he is foiled by Antonio's lawyer (in fact, a woman called Portia in disguise, who Bassanio is in love with), who argues that Shylock's contract permits him a pound of Antonio's flesh but none of his blood. Therefore, if Shylock sheds 'one drop of Christian blood', all his possessions will be forfeited to the state.[1] Crushed by this clever legal twist, Shylock is ordered to hand over his goods to Antonio and Bassanio and is forced to convert to Christianity for good measure.

The play is drenched in anti-Jewish invective. Shylock the Jew (he is referred to much more often as a Jew in the text than by his name) is materialistic, bitter and vengeful; Antonio, Bassanio and Portia represent Christian love and mercy. When Shylock's daughter Jessica elopes with another of Antonio's Christian friends, Shylock is as disturbed by the loss of her jewels as he is by the disappearance of his daughter. The dénouement evokes the medieval blood libel,[*] with the knife-wielding Jew denied his Christian blood by a miraculous intervention. The outcome for Shylock – humiliation followed by conversion – is what all Jews deserved.

This was written by Shakespeare in the late 1590s, over 300 years after Jews had been expelled from England by Edward I in 1290. The piercing force of the antisemitic stereotyping is all the more arresting given the almost complete absence of Jews from Shakespeare's England. There were a few Jews living in London in Shakespeare's time, mostly from Iberian families who had converted to Christianity to avoid persecution after Jews were expelled from Spain and Portugal a century earlier and who secretly maintained some elements of Jewish identity or practice.[†] One of these converted Jews, Roderigo Lopez, was Elizabeth I's personal doctor and was executed

---

[*] We will get to the blood libel in more detail in the next chapter.

[†] Converting to Christianity did not protect Spanish and Portuguese Jews from antisemitism: they just fell under further suspicion for not being true converts. In Lisbon in 1506, 2,000 so-called 'New Christians' were murdered over the Easter weekend by a mob egged on by Dominican friars who mistrusted Jewish conversions to Christianity.

in a high-profile case in 1594 for allegedly plotting to poison her. There is a theory that the character of Shylock was partly based on Lopez, but, even so, there had been no visible, openly Jewish presence in England for hundreds of years. It is highly unlikely that most of Shakespeare's audience would have had any meaningful contact with, or knowledge of, actual Jews, or would have known anyone who had. Nonetheless, the image of the Jewish moneylender was familiar enough that Shakespeare used it for one of his most enduring and acclaimed characters, and his audience would have understood exactly who and what Shylock was.

Shakespeare's England is one of many examples of a society in which anti-Jewish attitudes and stereotypes maintain a hold in the popular imagination despite the absence of any real Jews. Don't be surprised by this: antisemitism is a fantasy based on an imaginary notion of who Jews are and how they behave, so it can thrive perfectly well without any actual Jews being present. Even the motif of a pound of flesh would have resonated with the crowd as a familiar anti-Jewish tale. It derives from a late thirteenth-century poem called *Cursor Mundi*, in which a Christian defaults on a debt to a Jewish moneylender, who claims a pound of flesh in return but is denied because – you guessed it – his bond does not include the shedding of blood.[2] By the time Shakespeare made this phrase famous in English, there were similar dramatisations of Jewish lenders seeking payment via a pound of flesh in Italy, France and Germany.

Modern critics, actors and directors have gone to impressive lengths to try to overcome or explain away the antisemitism in *The Merchant of Venice*. The cruelty and hypocrisy of Antonio, Bassanio and the rest are played up and Shylock is presented sympathetically as a victim of the prejudices of his time. Solace is sought in Shylock's most famous speech, where he insists that Jews are – surprise, surprise – human beings:

> Hath not a Jew eyes? Hath not a Jew hands, organs, dimensions, senses, affections, passions? Fed with the same food, hurt with the same weapons, subject to the same diseases, healed by the same means, warmed and cooled by the same winter and summer, as a Christian is? If you prick us, do we not bleed? If you tickle us, do we not laugh? If you poison us, do we not die? And if you wrong us, shall we not revenge?[3]

I understand why people do this. Shakespeare is England's greatest literary treasure, loved and admired around the world. His work represents the very essence of Britishness, and *The Merchant of Venice* is one of his best-known and most performed plays. If its antisemitism is not an aberration or a clever satire, but rather is reflective of Shakespeare himself and the world he inhabited, well, that would be awkward. I also understand why British Jews would go along with this: how can you be fully part of Britain's national story if you cannot share in the unqualified celebration of Shakespeare, even if the man himself marked you out as a villain? But really, it is a grossly antisemitic play, full of spiteful contempt for Jews. It was even marketed as such: the title page of its earliest-known printing in 1600 reads: 'The excellent History of the Merchant of Venice. With the extreme cruelty of Shylock the Jew towards the said Merchant, in cutting a just pound of his flesh.'[4]

There is no evidence that Shakespeare intended to skewer the anti-Jewish prejudices of his time, nor would he have had any reason to do so. If modern audiences view Shylock sympathetically and recoil at the viciousness of his persecutors, that is more a reflection of contemporary values than of the play itself. It is typical of Shakespeare's genius that his work can be read in opposing ways, so a sympathetic reading of the play is available for those who are determined to find it, but that hardly means he had the anti-racist ideals of 21st-century Britain in mind when he wrote it. Shakespeare created an antisemitic caricature that has echoed down the ages, and it belongs in his canon not despite his totemic position in Britain's cultural history, but because of it.

'Shylock' has made its way from this sixteenth-century play into the lexicon of anti-Jewish insults, in this case denoting a particular kind of predatory financial practice. It was recognised as an anti-Jewish slur by a British court in 2016, when Highbury Magistrates' Court found a man called Herminio Martinez guilty of racially abusive words or behaviour for calling a Jewish property developer a 'Shylock' during a dispute.[5] If that seems trivial, how about the President of Argentina deploying this anti-Jewish insult to explain her country's credit problems? In 2015, Argentina was in the midst of a debt crisis that involved a US-based hedge fund called Elliott Management whose president, Paul Singer, is Jewish. Argentinian President Cristina Fernández de Kirchner tweeted that 'you have to read *The Merchant of Venice* to understand the vulture funds … Usury and bloodsuckers have been immortalised in the greatest literature for centuries.'[6] This was echoed the following year in a *Daily Telegraph* column that began 'latter day Shylocks at Elliott Management allowing, Argentina will soon have renewed access to international capital markets', and referred to 'aggressively litigious hedgies such as Mr Singer demanding their pound of flesh'.[7*]

---

* The *Daily Telegraph* removed these two antisemitic allusions following a complaint.

The contemporary association of Jews and money, just like the character of Shylock, draws heavily on the role played in medieval societies by Jewish moneylenders. This is the place to begin if you want to understand the origins of this enduring stereotype; its ubiquity today is a testament to how deeply embedded it became, yet the fact that Jews became known as moneylenders was itself a consequence of discriminatory restrictions placed on them in medieval Europe. The charging of interest on loans (known as usury – the same term used by President Kirchner) was seen as sinful in Christian teaching for a variety of reasons and was banned by the medieval Church, but it was allowed in Jewish law. Meanwhile Jews were banned from participating in several other professions. In many countries Jews were not allowed to own farmland, hold public office, employ Christians or join the Guilds that were at the heart of medieval trades. Where they could trade, it was rarely on equal terms and they were subjected to punitive taxes. The combination of these factors meant that in a lot of countries Jews filled the moneylending gap. There were still Christian moneylenders despite the Church's prohibition, and not all Jews were in this line of business, but in a lot of places the best-known, and richest, moneylenders and bankers were Jewish. The long involvement of Jews in moneylending gradually led to a belief that Jews and Judaism are particularly suited to finance and commerce.

This was central to the treatment of Jews in medieval England, a 200-year history that ended in catastrophe. This lost period is the subterranean bedrock upon which more recent anti-Jewish myths are layered, but it has largely been erased from our shared popular memory of Britain's treatment of minorities. This act of forgetting has left a vacuum in which modern antisemitism grows, and if we are to develop the tools to act against this phenomenon, we need to excavate its medieval imprint.

COMING AND GOING

The first significant Jewish settlement in this country came in the years after 1066, when Jews from Rouen followed William the Conqueror to act as his bankers. An English network of Jewish financiers developed during the twelfth century, lending money to the Crown and to lords, bishops, squires and other private individuals across the country. They also acted as Crown agents, making loans to the king and then collecting revenue on his behalf as repayment. There were Jewish doctors, goldsmiths, singers, traders and even crossbowmen in medieval England, but the moneylenders became the most prominent and important figures in the Jewish community and they were an integral, although never equal, part of the English state's financial apparatus. The greatest and most famous of the twelfth-century Jewish moneymen, Aaron of Lincoln, was probably the richest man in England when he died in 1186. His loans helped to pay for the construction of Lincoln and Peterborough Cathedrals as well as nine different abbeys, and he had property and other interests in twenty-five different English counties. His debtors included the King of Scotland, the Archbishop of Canterbury and several earls and bishops.

In this feudal society Jews were legally the property of the Crown, who kept them close for their banking services, and in turn Jews benefited from the king's protection. They provided a vital source of funds. Taxed more heavily and more frequently than others, the revenue they provided was used for, amongst other things, construction of part of the Tower of London and a chapel at Westminster

Abbey. In 1210 King John even ordered the arrest of every Jew in the country so that their possessions could be assessed and then taxed accordingly. The problem is that moneylenders tend to be unpopular, and the Jewish moneylenders of medieval England were disliked by many for the interest that they charged. They were ultimately expendable, because their powerful debtors always had the option of having them arrested or whipping up an antisemitic mob to get out of paying what they owed. It is an example of how social and economic tensions can add to religious bigotry in fuelling anti-Jewish sentiment.

Later in the thirteenth century they were targeted by a persecutory campaign over coin-clipping, a crime in which people shaved the edges off coins and melted the clippings down to turn into currency. Jews and Christians were both involved in this crime, but Jewish offenders were proportionately more likely to be arrested, and if arrested, they were much more likely to be hanged. Hundreds of Jews were executed for this offence in the late 1200s in a brutally oppressive crackdown. In 1275, the Statutes of Jewry made it completely illegal for Jews to lend money at interest. To compensate for this, the Statute allowed Jews for the first time to work as merchants, to lease land for farming and to engage freely with Christians (although it specifically barred Christians from living amongst Jews). In practice these concessions were meaningless because Jews were still prevented from joining the Guilds that controlled different trades, and any benefit they brought could not replace the income from the financial services they were now barred from practising. Fifteen years later the story of medieval English Jewry came to an end when all remaining Jews – around 3,000 people in total, a tiny fraction of England's population at the time – were expelled from the country.*

Unless you are Jewish or have a particular interest in medieval history this is unlikely to be familiar to you. There are towns around England with roads called Old Jewry or Jew Street that stand as ghostly reminders of this early Jewish presence, but I doubt many people who walk down those streets know much about the Jews who inhabited them when they acquired their names. Recent years have seen a renewed interest in reviving those forgotten lives. In Winchester, a statue of one of medieval England's most colourful Jewish moneylenders, a woman called Licoricia, was unveiled by King Charles in 2022. Worcester now has a blue plaque to commemorate its medieval Jewish community, 'who were persecuted and driven out of the City for their faith'.[8] The Tower of London has embarked on a project to catalogue the lives of hundreds of Jews who resided in the Tower during the Middle Ages, including both those who were imprisoned there and those who sought refuge from the anti-Jewish violence that periodically burst over London's Jews. There ought to be more efforts to revive these stories and place them where they belong: as part of Britain's long histories of both diversity and of persecution. Public debate about the history of racism and discrimination in Britain often starts in the twentieth century, either with fascist antisemitism in the first half of the century or the post-war treatment of black and Asian communities. Those with a

---

* When googling for a copy of this statute I quickly ended up on a British far-right website that has published the full text. I won't include the link here, but the 1275 Statutes of Jewry and 1290 Edict of Expulsion hold a particular fascination for those British antisemites who insist that these rulings have never been formally revoked: they cling to the fantasy that one day they will be re-enforced and Jews will once more be removed from this country.

longer perspective talk about slavery and colonialism. But before any of this, for 200 years from the eleventh to the late thirteenth centuries, the Jews of medieval England provided a prologue to our understanding of how our society has treated minorities. And it didn't end well.

MONEY TALKS

Unlike this history, the idea that Jews are rich hasn't been forgotten at all. If, like me, you have a surname that is also a regular word, you will probably be wearily used to people making jokes about it. Yes, 'Rich' is a good name for a Jew, according to one kid in my class at school. Or a good name for a Zionist, to stay up to date. No, friendly call-centre person, I'm not rich, but I wish I was. Thank you, Twitter trolls, for insulting me with 'Dave Bitch' or 'Rave Dich' or some other variation, as if I've never heard those ones before. You'll have to try harder in future. And then there are all the jokes about rich Jews and stingy Jews. But despite all of this there have always been plenty of Jews who are poor. The nineteenth century saw the rise of several hugely influential international investment banks started and run by Jewish families, including the Warburg family, the Loebs, Lehman Brothers, Goldman Sachs and the Rothschilds, but it was also a period of intense poverty in many Jewish communities, including amongst Jewish immigrants to the United Kingdom. I see this in my own family history. My maternal grandfather was an upholsterer in the East End of London who, like many in his generation, never earned much. My paternal grandfather was a doctor, but only because he managed to get scholarships all the way through secondary school and then medical school. He grew up in a poor Jewish community in north Manchester and there is no way his immigrant, working-class parents could have afforded any of it. This was not untypical. An article about 'the Jews in London' in an 1889 edition of *Graphic* weekly newspaper noted that 'the poor are very numerous. The proportion of poverty among the Jewish people generally is larger than among any other civilised people,' but added that this is balanced by the generosity of those at the wealthier end of the scale: 'Happily, to meet this state of things, there are, at the other extreme of the community, wealthy and well-to-do individuals … whose generosity to their poorer brethren and activity for their welfare are in a fair ratio with their wealth and responsibilities.'[9] Despite the stereotype that all Jews are rich, it is common sense that the Jewish community, like the rest of society, should be marked by uneven distributions of wealth and poverty.

The same applies today. British Jews are, on average, more likely to be higher earners than the population as a whole, but there are parts of the Jewish community where child poverty, poor housing, overcrowding and unemployment are common.[10] In the United States, a 2013 survey by Pew found that while a quarter of Jews had a family income above $150,000, a fifth had a family income below $30,000.[11] Beyond the prosperous West, Jewish communities often experience the same economic problems as the societies they live in. One of the biggest Jewish charities in Britain is World Jewish Relief, and one of their main projects is to support elderly Jews in post-Communist states like Ukraine, Georgia, Belarus and Moldova who have no savings, no social care and little more than £50 per month in their pensions.[12]

Maybe I shouldn't waste my energy getting bothered by this. Stereotypes about Jews are nothing if not tenacious, and this is probably the one thing that everyone 'knows' about Jews, even if they don't know anything else. But it is immensely frustrating, because the idea that Jews are miserly couldn't be further from the truth. If you were to attend the regular fundraising lunches and dinners held by the charities that make up much of the social, welfare, educational and political life of the UK Jewish community, you would soon understand that the whole show relies on the generosity of donors who repeatedly sign pledge cards and write cheques to keep everything going. Money talks, and in the Jewish community one of the things it says is 'you must give back'. There are estimated to be around 2,300 Jewish charities and foundations in the UK, which is a ridiculous number for a community of only around 300,000 people and way out of proportion compared to the country as a whole. A 2016 survey of Jewish charitable giving found that 93 per cent of British Jews had given money to charity in the previous year (compared to 57 per cent in the general UK population), and 77 per cent of British Jews said giving to charity was an important part of their Jewish identity. Jews with strong religious observance were the most likely to give, which should not be a surprise as donating to charity is a religious commandment in Judaism.[13]

Nor is this about Jews looking after their own. The same survey found that British Jews are more likely to give to general charities than to Jewish ones – only 8 per cent of Jewish givers donated exclusively to Jewish charities – and those who give to both tend to give the larger share to the same national or local charities as their non-Jewish friends and neighbours. In 2022 World Jewish Relief raised millions of pounds for Ukrainian refugees, while over 1,000 Jewish families in the UK registered to host Ukrainian families.

It sometimes feels like no amount of reality can shake these stereotypes from their moorings. Some antisemitic tropes are woven so tightly into the fabric of our world that people reach for them to explain all sorts of things, seemingly without having a clue where they come from. US Republican Congresswoman Marjorie Taylor Greene became a laughing stock when it emerged that in 2018 (before she was elected) she had posted on Facebook a bizarre theory that wildfires in California may be caused by 'lasers or blue beams of light' coming from 'space solar generators', rather than the usual reasons such as hikers dropping cigarette butts or failing to put out their campfires properly. She further speculated that these lasers from space were somehow linked to the Rothschild investment bank – and this is where antisemitism comes into the picture. The Rothschild bank was founded by a Jewish family in Frankfurt in 1760 and became a powerful and important institution in nineteenth-century Europe. Members of the Rothschild family were notable political figures in Britain, France and other European states and often took on leading roles in their Jewish communities. The Rothschild Bank is now a minnow compared to the giants of global banking, but for antisemites 'Rothschild' became a byword for their conspiratorial belief that Jews control the financial system and use it to influence and manipulate governments to act against their national interests. The role of the Rothschilds in the antisemitic imagination was exploited and reinforced by Nazi Germany, who made a feature film about it.

You can never have too many reminders that antisemitism can be comical as well as sinister, and everyone made fun of Greene. 'Jewish space lasers' trended on Twitter. There is even merchandise: I have a laser pointer toy for my cats with 'Jewish Space Laser' printed on it. Greene later claimed that she didn't know the Rothschilds were Jewish, which is entirely believable but also beside the point.

Antisemitic tropes enter the consciousness through osmosis more than conscious imbibing. The Rothschild name is a fixture in the conspiracist world, and Greene has a track record of endorsing conspiracy theories that are common on the hard right of US politics. The internet has a limitless supply of videos and social media posts using the name 'Rothschild' as a totem of exploitative, rapacious global financiers and Greene probably absorbed the message without realising.[14]

Even more improbably, the Rothschild conspiracy trope has been at the centre of a Football Association disciplinary hearing. In July 2020 the Port Vale footballer Tom Pope was suspended for six matches and forced to go on an education course after a fan asked him on Twitter to 'predict the #WWIII result', and Pope replied, 'We invade Iran then Cuba then North Korea then the Rothchilds [sic] are crowned champions of every bank on the planet the end.' When Pope was challenged by other Twitter users for repeating an antisemitic myth he doubled down, tweeting, 'It was saying they own every bank on the planet except them mentioned! That's a fact and there's nothing else to it!' The internet is full of claims that the Rothschilds own almost every other bank in the world (including the Bank of England and the US Federal Reserve) and start wars in any country that resists them, none of which are true.

The FA had to bring in academic experts to explain to them what the Rothschild conspiracy theory is all about. At his disciplinary hearing, Pope explained that it was after 'he had watched hundreds of conspiracy theory videos about the 9/11 attacks' that he got interested in the Rothschilds. One conspiracy theory leads to another, and no matter your starting point, you never need to go too far down the rabbit hole before you end up at antisemitism. Pope watched videos claiming that 'the Rothschild banking business had funded the invasions' of Afghanistan, Iraq, Libya and Sudan (they hadn't) and predicting that they would soon do the same with Cuba, Iran and North Korea (they won't). Pope insisted that 'he was not antisemitic and he was not racist', and he may well be right about that, but he still ended up tweeting an anti-Jewish conspiracy theory used by the Nazis.[15]

Here's the thing: Tom Pope did not tweet about the Rothschilds because of a personal grievance against them. His local branch hadn't turned him down for a loan; people don't blame the Rothschild Bank for wars and revolutions because they are angry about its interest rates. It isn't even that sort of bank, and this is not about anyone's real-life experiences. It's about people stepping into a heritage of anti-Jewish conspiracism of which the name 'Rothschild' is emblematic. Google searches in the UK looking for conspiracy theories about the alleged power and influence of the Rothschild family increased by 39 per cent from 2016 to 2019, and the prevalence of this conspiracy theory says more about the tenacity of antisemitism than anything to do with the Rothschild Bank itself.[16] Four of the five largest banks in the world in 2021 were Chinese, but you do not get conspiracy tropes about Chinese banks to match those about the Rothschilds.[17] This isn't because the Rothschilds are evil: it is because Western civilisation has a long tradition of conspiracism about Jews, and no amount of fact or experience will erase that inheritance.

The Rothschilds were not the only Jewish bankers to attract this kind of attention, but their name is the most enduring. By the late seventeenth century some of the leading bankers in Europe were Jewish, and they helped to pay for some of Europe's most significant and historic events. The successful Austrian defence of Vienna in

1683 from the Ottomans that turned back the high tide of Muslim advance into Christian Europe was financed largely by Samuel Oppenheimer, banker to the Habsburg Emperor. Five years later in 1688, a Jewish banking firm in Amsterdam helped to fund William III's capture of the British Crown. Monarchs and governments across Europe depended on finance to pay for their incessant warring, and the Jewish bankers who grew close to kings and emperors became the best-known, and most powerful, Jews in their countries.

These prominent Jewish financiers acquired titles and lands and built vast synagogues for their communities, whose opening ceremonies were often attended by royalty. The catch was that while their wealth gave them access to power it could never fully shield them from the vulnerability to that same power that was shared by every Jew, rich or poor. Rich Jews may have been rich, but they were still Jews. Money couldn't protect them when Jews were expelled from the whole of Bohemia and Moravia, including the jewel of Jewish Prague, in 1744, despite providing decades of banking to the imperial Habsburg throne. Jews were expelled from Vienna in 1670, and on this occasion they were invited back a few years later because their financial services were too attractive to do without – but this reversal just emphasises the vicissitudes of Jewish life under Christian rule at that time. No amount of money or service could bring true security. This is what all the conspiracy theories get wrong: even the most powerful Jews were only ever power-adjacent, and it could be quickly whipped away from them if the wind changed.

MAKING MONEY JEWISH

This association of Jews with money didn't just shape how people think about Jews: it worked in reverse, influencing how Europe's philosophers, politicians and theologians thought, wrote and argued about the role of money in society. Charging interest on loans had been made legal in the Netherlands in 1540 and in England by 1571, and over subsequent centuries many of Europe's greatest minds grappled with the question of how to control this 'Jewish' practice in a Christian society (*The Merchant of Venice* was, in part, a dramatisation of this question). 'You ask me if there are Jews in France,' wrote French political theorist Montesquieu in his 1722 satire *Persian Letters*. 'Know that wherever there is money, there are Jews.'[18] 'The Jews invented letters of exchange,' he wrote elsewhere. 'Commerce was transferred to a nation covered with infamy [i.e. the Jews], and soon ranked with the most shameful usury, with monopolies, with the levying of subsidies, and with all the dishonest means of acquiring wealth.'[19]

Edmund Burke's 1790 critique of the French Revolution contrasted 'men of rank' who 'sanctified their ambition by advancing the dignity of the people' with the supposed leaders of this revolution: 'Jew brokers contending with each other who could best remedy with fraudulent circulation and depreciated paper the wretchedness and ruin brought on their country by their degenerate councils.'[20] Burke's objection was that the revolutionaries were mainly lawyers, brokers and traders, all from lower classes than those he thought ought to rule. None of them were actually Jewish: there were barely any Jews living in France at that time, and the revolution was not led by Jews. But that wasn't Burke's point. He did not mean that the brokers and lawyers who had brought down the French monarchy and were seizing Church lands were actually Jewish by birth. It was their role in society selling stocks and shares, driven by material value rather than spiritual purpose, that he felt had a Jewish character.[21]

The best-known example of this way of thinking is probably Karl Marx's 1844 essay 'On The Jewish Question'. Marx was responding to another philosopher, Bruno Bauer, who had argued that Jews should not be accorded full civil rights until they had given up Judaism. Marx disagreed, but also chided Bauer for treating this purely as a religious question. Instead, Marx argued, you should look at the role of Jews in society. 'What is the secular basis of Judaism?' he asked. 'Practical need, self-interest. What is the worldly religion of the Jew? Huckstering. What is his worldly God? Money.' Consequently for Jews, 'emancipation from huckstering and money' would be emancipation from 'practical, real Judaism'. Furthermore, he argued, Christian society has been made Jewish by the adoption of these practices:

> The Jew has emancipated himself in a Jewish manner, not only because he has acquired financial power, but also because, through him and also apart from him, *money* has become a world power and the practical Jewish spirit has become the practical spirit of the Christian nations. The Jews have emancipated themselves insofar as the Christians have become Jews ... The god of the Jews has become secularised and has become the god of the world. The bill of exchange is the real god of the Jew.[22]*

Again, when Marx wrote that 'Christians have become Jews', he did not mean that Christians had converted to Judaism in a religious sense. He meant that Christian society had adopted financial practices that had a 'Jewish spirit'.

---

* There is an alternative interpretation that Marx used this passage to summarise prevailing attitudes about Jews rather than expressing his own personal views; to read this argument in more detail see Robert Fine and Philip Spencer, *Antisemitism and the Left: On the return of the Jewish question* (Manchester University Press, 2017).

There is an irony here, if you think back to the previous chapter. In modern Britain, people who are trying to be sensitive and avoid offensive terminology plump for 'Jewish people' rather than 'Jews', because 'Jew' is, for some, an insult. But as Marx and others show, 'Jewish' can be just as much of an insult depending on how it is used. Money became 'Jewish', trading became 'Jewish', stocks and shares and knowing the price of everything and the value of nothing all became 'Jewish'. Words are just words, in the end: it's the meaning you invest them with that matters.

Some, like Martin Luther, were unremittingly hostile to Jews and Judaism, with diatribes that would rival even the most vituperative social media troll. Others, like Kant and Hegel, equivocated over their attitude towards Jews. All were part of, and contributed to, a way of thinking that treated money and financial practices, and, more broadly, the world of material value, as having a corrupting 'Jewish' essence. This was not meant as a gratuitous insult, but as an adjective. By the end of the sixteenth century, Jews and usury had become virtually synonymous terms; by the modern period 'it is difficult to think of a financial innovation, practice or crisis that was not discussed in terms of Judaism in the nineteenth and the early twentieth century'.[23]

Meanwhile for some people, the idea that Jews are good at business is an opportunity to make some money for themselves. Amazon sells dozens of books promising to reveal the business secrets that Jews supposedly use to acquire their mythical wealth. How about a copy of *The Money Code: Become a Millionaire With the Ancient Jewish Code* by Howard Ward Charles, which promises to help you 'achieve long-term wealth and success in life' by copying Jewish methods of getting rich. 'Their secret lies not in their genetics or intelligence', it claims, 'but in their religion. Many of the wealthiest Jews use a code based on Judaism.' If that works for you (and, at the time of writing, 509 Amazon reviews with an average score of 4.4 out of 5 suggests a lot of satisfied customers), Charles – who does not appear to be Jewish but 'has a great interest in Hebrew, Jewish philosophy and interpretation of the Jewish bible' – has published a companion volume, *The Investing Code: Ancient Jewish Wisdom for the Wise Investor*. In China there is an entire mini-industry of get-rich-quick books that claim to use lessons from the Talmud and other Jewish religious texts to teach success in business.* These books market themselves in admiring terms ('Jews are estimated to make up less than 1 per cent of the world's population, yet approximately 25 per cent of the world's billionaires are Jewish ... No other ethnic group has even come close to matching the abilities and accomplishments of Jews,' says the blurb for one of them) but they rely on the same stereotypes that have fuelled resentment and hatred of Jews for centuries.[24]

This claim that Jews make up a disproportionate chunk of the world's billionaires is worth unpacking, because you see it in lots of places. I've been asked by Jewish students in the UK how they should explain it when their non-Jewish friends bring it up (as they do). It is usually based on the annual lists of the world's richest people published by *Forbes* magazine, and it is true that normally between 20 and 30 per cent of the people on that list are Jewish. At first glance that is impressive, and it is something that Jewish community websites and newspapers are often proud to point out. The problem comes when people assume that it is their Jewishness

---

* The Talmud is an ancient, very long and often contradictory and confusing set of religious commentaries and interpretations of Jewish laws. I wouldn't recommend trying to use it to write a business plan.

that explains the fact these people are billionaires, as if being Jewish somehow gives them special insight or talent for making money – which is the same thing that antisemites believe. It is probably more telling that almost all of them are men, most are American, and a lot of them inherited much of their fortune. In other words, the things that help some Jews become billionaires are the same things that influence wealth amongst non-Jews. Headlines about well-known Jewish tycoons like Mark Zuckerberg or Alan Sugar perpetuate the impression that Jews and money go together, but this ignores the large numbers of Jewish people around the world who, like most of us, can only dream of such wealth. There are many more poor Jews in the world than there are Jewish billionaires, but the billionaires are assumed to be typically Jewish because they fit the stereotype of what it means to be a Jew. This stereotype may have taken form in the distant past, when Jews were forced into moneylending and some became prominent bankers funding Europe's growing prosperity, but we are no freer from it today.

You might wonder why all this matters. It's only words after all, and at times it can seem fairly complimentary. Better to be thought of as clever in business than useless, and so what if people are wrong? But the danger with antisemitism comes in the uses to which it is put. These stereotypes do not float freely, but have been attached to political projects full of hatred and violence. All this thinking about Jews and exploitative finance found a sinister outlet in the ideologies that gripped Europe in the twentieth century. British fascist leader Oswald Mosley, in a speech at the Royal Albert Hall in March 1935, described 'international Jewish finance' as 'the enemy which Fascism alone dares to challenge'.[25] An antisemitic children's book published in Nazi Germany called *Der Giftpilz* (The

Poisonous Mushroom) included an image of a repulsive-looking Jewish banker sitting on a huge bag of gold, with the caption: 'Money is the God of the Jews. He commits the greatest crimes to earn money. He won't rest until he can sit on a great sack of money, until he has become king of money.'[26] A booklet published by a Soviet state-owned press agency in 1980 put it this way: 'Zionism is the ideology and policy of the Jewish bourgeoisie and forms part of the world-wide financial oligarchy ... The main aim of the Jewish bourgeoisie throughout the world is to consolidate its position in the system of monopoly capitalism.'[27] Fascism, Nazism and Communism may use different terminology, but they share the urge to put Jews, money and exploitation together as the enemy of ordinary people. Anti-democratic politics require an enemy and a scapegoat, and Jews are a convenient and traditional target.

It wasn't just that people thought Jews were more successful in business. The idea was that Jews were intrinsically, culturally and even biologically suited to making money. John Hobson was a radical nineteenth-century writer whose works on capitalism and empire have had a profound influence on left-wing thought for more than a century, and he argued that Jews' supposedly sharp business practices and financial acumen were rooted in their racial and religious characteristics. Hobson's work was thrust into the political spotlight in 2019 when it emerged that Jeremy Corbyn, at that time the leader of the Labour Party, had previously written a glowing foreword to a 2011 edition of Hobson's 1902 book *Imperialism: A Study*. Hobson had written in this book, which is widely taught in universities, that the finance houses propelling European imperialism were 'controlled ... chiefly by men of a single and peculiar race, who have behind them many centuries of financial experience' and 'are in a unique position to manipulate the policy of nations'. Who is this 'single and peculiar race' manipulating European governments? The clue is in the bank that Hobson identified as the prime string-puller: 'Does anyone seriously suppose that a great war could be undertaken by any European state ... if the house of Rothschild and its connections sets their face against it?'[28]

It is in a 1931 booklet called *God and Mammon* that Hobson revealed just how deeply he associated Jews with money. Discussing the relationship between capitalism and different religions, Hobson wrote of 'the characteristic qualities of the Jew as business man, his skilful profiteering as trader and money-lender, his steady pursuit of gain by careful planning, hard bargaining, and usurious loans'. Hobson concluded that Jews' religious practices and racial qualities

> have enabled them to seize the growing opportunities which a capitalism, ever more impersonal and financial in character and ever more international in scope, gives to a people who, scattered throughout the trading centres of the whole world, maintain common ties of religious and racial unity ... cultivating the sense of 'God's Chosen People'* as a fine instrument for money-making.[29]

In other words, accumulating wealth is something inherent to every Jew and to the condition of being Jewish, rather than just an acquired talent. Worse, the way Jews make their money involves shady and immoral methods such as usury and profiteering. Put all

---

* The phrase 'Chosen People' comes from a Jewish belief that the Jewish people were chosen by God to receive His commandments and live by His law. It is seen as an obligation and something of a burden rather than any kind of divine bonus. However, it is often twisted by antisemites to suggest that Jews think they are better than everyone else and even to falsely impute a Jewish theological doctrine of racial superiority – ironic, given that Jews have so often been victims of racial supremacist movements.

this together and you end up with the belief that Jewish behaviour is not just improper or unseemly but radically endangers everyone else. And to show just how weird antisemitism can sometimes be, this fear of Jewish amoral business practices takes us next, of all places, to Grenfell Tower.

CHAPTER THREE

BLOOD AND FIRE

On the morning of 14 June 2017, Britain woke to the horror of the Grenfell Tower on fire. Vivid footage of the giant residential tower block shrouded in flames, its thick smoke visible for miles across west London, gripped the nation's attention. Seventy-two people died in Britain's worst peacetime tragedy for over a century and many more were left homeless. As the scale of the tragedy unfolded, people across the country donated money, clothes, children's toys and household goods, while hundreds of volunteers gathered at the emergency shelters and charity distribution sites that sprang up in the immediate area around the smouldering tower.

One of those volunteers who rushed to help, a middle-aged woman from north London called Tahra Ahmed, believed she knew who was responsible for the unimaginable grief and loss that she witnessed. While others contemplated the devastation and wondered how such a disaster could possibly happen, Ahmed looked to blame a traditional scapegoat. 'I've been at the scene,' she wrote on Facebook, and have met many of the victims ... Watch the live footage of people trapped in the inferno with flames behind them. They were burnt alive in a Jewish sacrifice. Grenfell is owned by a private Jewish property developer just like the twin towers was owned by Jew Silverstein who collected trillions in insurance claims.

To emphasise the point, Ahmed underlined her post with a final sentence in full capitals: 'LONDON TOWER BLOCK FIRE: SINISTER CONNECTIONS WITH JEWISH RITUAL SACRIFICE EXPLORED.'[1]

This might seem bizarre enough – Grenfell Tower was owned by the local council and not by a 'private Jewish property developer', the fire started in someone's fridge-freezer, and what on earth is a 'Jewish ritual sacrifice' anyway? – but it was nothing compared to what Ahmed subsequently produced. She was prosecuted for stirring up racial hatred against Jews and, given her day in court, Ahmed drew on centuries of anti-Jewish fantasies and libels to make her case. She claimed that ancient Jewish religious texts, principally the Talmud, permit 'sacrificing children' and that medieval myths that Jews would kidnap Christian children and kill them in a religious ritual, known as the 'blood libel', might be true. She argued that 6 million Jews were not murdered by Nazi Germany in the Holocaust and that the 9/11 terrorist attacks in the United States were probably carried out by the Israeli intelligence agency Mossad, rather than by Osama bin Laden's al-Qaeda terrorist organisation. As for Jewish people themselves, Ahmed told the court that she believes there is a particular group of sinister, powerful Jews – 'I call them the cabal, I call them Talmudic, I call them Zionists' – who are responsible for satanic ritual abuse and other evils. When asked who these 'Satanic ruling Jews' are, she said they are 'the bankers, owners of media and corporations, they manipulate and control a lot of evil in the world and I want it to end and so I expose who they are'. Elsewhere on Facebook, Ahmed had written that 'Jews have always been the ones behind ritual torture, crucifixion and murder of children, especially young boys, as a way of atoning for their sins in order to be allowed back into Palestine', and to prove her point she posted a link to a website cataloguing 'a very brief history of these crimes they committed in Britain over the centuries'.[2]

It should go without saying that this is all complete rubbish. Jews have never ritually sacrificed children for satanic (or any other) purpose. Israel was not behind 9/11. The Holocaust really did happen as historians say it did. There is not a 'cabal' of Jewish media moguls and bankers secretly spreading evil. It would be tempting to dismiss these ridiculous claims as the paranoid delusions of an irrelevant fantasist whose views are so obviously repulsive and dangerous that she ended up in prison, were it not for the fact that Ahmed did not make any of this up herself. Every accusation she came out with – the claim that Jewish religious books encourage child murder, conspiracy theories about banks and the media and 9/11, denial that the Nazis murdered 6 million Jews, and the rest – have all been heard before, and often from people, parties, movements and governments of much greater consequence than Tahra Ahmed.[*] She expressed herself using buzzwords like 'Talmudic', 'cabal' and 'Zionist' that may seem obscure to the average reader but carry huge meaning for true believers in anti-Jewish folklore.

---

[*] To take just one example: Hitler warned repeatedly in *Mein Kampf* that the population was deceived by Jewish control of the press, writing that 'through the medium of his newspapers, the Jew is always spreading falsehood'. Not the kind of company anybody should want to keep, ideas-wise.

At different times and places in history these myths, lies and legends about Jews, however outlandish they may sound, have been believed by millions of people and have provided the fuel for unspeakable crimes. Right now, in Britain, they are more widespread than they have been for years. Stereotypes about unfamiliar minorities become accepted truths that people absorb from all sorts of places, perhaps a friend or family member, at work, at a party or online. If it sounds right then it sticks, especially when it concerns a small minority about whom negative beliefs have circulated for centuries, and when these beliefs have played a profound role in creating the society we live in now. Much of this is unthinking. People can be contradictory and incoherent when it comes to abstract issues like Jews and antisemitism, so they will believe antisemitic ideas even while disapproving of racism and bigotry. Antisemitism has been around for centuries and murdered millions, but for many it remains an obscure, and often misunderstood or unrecognised, phenomenon. This lack of understanding provides the space for antisemitism to keep returning, generation after generation, reflecting a failure to see what lies within as much as active and knowing antipathy.

Let's unpack Tahra Ahmed's Facebook post about Grenfell Tower being a 'Jewish sacrifice' to show what I mean. You might think that someone parroting such an obviously, and repulsively, antisemitic idea as this would have got it from the Nazis, but in this case you would be wrong, because the place Ahmed was channelling was not Nazi Germany but Norwich, and the history of this medieval myth shows just how enduring and adaptable antisemitism can be.

The story begins in 1144, when the body of a twelve-year-old boy called William was found in a wood outside Norwich. William's uncle blamed local Jews for his murder, but this came to nothing as there was no evidence of their guilt. This did not deter a monk called Thomas of Monmouth, who picked up the case a few years later and ran with it until the allegation took hold. At one level, it is a simple story of Jews being accused of murdering children, and it is difficult to think of a more despicable crime. Except Thomas of Monmouth did manage to come up with something even worse than child murder, because he and his fellow accusers designed their allegation to be a re-enactment of the charge that the Jews killed Jesus.

If you remember your bible stories, you will know that Jesus was a Jewish preacher who attracted a following for his radical sermons that were unpopular with Jewish religious leaders. He was arrested in Jerusalem by the Roman authorities on the eve of the Jewish festival of Passover, having been betrayed by Judas, who received thirty pieces of silver as a payment. The Roman prefect Pontius Pilate, so the story goes, gave the Jewish crowd an opportunity to ask for Jesus to be released, but they refused. Jesus was sentenced to death by crucifixion, which involved being nailed to a cross while wearing a crown of thorns before being stabbed in the side by a Roman soldier. After he died, Jesus was swiftly buried, only to miraculously rise from the dead three days later, ascend to heaven and give us all an excuse to eat chocolate eggs every Easter.

Whether or not this is an accurate account of real events is beside the point; what matters for us is how the details of Jesus's death shaped the accusation of Jewish child-murder in Norwich. First, the Jews who allegedly murdered young William were said to have put him on a cross and tortured him using the same methods by which Christ himself suffered. Second, the abduction and crucifixion of the child was said to have happened at Easter, in a further re-enactment of the Jews' biblical sin of deicide. Third, this was said to be a collective crime involving all Jews – meaning, as these blood libel cases spread, either all Jews in the towns where they occurred or all Jews in the whole country. Finally, it was believed that Jews were obliged by their religious commitments to commit this dreadful act. In other words, this was not just an allegation of child-murder, which would have been bad enough: it was very much specifically *Jewish* child murder, a collective crime carried out by a Jewish conspiracy, and motivated, so the allegation went, by a hatred of Christ and Christianity. This was the world's very first antisemitic blood libel charge, and it was invented right here in England.

It was in the Gospels, written a few decades after the crucifixion took place, that the incendiary charge of deicide was first laid at the feet of the Jewish people, with the added smear of Satanism thrown in. The Gospel of John described Jesus and the Jewish religious authorities as opposing forces in a cosmic struggle between God and the Devil. While Jesus speaks for God as his Father, John wrote, the Jews represent Satan himself: 'You are from your father, the devil, and you prefer to do what your father wants.'[3] The Gospel of Matthew tells the story of Jesus's life, arrest and eventual crucifixion, with the Jews firmly in the dock. Matthew depicts Jewish elders plotting to have Jesus executed and then inciting the crowd to call for him to be crucified. Matthew quotes Pilate, saying, 'I am innocent of this man's blood, it is your responsibility,' to which the Jewish people reportedly replied: 'His blood is on us and on our children.'[4] This is the *prima facie* evidence for perpetual Jewish guilt; for some people it really is on all Jews, for ever. Shortly after

Jeremy Corbyn's leadership of the Labour Party came to an end in April 2020, I tweeted a thread of allegations of antisemitism that Corbyn had faced throughout his leadership. A Twitter account called Interfaith For Palestine responded to me with the comment: 'JC was crucified by the extremist UK Jewish establishment. Another rejected Messiah.'

Now, your first thought might be that this is a novel approach to interfaith. And the coincidence that Jesus Christ and Jeremy Corbyn have the same initials was probably too much for this tweeter to resist. But there it is, the same 2,000-year-old charge in black and white: British Jews rejected Corbyn in the twenty-first century just like the Jews crucified Jesus back in ancient times.

Jesus and his disciples were all Jewish, but as time passed, adherents to his message started to reject the old ways and developed their own ideas about worship and belief. What began as an internal Jewish argument over Jesus's teachings gradually morphed into a hostile breakaway. The new religion of Christianity defined itself in opposition to Jews and Jewish practices, because that is what they were leaving behind, and Judaism came 'to possess for Christians a much more precise meaning, one that cast Jews as citizens of a presumed counter-point to Christianity'.[5] The vitriol circulated about Jews by some of the most influential and admired early Christian thinkers was truly appalling. Jews were accused of being murderers and child-killers, bloodthirsty devils known for cheating and thieving. Christians should have no contact with Jews, 'the common disgrace and infection of the whole world … they sacrificed their own daughters to demons'.[6] Even internal Christian debates over their new faith were sometimes framed in anti-Jewish terms. Christian protagonists would attack each other's doctrines and arguments by calling them 'Jewish' and accuse Christian rivals of 'Judaising' their beliefs, even when none of the people involved were Jews.

This might not have mattered, were it not for the fact that Christianity was adopted by the Roman Empire, became the dominant religion in all of Europe and subsequently spread across much of the world. Some of the most common anti-Jewish insults were already in circulation in Roman and Greek societies before early Christians picked them up, but it was through Christian writings that they became embedded. In time, a profound way of interpreting the world emerged in which Jews and Judaism were positioned as conceptually opposed to everything that is deemed good, wholesome, and humane. If you are asking where antisemitism comes from, why the Jews, and how it all began – this is as good a place as any to look for an answer.[7]

It is important to stress that Christianity is a vast and diverse religion. It would be grossly unfair and untrue to assume that most Christians today hold antisemitic beliefs or follow an antisemitic faith, and it is not my intention to imply any such thing. Even in the darkest times there have always been variations in how the Church engaged with, and responded to, Jews and Judaism, and different Christian denominations have made great efforts to repair the damage done by the history of anti-Jewish persecutions. In 1965 the Catholic Church made the historic announcement that Jews should not be held responsible for Jesus's death, declaring that while 'the Jewish authorities and those who followed their lead pressed for the death of Christ', it 'cannot be charged against all the Jews, without distinction, then alive, nor against the Jews of today', and 'the Jews should not be presented as rejected or accursed by God'.[8] Relations between the two faiths are very different now from how they have been in the past.

This good work is important and, hopefully, effective, but it cannot erase the fact that negative attitudes about Jews are part of the Christian baggage that Western civilisation carries around in almost everything it does – and certainly in anything relating to Jews. In May 2021, a protester was photographed on an anti-Israel demonstration in central London holding a home-made placard featuring an image of Jesus Christ carrying a large wooden cross with the word 'Palestinians' printed alongside. Underneath was the message, in bold capital letters: 'DO NOT LET THEM DO THE SAME THING TODAY AGAIN.'[9] It does not require a degree in theology to work out that 'them' means the Jews; the 'thing' they allegedly did was murder Jesus Christ, the son of God, who died on the Cross to save humanity; and the reason that Israel fights Palestinians in 2021 is, according to this placard, because Israel, the Jewish state, is the enemy of humanity now, just as Jews were back then. Even in our modern secular societies, the anti-Jewish motifs that early Christian writers developed nearly 2,000 years ago remain an essential piece of the puzzle if we are to understand why antisemitism has been around for so long and why it continues to take the forms that it does.

Tahra Ahmed isn't a Christian, but that isn't the point. Don't look for rationality when you are trying to work out how antisemites think. This is a story of myths and folk tales and traditional bogeymen being blamed for humanity's worst fears, and it can be applied to all sorts of scenarios. This was the beginning of a history we are all still living in today, one which 'encoded the threat of Judaism into some of the basic concepts of Western thought, regenerating that threat in new forms fitting for new periods'.[10] Two thousand years is a long time for the image of the Satanic, conspiring and merciless Jew to implant itself into the Western subconscious.

LITTLE SAINT HUGH

Allegations of Jewish child murder spread easily enough in medieval England. Often an invented tale of Jewish child-murder (they were all invented) was financially beneficial, attracting pilgrims and raising the status of a particular town or cathedral. The most famous English blood libel was in Lincoln in 1255, when the body of a young boy called Hugh, who had been missing for three weeks, was found at the bottom of a well near the home of a Jewish family. The owner of the house, a Jewish man called Copin, was tortured until he 'confessed' to murdering the boy, but this was not the end of the affair. Jews from all over the country were in Lincoln at the time to celebrate a wedding, and their presence was taken to be part of a murderous plot which, it was alleged, was performed on behalf of all the Jews of England. As in Norwich, the arrest of one Jew became an opportunity to put all Jews on trial. They were accused of holding young Hugh hostage for days, allegedly subjecting him to his own trial with 'a Jew of Lincoln as judge, to take the place of Pilate'. According to the most comprehensive account, the Jews were accused of crucifying Hugh, calling him 'Jesus the false prophet', and stabbing and beating him until he died.[11] The echoes of the original crucifixion story were hardly subtle. King Henry III came to Lincoln to investigate in person and ordered the execution of Copin and the prosecution of ninety-one other Jews. Eighteen of the accused refused to recognise the legitimacy of the trial and were immediately put to death; almost all the others were convicted and sentenced, but ultimately released. As for poor Hugh, he was buried in Lincoln Cathedral where his shrine became a well-known pilgrimage site, and his story inspired folk ballads and songs all the way into the twentieth century. You can still visit his tomb: it was only in 1959 that the cathedral put up a sign confirming that Hugh was not actually murdered by Jews and this was all an antisemitic myth.

There were other blood libel allegations in Gloucester, Winchester and other English towns, along with other persecutions. In Bury St Edmunds there was a blood libel charge in 1181, a massacre of fifty-seven Jews in 1190 (the day after the mass killing of 150 Jews in York) and soon afterwards all remaining Jews were expelled from the town. The fashion for accusing Jews of murdering children crossed the English Channel to France in 1171, where the entire Jewish community of Blois was wiped out following another false charge, and then on to Fulda, in central Germany, where it acquired its specifically bloody component. Thirty-four Jews were executed there in December 1235 because they were believed to have killed five boys who had been found burned to death. Crucially, the Jews of Fulda were accused of extracting blood from their victims, which they were said to have either consumed for medicinal purposes or used in some magical rite. Jewish dietary laws forbid the consumption even of animal blood, never mind human blood – try getting a decent medium-rare kosher steak and you'll see what I mean – but this did not stop future allegations of Jewish child-murder from incorporating this macabre element. Why let facts get in the way of a powerful, if completely baseless, myth?

Jews were said to need Christian blood either to use in religious rituals, or to bake the *matzo* (unleavened bread) that Jews eat at

Passover, or to drink neat because the Jews' own blood was somehow deficient. Either Christian blood had special properties desired by Jews, or the Jews were driven by their own hatred to defile the blood of Christ. The whole theatre of the blood libel, with its evocation of the crucifixion, would have been understood in the light of Catholic doctrine that the body and blood of Jesus become bread and wine through transubstantiation. In a sense, the idea that Jews had a physiological need to consume Christian blood as a way of supplementing their own physical inadequacies prefigured modern racial antisemitism's belief that Jews are biologically inferior.

Papal authorities never endorsed the blood libel charge and issued formal rulings condemning it as false, but they were regularly undermined by local bishops who benefited, both financially and status-wise, from having the shrine of an alleged child martyr under their control. Popular belief in blood libel myths was widespread and the child martyrs often attained the status of unofficial saints, celebrated via feast days and pilgrimages. There were dozens of blood libel allegations in central Europe in the two centuries following the murders of Jews in Fulda, often leading to the arrest, torture, forced confessions and executions or expulsions of Jewish populations.

This is horrible stuff and it all feels long ago, but elements of the blood libel are still very much with us. The spectre of vampires ghosting into people's homes and draining them of blood is constructed, in part, from these old blood libel stories. The most famous vampire of them all, Dracula, draws implicitly on anti-Jewish motifs, featuring as it does a diabolic figure from eastern Europe (written at a time of mass Jewish immigration from eastern Europe to Britain), mysteriously wealthy, with a hooked nose and beard, who drinks blood and shrinks from the sight of a Cross. The QAnon conspiracy movement, which has become very popular across the American far right and has made inroads into the UK, holds that politicians, celebrities and other powerful figures are part of a satanic conspiracy to kidnap and traffic children. This includes, in an echo of the blood libel, the suggestion that elite figures in American society either drink children's blood or harvest a specific chemical from it to inject into themselves for medicinal purposes. This derivative of the blood libel even made an appearance in the 2020 film *Borat Subsequent Moviefilm*, in a scene where two QAnon believers tell Sacha Baron Cohen (or rather, his alter-ego Borat) that Hillary Clinton and other Democrats torture children and drink their blood. In a surreal twist, the following year Hillary Clinton went public to insist that this rumour isn't true and ask people to stop spreading it. The fact she felt compelled to do so is a sign of how widely this bizarre belief had spread. Research by Media Matters for America identified fifty-nine Republican candidates for Congress in the 2022 elections who had endorsed or promoted the QAnon movement.[12]

Despite the similarities to the blood libel, QAnon does not always have an explicitly anti-Jewish element. This is not as strange as it sounds: antisemitic ways of thinking about conspiracies of power, child sacrifice and so on, often transmute into non-antisemitic versions while retaining the same distorted interpretation of how the world works. This is one way that antisemitism is harmful for society as a whole, not just for Jews: it messes with your brain and replaces rational thought with weird, improbable belief. What starts with calumnies about Jews ends up perverting national politics. And before anyone in the UK gets snooty about gullible Americans falling for crazy conspiracy theories, a 2020 poll by the anti-fascist organisation Hope Not Hate looking into potential QAnon support in the UK found 25 per cent of British people agreed that 'Secret Satanic cults exist and include influential elites', while a 2022 poll by the same organisation found 35 per cent of British people believe that '"elites" in Hollywood, politics, the media and other powerful positions are secretly engaging in large scale child trafficking and abuse'.[13]

The blood libel also colours some of the more lurid depictions of Israel as a uniquely, unfathomably cruel nation that delights in killing Palestinian children and has an unusual taste for bloodletting. Nation of Islam leader Louis Farrakhan has described American Jews as 'bloodsuckers', while former Egyptian President Mohamed Morsi used the same term to refer to Israel.[14] In 2012 the Supreme Leader of Iran, Ayatollah Khamenei, claimed that Iran is threatened by 'bloodsucker capitalists and Zionists'.[15] The implication is that Jews, Zionists or Israel are figurative bloodsuckers, draining the lifeforce from other nations, a modern political metaphor rooted in the Middle Ages. In May 2021, a student at Warwick University went to an anti-Israel demonstration with a home-made placard showing Israeli Prime Minister Benjamin Netanyahu as a devil ('Satanyahu', it was captioned) literally drinking from a bottle of blood. This student may not have been aware that they were perpetuating a 900-year-old anti-Jewish myth, but you can't understand that placard without knowing about the blood libel.[16]

There's a striking image on an Iranian cartoon website, drawn in 2006 by a Brazilian cartoonist called Carlos Latuff, of a Gaza-shaped swimming pool full of blood and skulls, from which then Israeli Prime Minister Ehud Olmert has just emerged, drying the blood off himself with an Israeli flag. The American figure of Uncle Sam is lounging in the pool while a waiter labelled 'United Nations' brings him a drink of pure blood in a cocktail glass. It is a stomach-churning image and it revolves around this same old idea: not just that Israel spills Palestinian blood – that happens in all wars – but that they luxuriate in the feel and taste of it. That they literally drink blood.[17] Carlos Latuff is a popular cartoonist whose work features prolifically across anti-Israel and anti-Western online spaces. Most notoriously, the same year that he drew this blood-soaked image, he also won second prize in an Iranian competition to draw cartoons about the Holocaust.

You can detect the echo of the blood libel in some of the more gruesome allegations of Israeli inhumanity. In 2009 the Swedish newspaper *Aftonbladet* claimed that Israel systematically harvested organs from Palestinians. That same year a version incorporating child-abduction began circulating in Arabic-language media, in which 'Jewish rings' supposedly kidnapped Algerian children and extracted their organs for export to America and Israel,[18] before appearing in English on Iran's Press TV under the headline: 'New Jewish organ theft gang busted.'[19] These stories were either completely untrue or wildly distorted stories of actual prosecutions for other crimes, but it was a neat case study in how a false tale like this can gain traction. This led to a minor political scandal in Britain in 2010, when the Liberal Democrat's health spokesperson in the House of Lords, Baroness Jenny Tonge, was sacked from her party role after calling for an inquiry into internet rumours that Israel had used its humanitarian aid programme in Haiti to harvest organs from victims of the devastating earthquake suffered by the Caribbean nation.

It would be easy to dismiss blood libels as medieval superstition and assume they have been left in the distant past, but the myth of Jewish child-murder retained its power to incite hatred and murder well into the twentieth century and the scientific age. It was prominently deployed in Nazi propaganda against Jews, especially in Julius Streicher's notorious *Der Sturmer* newspaper, but the Nazis were only reaping a well-watered crop. There were blood libel allegations and trials of Jews in Russia, Austria–Hungary, Germany and Bulgaria in the decades leading up to the Holocaust. They began to appear in the Middle East from the mid-1800s onwards, particularly in countries influenced by European colonialism, with blood libels in Syria, Egypt, Palestine, Iran and Turkey. According to one estimate, 'There were more recorded instances of the blood libel between 1870 and 1940 than in the entire preceding period of some 700 years.'[20]

Some cases achieved international notoriety. In 1911 the body of a Christian boy was found near a Jewish-owned brick factory in Kiev (then in Russia, now the Ukrainian capital Kyiv) and Mendel Beilis, the factory foreman, was arrested. His trial stirred up all the old folk tales about Jewish ritual murder and lasted for two years before he was finally acquitted (although the jury did not reject the idea of Jewish ritual murder *per se*). In a sign of how far the Christian establishment had shifted from its medieval forebears, a letter of protest declaring this trial to be an 'utterly baseless libel on Judaism' was jointly signed by the heads of UK Christian denominations, including the Archbishops of Canterbury, York and Armagh, the Cardinal Archbishop of Westminster, several bishops, peers, judges and the principals of eleven Oxford colleges.[21] Similar protests were written by Christian leaders in France, Germany and by many dignitaries within Russia itself. An earlier case in 1903 had seen the death of a Christian boy near Kishinev in Russia (now Chișinău, the capital of Moldova) become the pretext for a two-day pogrom* over Easter that left forty-nine Jews dead, nearly 500 wounded and around 2,000 homeless. The level of violence in Kishinev was horrific. According to one account, 'Nails were driven through heads; bodies, hacked in half; bellies, split open and filled with feathers. Women and girls were raped, and some had their breasts cut off.'[22] This occurred in the midst of large-scale Jewish emigration from increasing persecution under Tsarist rule. Two million Jews left Russia in the years between 1881 and 1914, around 150,000 of whom ended up in Britain, and Kishinev and other pogroms accelerated their departure. Just as blood libels had helped to create the atmosphere that saw Jews expelled from England in 1290, so they contributed to the flow of Jews back into this country over 600 years later.

The blood libel even became the subject of a British court ruling in 2012, when an immigration tribunal ruled that Sheikh Ra'ed Salah, an Islamic leader from Israel, had used a 'blood libel against Jews' in a speech in Jerusalem in 2007. Salah had been arrested on the orders of the then Home Secretary Theresa May, who had initially tried to prevent him from entering the country and wanted him deported. The case hinged on a few examples of Salah's writings and speeches that May said justified his exclusion, one of which was a speech from 2007 that included this blood libel reference:

> We are not a nation that is based on values of envy. We are not a nation that is based on values of vengeance. We have never allowed

---

* 'Pogrom' comes from the Russian word for devastation or violent destruction, and was the name given to widespread mob violence, often done with official sanction, against Jews in Russia in the late nineteenth and early twentieth centuries.

ourselves, and listen carefully; we have never allowed ourselves to knead the bread for the breaking [of] fasting during the blessed month of Ramadan with the blood of the children. And if someone wants a wider explanation, then he should ask what used to happen to some of the children of Europe, when their blood used to be mixed in the dough of the holy bread. God almighty, is this religion?[23]

Salah won his overall immigration case against Theresa May, but the tribunal ruled against him on the blood libel point. He had his supporters in this country, even after that ruling. He was subsequently sentenced to eight months in prison in Israel for inciting a riot with this speech, and the whole row was revived when Jeremy Corbyn, who had campaigned for Salah and maintained his support for him after the ruling, became Labour Party leader. Once again, the strangest of medieval myths about Jews held its relevance in 21st-century British politics.

I had a minor role in this affair because the organisation I work for, the Community Security Trust (CST), campaigned for Salah to be excluded from the country. As part of these discussions I met a senior *Guardian* journalist who had been due to meet Salah when he was arrested. This journalist was strongly critical of both the Home Secretary and CST's position, but promised that if it turned out that Salah had, as alleged, made a speech invoking the blood libel, he would be the first to condemn him for it. Ten years after a British court ruled that this was indeed the case, I'm still waiting for his condemnation. Another prominent journalist, writing about the case for a different left-wing outlet, asked me whether I really thought Salah was antisemitic or if this was just about his anti-Israel activism. It is difficult to convey how infuriating it was to have to justify, to avowed anti-racists writing for progressive media outlets, why Salah's invocation of the blood libel was such a problem for Jews. Why this wasn't just an excuse we'd come up with to slander a fierce critic of Israel, but a real, visceral fear of the influence Salah's medieval Jew-hatred could have on his British audiences. It felt very lonely.

MURDEROUS VERSE

I feel obliged to tell you that every allegation that Jews kidnapped and murdered children for some religious or cultural purpose was a fake. None of them ever happened. The world of antisemitism is an entire ecosystem of ridiculous, improbable and outrageous allegations about Jews which, despite their absurdity, nevertheless need refuting because they have sometimes been so widely believed. George Orwell wrote in 1945 that 'one of the marks of antisemitism is an ability to believe stories that could not possibly be true', and that is as true now as it was when he wrote it.[24] Every single allegation of Jewish child-murder or blood libel was invented, fabricated or simply imagined, with evidence concocted and false confessions extracted under torture. In some cases there was never even a dead body or a missing child on which to hang the story. Some conspiracy theories have a kernel of truth, which then gets twisted beyond recognition, but the blood libel was wholly invented out of thin air.

Despite this, blood libel stories became so well-known that they even made it into one of English literature's most celebrated works, Geoffrey Chaucer's *The Canterbury Tales*. Written in the late 1300s, *The Canterbury Tales* takes the form of a series of poems attributed to a group of fictional pilgrims: a knight, a cook, a physician, a merchant and various other characters, who entertain each other with stories as they journey to Canterbury. One of the poems, 'The Prioress's Tale', is set in a fictional town with a Jewish ghetto, through which a seven-year-old Christian boy walks to and from school each day. This boy sings hymns as he walks along 'the Jewish street', which, the Prioress tells us, enrages the local Jews who cannot bear to hear his pure Christian tones. These Jews are 'hateful to Christ and all his company', so they plot for a 'cursed Jew' to grab the child, cut his throat and dump him in a pit. However, in a heavenly miracle willed by Christ himself and enacted by the Virgin mother, the deceased boy continues to sing his hymns from beneath the ground. The evil deed is thus exposed and 'all the Jews' are arrested, tried and hanged.[25] Chaucer's version, like the original blood libels, is a straightforward reworking of Jesus's crucifixion and resurrection, with the Jews yet again in the dock. Hugh of Lincoln gets a mention at the end:

> Hugh of Lincoln, likewise murdered so
> By cursed Jews, as is notorious
> (For it was but a little time ago).

By the time Chaucer wrote these lines the Jews of England were long gone, having been expelled *en masse* in 1290 'because of their crimes and the honour of the Crucified Jesus'.[26] Their expulsion was preceded by another blood libel allegation, this time in Northampton in 1279. England was the first country in Europe to rid itself of all its Jews – another English contribution to the antisemitic toolkit – and Jews were not allowed to return to this country until Oliver Cromwell invited them back in 1656. Despite their physical absence from England for almost a century by the time *The Canterbury*

Tales was written, Chaucer (like Shakespeare 200 years later) must have been confident that the archetype of the child-murdering Jew would be familiar enough for his audience.

I have a lovely copy of *The Canterbury Tales*, given to me by my parents as a Chanukah gift when I was sixteen.* It is a beautiful hardback edition published in 1986 to mark the (approximate) 600th anniversary of the *Tales*, complete with almost 300 illustrations, many in full colour, and a foreword by Melvyn Bragg. It was exactly the kind of thing my parents liked to imagine their sixteen-year-old son wanted as a Chanukah present, and naturally, being a teenage boy, I dumped it on my bookshelf and didn't read it. But I'm reading it now, and I'm struck by how little the antisemitism of 'The Prioress's Tale' is acknowledged. It isn't mentioned in Melvyn Bragg's foreword or in the longer introduction. The blurb on the dust jacket remarks on how readers 'smile at his coy prioress who intones her prayers through her nose and speaks daintily in French', but there is no 21st-century trigger warning that the 'coy prioress' has something more sinister to share. Inside, 'The Prioress's Tale' is illustrated by a large colour picture, taken from a fourteenth-century manuscript, that is captioned as depicting 'a Jew who threw his own child into an oven because he had been contaminated by entering a Christian church'. The belief that Jews would murder their own children simply for entering a church was itself part of the antisemitic medieval mythology that Jews had a predilection for child-murder, but it is presented in my edition of *The Canterbury Tales* as fact. Even worse, the same caption insists by way of

---

* Chanukah is a Jewish festival when adults traditionally give children gifts. Like many Jewish festivals, it celebrates the defeat of ancient enemies: in this case, the Greeks who had occupied Judea in 167 BCE and, so the story goes, defiled the Temple in Jerusalem and banned many Jewish practices. Chanukah falls in winter, and the coincidence with Christmas has led to significant gift inflation in many Jewish households.

explanation that 'the hostility of the Christian world towards the Jews in the middle ages was fully reciprocated'.

Let's linger in medieval England a little longer to explore just how misplaced that phrase, 'fully reciprocated', truly is. The increasing fervour for the Crusades in the twelfth century led to an explosion of anti-Jewish violence in England in 1189 that spread with vicious speed across the country. The spark was the coronation of King Richard I at Westminster Abbey, which Jews had been banned from attending. Various Jewish notables turned up anyway to pay their respects but were set upon by the crowd, who beat around thirty of them to death before setting off to the Jewish quarter of London to seek further victims. The false rumour spread that the newly crowned Crusader king had ordered all Jews to be killed, and massacres of Jews duly followed in several towns around England. Richard I demanded an end to the violence and for a while it abated, but by 1190 the king was in France and bands of Crusaders who were assembling in towns across the country took advantage of his absence to go on the rampage once again. Why wait until you get to the Holy Land to slaughter unbelievers when you can start right here, so the thinking went. In Norwich seventeen Jews, including adults and children, were thrown down a well near to the Jewish quarter, where their bodies lay undisturbed for 814 years until builders digging the foundations of the Chapelfield shopping centre in 2004 found their remains. Borat's satirical song 'Throw the Jew Down the Well' was more accurate than its creator, Sacha Baron Cohen, probably realised.

The most notorious of all the massacres in 1190 came in York, where around 150 Jews were killed after seeking refuge in Clifford's Tower in the centre of the city (some took their own lives rather than face the mob). Amongst the bloodlust, their killers took the opportunity to burn all the bonds and debtors' notes held by the deceased Jews, conveniently freeing themselves from any records of money owed. It is a reminder that there was often an economic motive to killing Jews, either through plunder or the cancellation of debts.

In 1215 the Catholic Church's Fourth Lateran Council prohibited Jews from holding public office because 'it would be too absurd for a blasphemer of Christ to exercise power over Christians', and ruled that Jews and Muslims must wear special clothes to mark them out so that they could be identified in public.[27] You read that right. Pictures of Jews living under Nazi rule in the 1930s and 1940s wearing yellow stars is one of the most searing images of the Holocaust, but Nazi Germany did not invent the idea that Jews must wear special badges to mark them out. This was a feature of life for Jews in several European countries 700 years before the Nazis came up with it (and it originated in Muslim-ruled lands before that). In England the need for Jews to wear an identifying badge on their clothing was confirmed by royal decree in 1218. Four years later the Synod of Oxford issued a further raft of restrictions on Jewish life including details about the exact shape, size and colour of the identifying mark that Jews had to wear. In 2022 the Church of England marked the 800th anniversary of this Synod by issuing an apology to British Jews, to which I think the only appropriate response can be: better late than never.

This brings us to Leicester, where in 1231 Jews were expelled by Simon de Montfort, Earl of Leicester (followed over the next twenty years by similar expulsions in Newcastle, Derby, Wycombe, Warwick, Southampton, Berkhamsted, Cambridge and elsewhere).

Simon de Montfort was a notably enthusiastic champion of anti-Jewish measures and was responsible for multiple massacres of Jews in 1264, including the murder of up to 500 Jews in London. Despite this he now has a university named after him in Leicester, and you will struggle to find any mention of his role in the mass murder of English Jews on De Montfort University's website. Every now and again this becomes a minor local controversy, most recently in November 2020 when the Students' Union called for a name change because 'this is not a name which is reflective of our core values and beliefs'. I assume De Montfort University did not name itself after an antisemitic mass murderer *because* he had murdered hundreds of Jews, and Simon de Montfort did lots of other things that would legitimately justify having things in Leicester named after him. But I do think they could be more open about the darker side of de Montfort's record than is currently the case. Being a university, perhaps they could see their way to teaching a course about England's medieval persecutions of Jews and their namesake's role in that history.[28]

I'm always conscious, when talking and writing about antisemitism, that there is a temptation to only discuss the worst aspects of our existence, and there was much more to Jewish medieval life than these horrors suggest. However, this is a book about antisemitism, not a history of Jewish life in the round, and there are aspects of Britain's contribution to this sordid history that have never been fully absorbed into our sense of who we are as a country.

The events of 1290, when the Jews were finally expelled by Edward I, were the culmination of a slow deterioration in status, marked by new methods of persecuting and libelling Jews that would, in time, be taken up across the world. This was not a planned or coordinated campaign and it happened over more than a century, but with hindsight the pattern of English persecution, from defamations, to mob violence, legal oppression and finally elimination, took a form that loosely resembles the incremental steps taken by Nazi Germany over a much shorter time period hundreds of years later. I'm not claiming that one inspired the other, but the imprint of medieval antisemitism is detectable centuries later, like a fossilised footprint in the rock in which water pools the same way every time it rains. This history matters.

I think about all of this sometimes when I walk past the Houses of Parliament. At one end, outside the House of Lords, is a statue of Richard I, posing majestically on his horse with sword raised. At the other, outside the House of Commons, stands Oliver Cromwell looking rather less regal. These two figures bracket the demise of English Jewry in the Middle Ages and its rebirth and renewal in modern Britain; there they both are, outside the home of British democracy, entirely mute about the pivotal roles they played in the fate of Jews in this country. It is proposed that the UK's Holocaust Memorial and Learning Centre will be built just along from Parliament, within shouting distance of these two statues, yet the role played by this country in inventing and exporting the antisemitism that led, ultimately, to genocide, is almost completely unknown. It ought to be part of our telling of why the Holocaust happened, and why, in the twentieth century, so many Europeans tried to exterminate the Jews. Which brings us, amongst other things, to motor cars.

CHAPTER FOUR

CARS, CONSPIRACIES AND COVID

You can't go far wrong buying someone a book, if you know what they are interested in. People usually buy me books about history, politics, music or football, and the more of those subjects that any book includes (ideally all in combination) the happier I am. A few years ago, a friend was flying home via Dubai and bought me a book by Henry Ford – that's Ford as in Ford cars – that he saw in the airport bookshop. It includes a lot about history and politics, there's a chapter about jazz, and while it doesn't mention football there is a chapter about baseball, so sport is covered, sort of. Henry Ford was one of the greatest industrialists of the twentieth century and the creator of mass-produced motor cars. He introduced assembly line production and a whole host of other innovations that we take for granted today. Ford also took a keen interest in the world at large, including things you would expect, like the state of the economy and America's foreign policy, and other subjects you might not, like traditional culture, nature conservation and the preservation of American rural life. In 1919 he took over a weekly newspaper called the *Dearborn Independent* (Dearborn, Michigan, is where his car plant is based) and used it to set forth his views on the world, in a weekly column that was ghost-written in his name. These columns were compiled and published as a book, which is what my friend saw on sale in Dubai airport. And he knew I would be interested in reading it, because it had an eye-catching title: *The Complete International Jew: The World's Foremost Problem*.

Yes, that's right: the guy who made Ford cars the most famous vehicles on earth was also one of the twentieth century's most influential antisemites. He was a hero to Adolf Hitler, who kept a photograph of him on his desk (Hitler called him 'Henrich Ford', which I can't help imagining in a comedic, Basil Fawlty accent). Let me reassure you that I am not about to suggest you boycott Ford cars. I have owned a couple myself in the past without any complaints, so if you are keen to keep hold of your Ford Fiesta, don't worry – it doesn't make you an accomplice to anti-Jewish hate. But the story of why Henry Ford became America's leading propagator of antisemitism in the 1920s is a tale about what people use antisemitism for, and the usefulness of antisemitism is a crucial part of its enduring appeal.

There were a lot of problems exercising Henry Ford during that period of his life. He opposed America's involvement in the First World War, lost a political campaign to become the Democrat Senator for Michigan, fought a bruising libel suit against the *Chicago Tribune* who called him an 'ignorant idealist' (Ford won, but was humiliated in the process) and had various industrial problems as he tried to push forward with his visionary production methods. Further afield, political instability following the end of the Great War and the Russian Revolution troubled him, as did ongoing immigration into the United States. Ford became increasingly convinced that the source of all these problems was the Jews, and he gathered a group of investigators to compile material for a weekly column explaining this to his readers. From May 1920 until January 1922 they focused on nothing else. The *Dearborn Independent* had a circulation of 300,000; in book form, *The International Jew* sold half a million copies in the United States and was translated into several languages for sale abroad. You can still buy it online from Waterstones, Foyles and Barnes & Noble (it exposes 'Jewish-inspired evil', according to the blurb on the Barnes & Noble website),[1] but I wouldn't bother.

The range of subjects it covers is extraordinary. Jews, according to Ford, have a malign influence across business, politics and the media. They control Hollywood and were behind the Russian Revolution. Political corruption, alcohol and gambling in America are all down to the Jews; they even incite rowdy behaviour at baseball matches and fix American wrestling. Ford painted a picture of America in which every social or political problem was due to Jewish meddling:

> In baseball corruption – a group of Jews. In exploitative finance – a group of Jews. In theatrical degeneracy – a group of Jews. In liquor propaganda – a group of Jews. In control of national war policies – a group of Jews. Absolutely dominating the wireless communications of the world – a group of Jews. In the menace of the movies – a group of Jews. In control of the Press through business and financial pressure – a group of Jews. War profiteers, 80 per cent of them – Jews. Organisers of active opposition of Christian laws and customs – Jews.[2]

My absolute favourite is Ford's conviction that Jews are to blame for jazz. 'Jazz is a Jewish creation,' he writes. 'The mush, the slush, the sly suggestion, the abandoned sensuousness of sliding notes, are of Jewish origin.'[3] If only. There have been many Jewish jazz greats, but I don't think my people can truly take credit for this most sublime of artforms, any more than we were to blame for drunken baseball fans booing opposing players.

It is easy to look down on conspiracy theorists as fantasists and cranks who cannot keep up with the demands of modern life, or are resentful at the achievements of their peers and need a way to avoid responsibility for their failures. Losers tend to look for scapegoats to blame for their problems. Conspiracy theories offer this, with the added sense of prestige and fascination that comes with hidden knowledge. They provide a different route to expertise, one that is not acquired by the orthodoxy of the school curriculum, university study or listening to recognised authorities. In this way conspiracy theories become an alternative elitism: only we are smart enough to see through the fog of misinformation and perceive the real truth, so the thinking goes. The appeal is especially strong when it feels like everything you took for granted has suddenly, inexplicably, collapsed, because in such circumstances the promise of an explanation – any explanation, however farfetched or apocalyptic – can be comforting.

However, this doesn't account for why antisemitism grabs the imagination of people across all strata of society, including those at the very top. Henry Ford was, at that time, one of the most famous, successful and influential people on the planet, yet even he, faced with the complexity of an unstable world and the fractures of a growing, modern society, reached for the simplicity of antisemitism to explain it all. Perhaps, deep down, he felt partly responsible for creating some of these problems himself, given his role in America's industrial, urban growth, but still: why do people fall for this stuff?

Perhaps the thing that gets you going in today's world is immigration. Why are there so many non-white people coming to live in Europe or the United States, with their strange languages, customs and religions? A rational answer to this question is that they may be fleeing poverty, war or persecution. Perhaps they are ambitious people who admire the relative prosperity, stability and freedom in the West and want to build a better life for themselves and their families than they can get in their home countries. There is usually a combination of reasons why people leave everything they know behind and try their luck in a strange land. That was the case for my great-grandparents, who left Russia over a century ago, and it is why so many migrants continue to make perilous journeys around the world today. But an American called Robert Bowers had a different answer. He believed that immigration into the United States was orchestrated by Jews who wielded it as a weapon to undermine, and ultimately replace, the white race. This is a common belief across the far right, and it even has a name: the Great Replacement Theory.* A convinced neo-Nazi, Bowers was enraged when he saw that his local synagogue in Pittsburgh, USA, was working with a refugee charity called the Hebrew Immigrant Aid Society (HIAS), which had originally been set up in 1881 to support Jewish immigrants

---

* The idea that Jews are behind non-white immigration has been around for a long time, well before it had the name 'Great Replacement Theory'. You can even find an example of it in *Mein Kampf*, where Adolf Hitler railed against the presence of black people in Germany by blaming it on – well, you can probably guess. 'The Jews were responsible for bringing negroes into the Rhineland, with the ultimate idea of bastardising the white race which they hate and thus lowering its cultural and political level so that the Jew might dominate,' he wrote. Hitler was infuriated by the idea that black people might dilute the so-called racial purity of white Europe, and he thought this was all part of a Jewish plot.

to the United States and now assists immigrants and refugees of many different backgrounds. 'HIAS likes to bring invaders in that kill our people,' read his final post on Gab, a fringe social media site favoured by far-right extremists, shortly before he set off for the synagogue on that Saturday morning. 'I can't sit by and watch my people get slaughtered. Screw your optics, I'm going in.' So in he went, armed with an assault rifle and several handguns, and shot dead eleven Jews at the Tree of Life Synagogue in October 2018. During the subsequent shootout with police, Bowers apparently said: 'They're committing genocide to my people. I just want to kill Jews.'[4]

Or maybe you are a young man who struggles to find a girlfriend and feminism is the thing that makes your blood boil. Almost exactly one year after the Pittsburgh synagogue murders, another neo-Nazi called Stephan Balliet tried to shoot his way into a German synagogue on the Jewish holiday of Yom Kippur. Balliet was a pathetic character in many ways, who blamed Jews for his personal failures in life. Before leaving his car to attack the synagogue he made a video in which he blamed Jews for feminism, which, he argued, threatened the birth rate of white Europeans (he also espoused a wider range of antisemitic and racist views). In the end Balliet didn't kill any Jews because his home-made gun couldn't blast through the synagogue door, so instead he murdered a random passer-by and then drove to a nearby kebab shop, where he shot dead one of the customers.

Bowers and Balliet both bought into the fundamental utility of antisemitism. It won't tell you what is wrong with the world, as that depends on your own fixations and prejudices, but it will tell you *why* that thing happens, and the answer is reliably the same, every time. They both started out with a hatred of something that isn't Jewish – immigration for one, feminism for the other – and both ended up hating Jews because they blamed them for these supposed problems. This is the secret knowledge that antisemitism promises to its adherents, and blaming a hidden Jewish hand is much simpler than navigating the complex factors that lie behind gender relations or the global flow of migrants and refugees.

Most antisemitism comes down to the idea that Jews are always up to something. It is not enough simply to dislike Jews: antisemites will believe that whatever Jews say and do, they must have some ulterior motive or hidden purpose that explains their real intentions, and this secret Jewish purpose will be harmful to humanity. Or, to flip it around, if something terrible, dangerous or frightening is happening in the world, whether it is war, terrorism, an economic crash or a global pandemic, some people cannot resist the temptation to find a Jew (or a bunch of Jews) who they can either blame for making it happen or accuse of benefiting from it. It is a fantasy about the fearsome danger of Jewish wealth and power, combined with an assumption of Jewish malevolence, that is deployed to explain why things go wrong. Antisemites find 'the existence of the Jew absolutely necessary',[5] wrote Jean-Paul Sartre, because this fantasy about a Jewish conspiracy explains away their own fears and failings. This conspiracism is antisemitism's defining characteristic, an extra dimension that differentiates it from other forms of prejudice. Sometimes these conspiracy theories focus on specific Jewish individuals such as the Rothschild banking family. Sometimes they draw in large numbers of Jews. In modern times these conspiracy theories tend to focus more on Israel, but they derive from the same underlying way of thinking about Jews.

Needless to say, if your answer to why things are going wrong is to blame the Jews, you aren't going to find a genuine solution to your problems – but for some people it seems like any answer is better than none. Few of us, I imagine, had spent any time thinking about lockdowns, masks, vaccines, school closures, social distancing and the rest before Covid-19 swept across the globe in early 2020. Most people were completely unprepared for the bewildering, restrictive and at times deeply destabilising impact of the pandemic, but, as ever, antisemitism was available as an explanation for anyone who wanted to reach for it. The counter-extremism think tank Moonshot looked at millions of tweets about Covid in the first two months of the pandemic and found that, while conspiracy theories about Chinese responsibility predominated,

> there has also been a clear, albeit much smaller rise in the use of anti-Semitic hashtags ... These Tweets typically employ anti-Semitic tropes, such as the notion that a Jewish-led 'world government' or 'deep state' is using the virus to suppress and kill large swathes of the population in an effort to control the global economy.[6]

An investigation by the British government's independent adviser on antisemitism found antisemitic posts in twenty-two out of twenty-eight Facebook groups dedicated to Covid conspiracy theories or anti-vaccine propaganda.[7] In Germany, antisemitic posts increased thirteen-fold across Twitter, Facebook and Telegram during the pandemic; in France they increased seven-fold.[8] The pandemic boosted interest in, and exposure to, conspiracy theories in general, and this rising tide inevitably carries antisemitism with it. It would be naive for us to wonder why antisemitism has surged when current conditions seem perfectly designed to encourage it.

Some antisemitic posts argued that the virus was a hoax designed to instil fear and allow governments (secretly controlled by Jews, naturally) to impose draconian restrictions on daily life. Others posited that the virus was real and was developed and spread by Jews to kill off a large chunk of the non-Jewish population. These might seem contradictory in their details – either the Covid-19 virus exists or it doesn't – but they serve the same purpose, because both ultimately blame it all on a Jewish conspiracy. When vaccines became available in late 2020, the focus of pandemic antisemitism shifted from blaming Jews for the virus to claiming that vaccines are being developed by Jewish scientists to poison the population. An investigation of eleven different anti-lockdown or anti-vaccine Telegram channels, with a combined membership of around 60,000, found they all included antisemitic posts.[9] 'Covid is a lie, the Holocaust is a lie, Fuck the Jews,' read one piece of graffiti in London in 2021.[10]

POISONING THE WELLS

The reason why some people believe these ideas today is because, like hikers following a trail across unfamiliar terrain, they are walking a path trodden into our world by millions of people before them in times long forgotten. In the late 1340s the Black Death ravaged Europe, killing between a third and a half of the population, and in many locations Jews were blamed for spreading the plague by poisoning wells. Some towns, such as Zurich, banned Jews before the plague arrived in a futile attempt to prevent it from entering the city; in others they put Jews on trial after it had arrived. By 1349 a wave of anti-Jewish violence spread into Germany and several places witnessed awful atrocities. In Strasbourg, 900 Jews were burned and the rest were banned from the city. In Basel, Jews were rounded up and imprisoned in a house which was then burned down, killing all inside. Bonn, Mainz, Cologne and a dozen other German and Swiss towns saw Jews hounded, arrested, burned and banished, with whole communities devastated. Alleged poisoners were tortured into 'confessing' that their crimes were part of a wider Jewish plot. The image of Jews as poisoners, either literally or metaphorically as a threat to the health of the nation, became fixed.

I don't want to give the impression that Jewish history is nothing more than a story of persecution and suffering. There is much more colour and life to it than that, both today and in the past, but the rise and fall of Jewish communities are often bookended by tales of violence, discrimination, expulsion and flight. By 1500 western Europe was largely emptied of its Jews, the Black Death persecutions finishing a process begun by England in 1290, and a lot of these displaced Jews found sanctuary in Poland and Lithuania, who welcomed Jewish settlement. This became the great Jewish civilisation of eastern Europe, the centre of the Jewish world, until it was itself annihilated in the Nazi Holocaust; the Nazis, following in this tradition, described Jews as a virus. In a detail that remains astonishing however many times you read it, antisemitic violence and support for the Nazi Party in Germany in the 1920s and 1930s was higher in towns and cities that had also seen well-poisoning allegations and anti-Jewish pogroms during the Black Death 600 years earlier. We know this because a pair of German economists decided to compare records of anti-Jewish violence in Germany during the Black Death with levels of anti-Jewish sentiment and pro-Nazi activity in Nazi Germany. What they found was a remarkable persistence of anti-Jewish attitudes across six centuries. Even when they accounted for the size, location, demography and politics of different towns,

> places that witnessed violent attacks on Jews during the plague in 1349 also showed more anti-Semitic attitudes more than half a millennium later: their inhabitants engaged in more anti-Semitic violence in the 1920s, were more likely to vote for the Nazi Party before 1930, wrote more letters to the country's most anti-Semitic newspaper, organised more deportations of Jews, and engaged in more attacks on synagogues.[11]

It's a warning against complacency. If you live in a place that has persecuted Jews in the past – and if you live anywhere in Europe, you almost certainly do – this inheritance of antisemitic potential lies dormant beneath the soil. Don't let it awake.

FAKE NEWS FROM RUSSIA

The great codifier of all antisemitic conspiracy theories was a book called *The Protocols of the Learned Elders of Zion*, which originated as a hoax cooked up by Russian intelligence officers at the beginning of the twentieth century. It inspired Henry Ford, amongst others, and became the most notorious and influential conspiracist text ever written: by one estimate, in the two decades prior to the Second World War it sold more copies worldwide than any book other than the bible.[12] The *Protocols* claimed to be the minutes of clandestine meetings held by the leaders of the secret Jewish conspiracy that revealed their plans to dominate the world, but in fact it was plagiarised from a much older French political satire that had nothing to do with Jews. It was not the first effort of its kind, but it was the most popular, and it had some novel features that have made it a template for conspiracy theories ever since.

Rather than limiting itself to accusing Jews of conspiring to commit individual crimes as happened in the Middle Ages, the *Protocols* constructed an all-encompassing theory of a Jewish plot, not just to murder a child or poison a well, but to take over the entire world. Accordingly, either the Jews controlled every lever in society – the media, the economy, education, the law – or they would do so once they took power. All the modern ideas that threatened traditional elites, like Marxism, Darwinism, socialism, liberalism, democracy, and so on, were invented by Jews to dupe non-Jews into giving up their power. Pornography and other forms of degeneracy were used to debase society's morals. Things that appear to be opposites, like capitalism and Communism, are just different tentacles of the same Jewish octopus. And like a deepfake video on YouTube, the *Protocols* put the evidence of the conspiracy into the mouths of the alleged conspirators themselves, via a fraudulent record of their supposed secret discussions.

The result was a meta-conspiracy that can explain anything and everything. The *Protocols* became the handbook of the antisemitic conspiracy theorist: media control, money manipulation, political string-pulling, cultural debasement, economic collapse, globalisation, war, revolution, terror and exploitation of workers are all included. There had been other, similarly expansive, conspiracy theories before the *Protocols*, mostly focused on secret societies like the Freemasons or the Illuminati. But it was the antisemitic version that caught fire, because it built a bridge into modernity for Europe's traditional anti-Jewish mythology. The idea that all of Europe's problems were caused by Jews simply made more sense than the idea they were caused by anyone else, because Jews had long been fitted for the outfit marked 'eternal villain'.

It was the *Protocols*' translation into English, German and French in 1920 that launched its international fame. The timing was everything. The First World War threw the entire world order into flux, and the suggestion that a hidden hand was behind the turmoil had some appeal. The Bolshevik Revolution that seized power in Russia in 1917 was believed by many to be the work of the Jews – including by Western diplomats and politicians – and the fantasy of a Judeo-Bolshevik conspiracy fuelled the murder of over 100,000 Jews in the Russian civil war that followed. Extracts from the *Protocols* were distributed to soldiers in the White Russian army that was fighting against the Bolshevik Revolution, with the slogan 'Kill the Jews, Save Russia' deployed to justify the slaughter.[13] As well as being used to provoke mass murder, the *Protocols* reached the highest levels of society. The last Tsar of Russia, Nicholas II, was fascinated by its revelations. When he and his family were executed in 1918 following the Russian Revolution, the Tsar's wife had only three books in her possession: the bible, *War and Peace* and an edition of the *Protocols*. The German royal family, too: Kaiser Wilhelm II, in exile in the Netherlands after the First World War, reportedly read chapters of the *Protocols* to guests over dinner. In 1922, General Ludendorff, who had led Germany's army to defeat in the First World War, wrote that 'the supreme government of the Jewish people was working hand in hand with France and England. Perhaps it was leading them both.' He was wrong, of course. There was no such thing as the 'supreme government of the Jewish people', but the *Protocols* convinced some of the most powerful, well-informed people in Europe that it not only existed, but was the true power in the continent.[14]

The *Protocols* landed on a Jewish world that was very different from that of the medieval persecutions. The Enlightenment had seen European Jewish communities emancipated in many countries, starting with French Jews following the Revolution in 1789. Ghetto gates were flung open and Jews were admitted into a range of professions from which they had previously been excluded. This was grudging at times and there was still much formal and informal discrimination. Often Jews had to convert to Christianity as the entry ticket to the higher reaches of European society, but emancipation nevertheless created opportunities for Jews to assimilate and make their mark, and many took up the challenge. This meant that, for antisemites, Jews were less visible and posed a more insidious threat. No longer were they safely confined behind walls or easily identifiable due to their traditional clothing and religious behaviour. Conspiracy theories were increasingly popular in the nineteenth century anyway, largely as a reaction to the spread of revolutionary politics and economic and social modernisation, and the newly emancipated and liberalised Jews, along with the Freemasons, were in the frame.

The *Protocols* had more mainstream appeal in Britain than we would probably like to admit. *The Times*, *The Spectator*, the *Morning Post* and other respectable newspapers ran excitable articles debating whether the *Protocols* were genuine; perhaps they revealed a truth about the world irrespective of their accuracy. *The Spectator* even called for a Royal Commission to be appointed to investigate. 'Whence comes the uncanny note of prophecy,' *The Times* asked.

> Have we been struggling these tragic years to blow up and extirpate the secret organisation of German world dominion only to find beneath it another, more dangerous because more secret? ... The 'Elders of Zion', as represented in their 'Protocols', are by no means kinder taskmasters than William II and his henchmen would have been.[15]

The Times was also the first to reveal the fraudulent nature of the *Protocols* in a series of articles in August 1921. There have been numerous efforts to counter its appeal since, including court cases in several countries, none of which killed it off because the appeal of its antisemitism lies not in its accuracy but in its utility. Antisemitic agitators and fascist supporters in Britain in the 1930s were convinced that the *Protocols* proved the Jews were planning another World War, and when that war came, they felt vindicated. Two editions of the *Protocols* were published in Britain during the Second World War and its authenticity was discussed once again, this time in the *Catholic Herald* and *Scotsman* newspapers. Although few people ever read the *Protocols* its conspiracy theories about Jews were widespread, even while those same Jews were being slaughtered on the European continent. There was in Britain during the 1940s a 'common belief that Jews controlled public opinion via the press, or culture via dance bands, comedy and the cinema ... a society where the concept of Jewish power was almost taken for granted'.[16]

Hitler was, predictably, a fan, writing in *Mein Kampf* that the *Protocols* provide a reliable guide to 'the mentality and methods of action characteristic of the Jewish people ... the Jewish peril will be stamped out the moment the general public come into possession of that book and understand it'.[17] The *Protocols* went through numerous editions in Germany, selling 120,000 copies in its first year, and became a compulsory text taught in German schools after the Nazis came to power in 1933.[18] Even when it became clear the *Protocols* were fake, the Nazi leadership clung to it as revealing an 'inner truth' about the Jews. In modern terms, the *Protocols* was fake news and the Nazi use of it was post-truth.[19]

You can see the legacy of the *Protocols* in the super-conspiracies that circulate today, even if they are not primarily about Jews. Covid conspiracists talk about the Great Reset or the 'Plandemic' to imply that the Covid-19 pandemic was deliberately manufactured to usher in a reshaping of the entire world. There is a genuine project called The Great Reset, developed by the World Economic Forum to encourage governments 'to build a new social contract that honours the dignity of every human being' as we emerge from the Coronavirus pandemic.[20] You can be cynical about whether our political leaders are really motivated by honouring human dignity, but that isn't the point: the conspiracist version is that the pandemic was planned all along to give governments the excuse to take away our fundamental rights. For true believers, it is no coincidence that a war in Ukraine began just as the pandemic was winding down in Europe, because the plotters need to keep the world in turmoil.

The conspiracist world is dotted with acronyms like ZOG (Zionist Occupied Government) and NWO (New World Order) to express this idea in short-form. These systemic conspiracy theories do not always involve Jews at the outset, but the architecture is designed in such a way that antisemitism can be easily accommodated. A 2010 examination of over fifty different extremist groups by the think tank Demos, encompassing far right, far left, eco, anarchist and cult-based organisations and movements, found that 'the most commonly held conspiracy theory was variants on ZOG, the belief that Jews secretly control major world governments'.[21]

The popularity of the *Protocols* receded after the Second World War, but it planted the idea that Jews have hidden power, and the fruits of this seeding continue to sprout. The *Protocols* and Ford's *International Jew* have both been translated into dozens of languages and published around the world, and their appeal has nothing to do with real Jews and their actual lives. I have a copy of the *Protocols* published in Pakistan in 1984 under the title *Zionism and Internal Security*, in which the publisher's Preface declares: 'The movement for the domination of the whole world by the Jews, using all forces of terror, coercion and intimidation is called Zionism.'[22] Another edition, published in Malaysia in 1991 as *Jewish Conspiracy and the Muslim World*, promises that the *Protocols* explains the threat posed by Israel and India to Muslim countries. Yet the *Protocols* does not mention Israel, India, Pakistan or Malaysia: unsurprising, since none of those countries even existed as independent states when the *Protocols* was written. Nor is there any visible Jewish presence of any significance in Pakistan or Malaysia today. This doesn't seem to matter, because the reason why the *Protocols* can always be made to seem relevant does not lie in the detail of any secret information it claims to reveal about Jews, as that information is completely bogus anyway. The longevity and global appeal of the conspiracy theory at its heart relies on its ability to provide a framework for people to interpret their own world and explain its problems and dangers in a way that scapegoats Jews, whether that world has Jews in it or not. Publishers of new versions just write their own preface explaining how the conspiracy applies to their own time and place, and the work is done.

The *Protocols* are still very much alive in the conspiracist world. Britain's leading conspiracy theorist, David Icke, quotes them extensively. 'Almost everything these documents proposed to do has happened in this century,' he wrote in one of his books. Icke renames them the 'Illuminati Protocols' to distance himself from their explicit antisemitism, but he still can't resist their lure.[23] When Iran's Press TV lost its Ofcom licence in 2011 for broadcasting the forced interrogation of an imprisoned Iranian opposition activist, their response was, unbelievably, to quote the *Protocols* as supposed proof that the world's media is controlled by 'the American Jewish Lobby'.[24] There is a conspiracist channel on Telegram with the impressive name 'Covid-1984 Jew World Order' that posted the full text of the *Protocols* online as an audiobook in December 2021. The *Protocols* were also written into the 1988 charter of the Palestinian terrorist organisation Hamas, which claimed:

> The Zionist plan is limitless. After Palestine, the Zionists aspire to expand from the Nile to the Euphrates. When they will have digested the region they overtook, they will aspire to further expansion, and so on. Their plan is embodied in the 'Protocols of the Elders of Zion', and their present conduct is the best proof of what we are saying.[25]

It might seem odd that the idea this tiny religion is the true hidden force behind world events fools anybody, but antisemitism has always revealed more about antisemites than about the Jews they claim to expose. I've always thought that if Jews really did have the power that antisemites claim, there are lots of things we'd do with it before trying to ruin everyone else's lives. Reducing the price of kosher food. Not scheduling football matches on Yom Kippur.

Sorting out the parking outside Jewish schools at drop-off time in the mornings. That kind of thing. Instead, the Jew of the *Protocols* has nothing to do with what actual Jews think, feel and do. It is a fantastical invention, a filter through which antisemites explain their own failings and a screen onto which they project their own hatreds. 'Tell me what you accuse the Jews of – I'll tell you what you're guilty of.'[26] It is antisemites who try to subvert moral norms in their societies, not the Jews they blame for liberalism and atheism. It is antisemites who incite conflict, not the Jews who they accuse of plotting war, revolution and terrorism. This all has a purpose, because antisemitism is not merely a bad idea or a nasty prejudice: it is an organising principle for extremist, violent, deadly politics. Throughout history, it has been deployed by dictators, demagogues and politicians of all stripes as a way of mobilising support and focusing popular anger onto a traditional and familiar target.

THE ECHO OF THE PROTOCOLS IN CONTEMPORARY POLITICS

Nowadays you rarely find mainstream politicians referring openly to *The Protocols of the Elders of Zion*, but the ideas it laid out – the image of Jewish peril threatening the nation – is very much alive. You would be wrong to assume that the phenomenon of authoritarian politicians exploiting anti-Jewish fears for political gain is consigned to Europe's past. The Prime Minister of Hungary, Viktor Orbán, has conducted a campaign against the Jewish financier and philanthropist George Soros in unmistakably antisemitic, conspiratorial terms. 'We must fight against an opponent who is different from us,' is how he has put it.

Their faces are not visible, but are hidden from view. They do not fight directly, but by stealth. They are not honourable, but unprincipled. They are not national, but international. They do not believe in work, but speculate with money. They have no homeland, but feel that the whole world is theirs.[27]

In an echo of the Great Replacement Theory, Orbán has claimed that 'Grandmaster George Soros' uses his 'unlimited financial and human resources' to promote immigration, with the goal of creating 'societies of mixed ethnicity, to tear down national decision-making and to hand it over to the global elite'.[28] Government posters have depicted Soros as a puppeteer and Orbán's anti-immigration legislation was even called the 'Stop Soros' law.[29] Anyone who has ever been funded by Soros's Open Society Foundations is dragged in to this supposed conspiracy. When Orbán won the 2022 Hungarian election, he listed 'the money of the Soros empire' and 'the international media' alongside the EU and the Hungarian left as the opponents he had defeated.[30] Orbán insists his problem with Soros has nothing to do with the fact Soros is Jewish, but then he has also said that 'Hungarians can only survive as Christians'[31] and 'a Christian politician cannot be racist', neither of which is especially reassuring for Jews.[32]

George Soros has become something of a demonic figure in right-wing politics. He was born to a Jewish family in Hungary in 1930, survived Nazi occupation, then lived in London and the US before making a fortune speculating on financial markets, and he now uses that wealth to support progressive causes. He funded campaigns against Communism in eastern Europe during the Cold War and is now a supporter of liberal movements and initiatives in those same countries. It is as if he was designed in a laboratory to trigger anyone drawn to conspiracist antisemitism, and in a way, he was. Orbán's campaign against Soros was devised by his campaign strategists after he had won the 2010 Hungarian elections with a huge majority. Orbán was now so powerful domestically that 'there was no real political enemy' left for him to fight; so his team simply invented one, pouring into it all the old fears and hatreds that had animated populist movements in Europe for centuries. All politicians like to have an opposition to define themselves against, and populism demands that they should be depicted not just as an opponent of the government, but as an enemy of the people. The twist is that the two strategists who devised the anti-Soros campaign, George Birnbaum and Arthur Finkelstein, are both Jewish. Neither of them imagined they were creating an antisemitic monster. They just thought, 'Soros was a perfect enemy. It was so obvious. It was the simplest of all products, you just had to pack it and market it.' They knew that painting Soros as a sinister string-puller, using his money to manipulate and distort Hungarian politics and undermine national identity and traditional values, had immense appeal; it never occurred to them that it worked so well because it activated so many antisemitic touchpoints.[33]

And not just in Hungary. At David Icke's live show in Watford in 2018,

> an image of the billionaire philanthropist George Soros (who is of Jewish heritage), depicted as a fiery demon with reptile eyes, was displayed on screen next to images of refugees and of the Arab Spring. Another image depicted Soros as a controlling puppet master, and another alleged that 'Rothschild Zionism' was a constituent part of a supposed ring of global manipulators.[34]

In 2019, three different general election candidates for the Conservative Party and the Scottish National Party were investigated by their parties for sharing conspiracy posts online about Soros. One of these involved a cartoon originally published by the Russian TV channel Sputnik News in 2016 depicting Soros as a puppeteer, controlling US President Obama and German Chancellor Merkel.

It is Nigel Farage who, more than any other British politician, has drunk from the conspiracist well when it comes to George Soros. In a 2018 interview with Tucker Carlson on Fox News, Farage claimed that Soros sought 'to undermine democracy and to fundamentally change the makeup, demographically, of the whole European continent'. He said that Soros

> wants to break down the fundamental values of our society and in the case of Europe, he doesn't want Europe to be based on Christianity … all of this is based on some kind of self-loathing, some sort of guilt trip about the past. And in Soros's case, it's a guilt trip of course about America's, about, sorry Germany's wartime actions. The way the Jews were treated … It's all based on guilt, but it's not based on reality.[35]

The same year, at a conference of the US Conservative Political Action Committee, Farage encouraged the audience to boo the name of George Soros before claiming that he

> is attempting to intervene and disrupt in every single election and cause and campaign that is taking place across the Western world. These people don't believe, people like Soros don't believe in the existence of the nation state. They don't believe as we believe, don't we,

in basic patriotism and believing in who we are. They don't believe in national identity. They want us to live in a world with open borders.[36]

Farage was not the only pro-Brexit campaigner to use this kind of conspiracist language about Soros. The Leave.EU campaign accused 'globalist billionaire George Soros' of using 'filthy money' to try to stop Brexit.[37] One of their tweets depicted Soros as a puppeteer controlling Tony Blair – in an echo of the Sputnik cartoon of Soros from two years earlier – with the slogan: 'The face of the People's Vote campaign'; a reference to the campaign for a second Brexit referendum.[38]

Brexit had nothing to do with Jews or with antisemitism. People did not vote to leave the European Union because they wanted to rid themselves of the imaginary yoke of Jewish financial manipulation. But it did stir up questions of national identity, sovereignty and immigration, and campaigners regularly depicted Britain as a powerless plaything of faceless Brussels. There is nothing wrong with wanting lower immigration or with seeking to identify the funders of anti-Brexit campaigns, but the suggestion that Soros, who is Jewish, did this because he hates Christianity, opposes the existence of nation states and wants to destroy our fundamental values, takes the critique of his actions onto antisemitic territory. I don't believe Farage thought there were many votes to be won by flirting with antisemitism. I just think talking about Soros in this way came naturally, because that is how our society has taught people to think about wealthy Jews who get involved in political campaigning. Less of a conscious conspiracy theory, more of an assumed fact. The kind of thing that 'everyone knows' about Jews, simply because it's the kind of thing people have said and thought about Jews for centuries.

ZIONISM IN THE FRAME

It is easy to get lost in trying to distinguish between antisemitism, anti-Zionism, criticism of Israel and everything in between. There are important differences between each, but one fact that often gets lost is that the *Protocols* tied antisemitic conspiracism to anti-Zionism from the outset. The Zionist movement had only just got going when the *Protocols* were written. Hardly anybody had heard of Zionism at that time and even most Jews were not interested. But the first Zionist Congress had taken place in Switzerland in 1897, and any gathering of important-sounding Jews was a perfect hook for the conspiracy outlined in the *Protocols*. Proponents of the *Protocols* therefore claimed that their text was a record of secret meetings that took place at that first Zionist Congress, and as the Zionist movement grew in reach and influence, so it was natural for antisemites to see it as the vehicle for the global Jewish conspiracy that they imagined existed. After all, it is called *The Protocols of the Learned Elders of Zion*, not *The Protocols of the Learned Elders of Judaism*. Once Israel was created in 1948 – giving Jews a state with actual power, rather than the mythical power of the *Protocols* – it followed that Israel and its supporters around the world should get roped in. It made perfect sense to believers in a worldwide Jewish conspiracy that Israel should be the HQ of this mythical global network, and it is no coincidence that Hamas quotes the *Protocols* as if they are accurate in its founding charter.

Israel is, obviously, a country, with a government that does things worthy of criticism like any other. It has been embroiled in different conflicts since it was created in 1948 (in fact, since well before then), there are legitimate questions to be raised about its treatment of Palestinians living under Israeli rule in the West Bank, and its military activities are also subject to scrutiny like that of any other country's armed forces. That much is all pretty straightforward. Zionism, meanwhile, is the political movement that campaigned from the late nineteenth century onwards to create a Jewish homeland in what is now Israel. It rested on two fundamental ideas: first, that the Jews are a single, coherent people, dispersed around the world; second, that national self-determination for Jews, gathered together in their ancient homeland, would be the best way to ensure the future existence and well-being of the Jewish people. There were different visions for what this might look like, reflecting different political and religious strands within the Zionist movement itself, but these two ideas are the essence of what Zionism was, and what it remains today. Being a Zionist does not tie someone to a particular political outlook or to supporting one Israeli party or set of policies or another. It means that somebody supports what Israel is, irrespective of whether they support what it does.*

This is the back-and-forth of regular politics and lends itself to ordinary political criticism and debate. That's very different from conspiracy theories about Israel that are couched in starkly similar terms to the absurdities the *Protocols* suggested about Jews. When Anders Breivik murdered seventy-seven people in a terrorist attack in Norway in 2011, the idea that it was a 'false flag' attack carried out by Israel or Zionists was suggested by a diverse bunch of conspiracy theorists, including the chair of a local Palestine Solidarity Campaign branch in London; former Israeli jazz musician Gilad Atzmon; the British National Party; and the magazine of the Islamic Centre of England, which is the main Iranian mosque in London.[39]

---

* We'll come back to all this in more detail in Chapter Seven.

In 2012, following an attack by jihadists on Egyptian soldiers in Sinai, Jeremy Corbyn speculated on Iranian TV that 'the hand of Israel' may have been behind the attacks.[40] The same year, he agreed with another interviewer that Israel might create a 'false flag event' in order to trigger a war with Iran.[41] The idea that ISIS terrorism is really done by Israel is surprisingly common, with the clue being that ISIS stands for 'Israeli Secret Intelligence Service' (if the Israelis are that sneaky, surely they would come up with a better cover name than that). This hunt for Israeli 'false flags' maps directly onto the much older tradition of blaming a supposed Jewish conspiracy for whatever is deemed most threatening, or most repugnant, in society, and it is not limited to one part of the political spectrum or another. Former Labour and Respect MP George Galloway and former British National Party leader Nick Griffin have both suggested that Israel may have given chemical weapons to jihadists in Syria that they used in 'false flag' massacres of Syrians that could be blamed on President Assad.

This is not a case of people criticising Israeli government policies or practices and slipping accidentally into antisemitic language. We are dealing with an entirely different category of thought, one based on conspiracist fantasies rather than reality, of a type that is reserved for Israel and not projected onto any other government. The malevolent actor may be identified as Israel rather than Jews, but you need to look beyond the words used to get to the true meaning of the message. Conspiracy theories about Israel and Zionism take the form they do, and gain the purchase they have in the popular imagination, because Israel is Jewish. They latch onto pre-existing beliefs about how Jews behave, like a climber using footholds cut into the rock by those who have scaled the same mountain centuries before.

The Twitter account of the Supreme Leader of Iran, Ayatollah Khamenei, is an object lesson in using the words 'Zionist' and 'Zionism' in an antisemitic way. Try this one, from June 2022: 'Today, #Zionism is an obvious plague for the world of #Islam. The Zionists have always been a plague, even before establishing the fraudulent Zionist regime. Even then, Zionist capitalists were a plague for the whole world. Now they're a plague especially for the world of Islam.'[42] Or this, a month later: 'The Western powers are a mafia. The reality of this power is a mafia. At the top of this mafia stand the prominent Zionist merchants, and the politicians obey them. The US is their showcase, and they're spread out everywhere.'[43] 'Zionists' as a plague, responsible for global capitalism, with 'Zionist merchants' controlling politicians? It's well-poisoning, the *Protocols* and Shylock rolled into one. Khamenei may have been speaking about Zionism, a political movement, rather than about Jews, but he wouldn't do so in this language, hitting all these buttons, if Zionism wasn't a Jewish movement and antisemitism had not created this anti-Jewish vernacular to draw upon.

I can't think of a better example of this conspiracist antisemitism-as-anti-Zionism than a 2022 TV series (on Iran's Press TV channel) called *Palestine Declassified*, produced by former Bristol University Professor David Miller and presented by former Labour MP Chris Williamson. Both lost their positions in academia and politics respectively after controversies over their antisemitism and they have no doubt who to blame. *Palestine Declassified* calls itself an investigation into 'the Israeli regime's global war against solidarity with the illegally occupied people of Palestine', but it spends much more time talking about Jews than about Palestinians. Their method is to identify Jewish people and organisations with any connection to Israel, however tenuous – enough to account for all but the most anti-Israel Jews, anywhere in the world – and claim that they are 'Israeli assets', working as part of a global plot to destroy free speech, subvert democracy, and generally do all the stuff that antisemites accuse Jews of doing.

As with all alleged conspiracies involving Jews, you'll find it, according to *Palestine Declassified*, in the places you'd least expect. The Bradford Literary Festival is 'funded by Israel lobbyists, funders of settlements and the Israeli military'.[44] 'Zionist groups ... have an effective stranglehold over what is deemed permissible on Twitter.'[45] There is 'Zionist infiltration of the media' and academics are bullied and threatened. Muslim–Jewish interfaith is a trojan horse designed to trick well-meaning Muslims into befriending 'Zionists'. And just as Henry Ford was obsessed with 'Jewish Jazz', so Miller believes there is a 'Zionist stranglehold over the top of the music industry'.[46]

The playbook is familiar. Take any area of society, identify the people active in it who are Jewish, look for your 'evidence' of malpractice or misbehaviour – in this case, any kind of connection to Israel, whether it is political, cultural, charitable, professional or personal – and link them all together as if they are acting in concert, ruthlessly pursuing some supposed Jewish (or in this case, 'Zionist') agenda. The individual fact may be true in isolation – it isn't unusual that such-and-such Jewish person who gave money to some interfaith group in Britain had also in the past funded something in Israel, met someone from the Israeli government or worked with someone else who did. The Jewish world is small, and most Jews can be linked to Israel one way or another. The deceit comes in the implication that all Jews think and move as one as part of some grand and sinister plan that requires uncovering or that anything Jews do can't be taken at face value but is probably a subterfuge to promote Israeli and Jewish interests. In other words, that Jews are always up to something. That's the point where the language of anti-Zionism maps directly on to the thought structures of antisemitism.

David Miller was, until late 2021, a professor at Bristol University, and before that he was a respected academic at Bath and Strathclyde Universities. He was sacked by Bristol after saying that there is 'an all-out onslaught by the Israeli government' to 'impose their will all over the world', in which Jewish students – including at his own university – were being 'directed by the State of Israel' as part of a campaign to suppress free speech, subvert democracy and spread anti-Muslim hatred.[47] Since then, he has suggested that 'there's a long history of the Zionist movement trying to penetrate the British elite culture … there has been a long, long history of Zionist attempts to penetrate this country and to take on and to colonise parts of the power structure of this country' and 'they want to colonise every single public institution' in Britain.[48] Nor are these Miller's only conspiracy theories. He has claimed that Syrian White Helmet rescue workers, working with Western intelligence, faked some of the chemical attacks on Syrian civilians by the Assad regime during that country's civil war.[49] He wrote it is 'unlikely' that the Russian state would have tried to poison Sergei and Yulia Skripal in Salisbury in 2018 and that 'other actors' may have been responsible.[50] He has even argued on Russian TV that the Russian bombing of the theatre in Mariupol, Ukraine, which an Associated Press investigation estimated killed 600 people, was a propaganda hoax that never actually happened.[51] This is the other thing about antisemitism: it makes you stupid. Conspiracy theorists might like to think they are getting to the truth, but really all they are doing is convincing themselves of ever more ludicrous and fanciful stories that stray as far from reality as it is possible to go.

Miller is not, himself, that interesting. He lost his job, eventually, and is now an outcast reduced to Iranian television for his audience. Of much greater concern is that hundreds of other academics, in the UK and around the world, supported him. There is a website full of their names, all signed up to statements defending him as 'an eminent scholar' producing 'crucial' and 'respected' work.⁵² I know some people sign these letters without reading them properly,* but nevertheless, it is disturbing to see how many of those tasked with teaching students how to interpret facts and interrogate data couldn't see Miller's antisemitic conspiracy-mongering for what it was. Nineteen academics from Miller's own University of Bristol signed a letter in his support, sixteen from King's College London, fifteen from University College London, four from Oxford University, five from Cambridge, seven each from Edinburgh and Warwick and many, many others.

JEWS BEING ANTISEMITIC TOWARDS JEWS

I know, it sounds crazy. You may have noticed that the examples of conspiracist antisemitism I've included in this chapter come from across the board. Right-wing, left-wing, Muslim, Christian, European, American, and Middle-Eastern. Antisemitism is habitually associated with far-right politics, for understandable reasons – the most notorious exponents of anti-Jewish hate were the Nazis, and

---

* I have personal experience of this. I helped to write and organise a rival letter for academics to sign condemning Miller, and one very famous and lauded academic signed both letters, for and against Miller, and then when this was pointed out they withdrew their name from both.

you don't get more right-wing than that – but in fact it goes much further. You will find antisemitism alongside racism, anti-Muslim hatred, xenophobia and a range of prejudiced and bigoted attitudes towards minorities that, again, are usually associated with extreme right-wing politics; but you will also find it alongside anti-capitalism, anti-imperialism, even anti-racism and other ideas more commonly found on the political left. Antisemitism transcends political, national and cultural boundaries, partly because conspiracy theories and stereotypes about Jews are so varied and not tied to any single ideology or type of politics.

There is even a phenomenon of Jews being antisemitic towards other Jews, which you might think is the maddest of the lot. This tends to involve a minority of Jews who have left the fold, either by converting to another faith or by adopting political ideologies hostile to collective Jewish identity, and who then use their new allegiance as a platform to attack the community they have left behind. When Thomas of Monmouth wrote his account of the alleged ritual murder of William of Norwich, he claimed to have an informant called Theobald of Cambridge who had converted from Judaism to Christianity. In the Middle Ages, when public disputations were held in which leading rabbis were compelled to debate the validity of Jewish teaching against a battery of learned Christian scholars – effectively putting the Jewish religion on trial – it would often be a Jewish convert to Christianity who would lead the prosecution case. In the years following the Russian Revolution in 1917, it was the Jewish section of the Soviet Communist Party, known as the Yevsektsiya, that led the campaign to crush Zionism in the newly formed Soviet Union. Zionist offices were shut down, their activists arrested and exiled or imprisoned. The Yevsektsiya even 'branded as counter-revolutionary' Moscow's Hebrew-language theatre company, Habima, which ended up relocating to Tel Aviv in 1931.[53]*

This obscure phenomenon of Jewish leftists attacking Jewish Zionists, and doing so in antisemitic terms, was something that British politics had to get its collective head around during Jeremy Corbyn's time as leader of the Labour Party. Corbyn had Jewish allies on the left of the party who represented only a small slice of Jewish opinion in the country as a whole, but who acted as Corbyn's praetorian guard in defending him from allegations of antisemitism. These activists formed various groups with broadly similar memberships and a conspiratorial line that allegations of antisemitism were deliberately faked, inflated or weaponised. 'Israeli propagandists deliberately, yes deliberately, conflate anti-Zionism with anti-Semitism in order to discredit, bully, and muzzle critics of Israel' and 'suppress free speech,' wrote Avi Shlaim.[54] Complaints of antisemitism in Labour are a 'manufactured moral panic' based on 'mischievous or false charges', according to a group called Free Speech on Israel.[55] 'Antisemitism would be the baseball bat of choice for internal as well as external attacks on Jeremy Corbyn and his project,' wrote Jonathan Rosenhead, who has even speculated that antisemitic social media posts by people claiming to support Corbyn might be the product of 'false flag operations' by the Israeli government.[56] The consequence of all this alleged plotting and deception against Corbyn was that 'the Labour Party has become

---

* Habima became Israel's national theatre and will make another appearance in this book in Chapter Seven.

a pawn of Zionist organisations', wrote Jewish Voice for Labour secretary Mike Cushman.[57]

These are not run-of-the-mill political criticisms: they are suggestions that Zionists – which in this context means mainstream Jewish organisations like the Board of Deputies of British Jews and others – have conspired to hijack the Labour Party, dupe the British electorate and subvert democracy, and to do so through a campaign of knowing and deliberate dishonesty. It's worth noting that this allegation has been rejected by three different, very substantial, investigations. The 130-page Equality and Human Rights Commission report on Labour's antisemitism crisis warned that 'suggesting that complaints of antisemitism were fake or smears' is itself a form of unlawful antisemitic harassment.[58] The 138-page Forde Report saw 'no evidence that claims of antisemitism were fabricated' and concluded about antisemitism itself that 'the problem within parts of the Party was clearly of major significance'.[59] Most striking of all, an 851-page report written by supporters of Corbyn working within the Labour Party machine, who had every incentive to try to exonerate their leader, nonetheless insisted

> this report thoroughly disproves any suggestion that antisemitism is not a problem in the Party, or that it is all a 'smear' or a 'witch-hunt'. The report's findings prove the scale of the problem, and could help end the denialism amongst parts of the Party membership which has further hurt Jewish members and the Jewish community.[60]

It isn't only left-wing Jews who use antisemitic motifs to attack their Jewish political opponents. In 2017 Yair Netanyahu, son of Israeli

Prime Minister Benjamin Netanyahu, posted on Facebook a cartoon that merged a picture of George Soros with the antisemitic Happy Merchant meme, alongside a reptilian lizard, all of whom were controlling the world. It was an outrageously antisemitic image and was roundly condemned by Jewish organisations and Israeli commentators (and welcomed around the world by neo-Nazis).[61] The reason that Jews use the lexicon and imagery of antisemitism to criticise or condemn other Jews is the same reason that non-Jews do it. This is the anti-Jewish vocabulary that is most familiar, that resonates most strongly, as the way to interpret and explain alleged Jewish wrongdoing. We all inhabit this world, whether we are Jewish or not, and although Jews are obviously less likely to be taken in by these ideas, they are not completely immune. Some may even have an added incentive, because one way to inure yourself from the pressures of an antisemitic environment is to separate yourself from the wider body of Jews. 'They deal with their situation by running away from it,' wrote Jean-Paul Sartre about Jews who express antisemitic views, but their antisemitism is only 'borrowed'; they are 'first victim' of antisemitic propaganda. It is the antisemitism of wider society that creates the antisemitic Jew, according to Sartre.[62]

The type of antisemitism that draws heavily on conspiracy theories about Jewish wealth and influence has a particular appeal for those who view themselves as leading a liberation struggle against imperium. Left-wing antisemitism may seem an oxymoron if you only think about it as a form of racial prejudice; it is the utility of antisemitism as a fantasy about how power and influence operate in the world that explains its appeal to people who dream of a world free from oppression. Even the great Keir Hardie, a founder of the

Labour Party, wrote in 1900 that 'modern imperialism is really run by half a dozen financial houses, many of them Jewish, to whom politics is a counter in the game of buying and selling securities'.[63]

This appeal works for all sorts of politics that claim to be resisting global power. There is a conspiracy theory put about by Louis Farrakhan's Nation of Islam organisation that Jews were involved in the trans-Atlantic slave trade 'disproportionately more than any other ethnic or religious group in New World history', a claim that was condemned as 'false' by the American Historical Association.[64] In 2002 al-Qaeda leader Osama bin Laden wrote a 'Letter to the American People' in which he tried to explain, and justify, the 9/11 terrorist atrocities. Amongst a long, rambling set of grievances and self-justifications came this antisemitic nugget:

> You are the nation that permits Usury, which has been forbidden by all the religions. Yet you build your economy and investments on Usury. As a result of this, in all its different forms and guises, the Jews have taken control of your economy, through which they have then taken control of your media, and now control all aspects of your life making you their servants and achieving their aims at your expense; precisely what Benjamin Franklin warned you against.[65]

Usury is the charge that was laid at Jewish moneylenders during the Middle Ages and has stuck to Jews ever since. The notion that Jews control America's economy and media comes from *The Protocols of the Elders of Zion*, or perhaps Henry Ford's *International Jew*; either way, they are common antisemitic conspiracy theories. As for bin Laden's claim that US Founding Father Benjamin Franklin supposedly warned Americans not to let Jews take control of their country: that was another Nazi forgery, one that claims to be from a speech Franklin supposedly made in 1787 but really was written in 1934 by an American Nazi called William D. Pelley. No matter: for antisemites, the message works wherever it comes from. It sometimes feels like every ideology or political movement has its own version of antisemitism, and they are usually happy to share.

Antisemitism rhymes through the centuries, and in every generation there are people ready to write another verse. In 2003 the Labour MP Tam Dalyell, who was at that time the Father of the House of Commons, suggested that Tony Blair was 'unduly influenced by a cabal of Jewish advisers' in his decision to go to war in Iraq. Dalyell named Lord Levy, Peter Mandelson and Jack Straw as the three 'Jewish advisers' involved – only one and a half of whom (at most) are actually Jewish.* *The Guardian*'s Paul Foot defended Dalyell against complaints of antisemitism by explaining that 'obviously he is wrong to complain about Jewish pressure on Blair and Bush when he means Zionist pressure' – as if simply swapping a word can change the antisemitic way of thinking in Dalyell's claim that the British Prime Minister was not in control of his own policy but was manipulated to act in support of perceived pro-Israel interests.[66]

I found an extraordinary example of this thinking in the records of the Foreign and Commonwealth Office (FCO). In the early 1970s the FCO launched a secret research project into 'Zionism and its influence in USA and Western Europe'. This wasn't an attempt to

---

* The word 'cabal' – meaning a sinister private intrigue, not big enough for a conspiracy but of a similar character – carries an extra note of antisemitism as it derives from the Hebrew word Kabbalah, which is an esoteric form of Jewish spiritualism.

map Israeli diplomatic activity: it was an investigation into Jewish financial power and political influence across several countries. One Washington-based diplomat (reflecting on the United States) wrote of the 'enormous influence (which can scarcely be exaggerated) of the Jewish intellectuals ... much of the intellectual thought and discussion, certainly on the East Coast, is dominated by Jewish savants.' The political use of 'Jewish money' in America was of particular interest. An FCO official asked if 'we might try and explain why the American Jewish Community has become so rich and powerful'. The British embassy in Tel Aviv suggested examining 'the alleged link between the financial contributions of American Jews to Israel and the profits of crime syndicates.' Civil servants in London swapped memos discussing whether the 'Jewish lobby' was more able to inhibit Conservative or Labour policy on the Middle East. I'm sure the mandarins involved would have been horrified to think they were trafficking in antisemitic tropes, but it seems that some could not resist the natural pull of conspiracist ideas when discussing Jews and Israel. In contrast, British diplomats in West Germany were baffled by the request to contribute their thoughts, given that the Jewish community in that country had been exterminated in the Holocaust less than thirty years earlier. 'There is really no Jewish life as such in the Federal Republic, and nor do the Jews form any kind of unified pressure group,' was their poignant comment.[67]

It's exhausting, isn't it? This is just a sample, nowhere near complete, of antisemitic thoughts and statements from significant, powerful and influential politicians, leaders, journalists and opinion formers, in Britain and around the world. The point is not that all these people are knowingly hostile to Jews – although some undoubtedly are. It is that people reach for antisemitic ideas because this is how society, over many centuries, has taught them to think about Jews and about Jewish things. These are not esoteric concepts only accessible after years of study. They are common ideas, readily available, easily absorbed, floating in the atmosphere when Jews are discussed.

The thing that always strikes me about these conspiracy theories is what they would imply about human nature if they were true. One of the main conspiracy theories about 9/11 is that 4,000 Israelis (or Jews – antisemites are rarely fastidious about the difference between the two) who worked in the World Trade Center were warned not to turn up to work that day. For this to be true, not only would it mean they saved themselves while allowing friends and colleagues to die, but they must also have kept quiet about it for over twenty years since.* The various conspiracy theories of QAnon allege the involvement of huge numbers of evildoers, while the suggestion that Covid-19 is a hoax or that vaccines are either useless or poisonous would require millions of doctors, scientists and other health professionals the world over to be part of a vast conspiracy on a scale never before seen. It would mean that the people we trust the most are deceitful beyond compare. All of these ideas, I think, reveal a deep fear about the nature of humanity. The opening page of the *Protocols* tells us that 'men with bad instincts are more in number than the good', and I think at some level, you have to have

---

* For the record, it is estimated that between 270 and 400 Jews died in the WTC on 9/11, comprising 10–15 per cent of the overall victims, which is roughly in line with the proportion of the New York population that is Jewish.

a similarly dim view of your fellow human beings to buy into some of these conspiracy theories.[68]

Few people today have heard of the *Protocols* or read *The International Jew*, but the idea that Jews have power and influence out of all proportion to their number is set in stone. According to a 2015 opinion poll in six European countries, 35 per cent of respondents thought that Jews have too much power in the business world and in financial markets, 27 per cent thought Jews have too much control over the United States Government and 21 per cent thought that Jews have too much control over the global media. This isn't limited to people who bear ill will to Jews and it is found in the most surprising of places. A few years ago, I was invited to an impressive-sounding summit about racism in football, hosted by a government minister in Parliament. I took my place around the table alongside current and former professional footballers, officials from various football authorities and leaders of other anti-racist groups. It was an eye-opening and heartfelt discussion, and as we were wrapping up, I got chatting to the person next to me, a well-known ex-player who has since built a successful media career and speaks repeatedly about racism he has faced. We got onto discussing the problem of Spurs fans using the word 'Yid' (an offensive racist slur for Jews) as a nickname for themselves, and he declared, 'The Jewish community could stop this in an instant.' 'We've tried,' I said, 'but Spurs seem reluctant to act.' 'Come on,' he replied with a knowing smile, 'you have the power to bring down governments all around the world. Just look at what you are doing to Jeremy Corbyn!'

I am used to being told by antisemites and online cranks that Jews destabilise governments and manipulate politicians to get whatever they want. Yet here I was, at an anti-racist summit in the heart of government, getting it first-hand – as a friendly piece of advice about how to tackle antisemitism from somebody I used to watch on *Match of the Day*. I expect this person was completely ignorant of the antisemitic nature of what he was saying, and I am sure he is genuinely opposed to racism. He probably thought he was being helpful. Britain is full of people who say they are genuinely opposed to racism but don't recognise or understand antisemitism. Companies have anti-racist policies and diversity statements, and stories of famous people suffering racist abuse get a much more sympathetic hearing in the media than was ever the case previously. But all this effort to reduce racism in our society will fail if it doesn't include antisemitism, and it is impossible to tackle antisemitism if people can't recognise it.

Antisemitism is most obvious when terrorists attack synagogues or when people beat up Jews or shout antisemitic insults in the street, but these are not superficial acts of blind hatred. They are the physical expression of a realm of ideas and beliefs about Jews that are deployed to explain why things happen and who is to blame. It is a way of viewing the world that makes sense to lots of people who do not think of themselves as antisemitic or racist. This is partly because these ideas have been around for so long, but it is also because of a growing confusion over whether Jews can even suffer racism at all. To help explain that one, I'm going to enlist the help of one of Britain's best-loved film stars.

CHAPTER FIVE

ALIENS AND THEIR FAMILIES

The last few years have seen a flourishing of Jewish characters and plots on screen and stage, with Jews and Jewish storylines featuring in plays, films and TV series to an unprecedented degree. It feels like a shift after years of being hidden away, as if Jews are now a subject interesting enough to be part of the cultural mainstream. Historic dramas *Ridley Road*, *Vienna Blood*, *Peaky Blinders* and *Paris Police 1900* have all featured antisemitism in different ways. *Friday Night Dinner* turned the weekly Shabbat dinner that takes place in typical Jewish homes into a six-series TV comedy, while the play *Bad Jews* has its own, more acerbic, take on the internal dynamics of modern Jewish families. In theatres, *Leopoldstadt*, *Good*, *Indecent*, *The Doctor*, *Love and Other Acts of Violence* and *Jews. In Their Own Words* all explore antisemitism in different ways. There have been two separate productions of the musical *Fiddler on the Roof*, one at Chichester and the other in London's West End, which tells the story of Anatevka, a Jewish *shtetl* (village) trying to maintain its balance through persecution and revolution in Tsarist Russia. But of all the Jewish characters brought to life in recent years, my favourite isn't officially Jewish. In fact, he isn't even human. It's Paddington Bear.

As every British child knows, Paddington was a bear from darkest Peru who turned up unaccompanied in London, was taken in by the Brown family and spent the next few decades getting into all sorts of scrapes and adventures from which he invariably emerged unscathed. When I re-read the Paddington books as a parent, I thought he was a metaphor for the lovable, if slightly maddening, chaos that envelops all households with young children. But according to Paddington's creator, Michael Bond, he was very much intended to be a refugee, and Bond was inspired by the sight of Jewish children arriving unaccompanied in Britain in the late 1930s. 'I remember their labels round their necks,' Bond told an interviewer in 2014, 'and then I remember going to the cinema and seeing on the newsreel that Hitler had moved into some new country and seeing footage of elderly people pushing prams with all their belongings in them. Refugees are the saddest sight, I still think that.'[1] Paddington represents a child-friendly version of the traumas faced by many who are displaced from their homes and forced to rebuild their lives in an unfamiliar land. He struggles to settle and faces prejudice from a neighbour, but he gradually finds his place thanks to the loving support of the Browns and their friends; one of whom, Mr Gruber, was based on a real-life Jewish refugee from Nazism who was Bond's first literary agent. Paddington's story presents an ultimately optimistic vision of integration, emphasised in the conclusion to the 2014 film *Paddington*: 'Mrs Brown says that in London everyone is different, and that means anyone can fit in. I think she must be right, because although I don't look like anyone else, I really do feel at home.'[2]

Those child refugees whose arrival Michael Bond witnessed had come via the Kindertransports that brought up to 10,000 German, Austrian and Czech children, almost all Jewish, to Britain from late 1938 until the outbreak of war in September 1939. To get on one of the Kindertransport trains the children had to be sixteen or younger, sponsored by somebody in the UK (so they wouldn't be a financial burden) and, crucially, unaccompanied by any adult family members. The Kindertransport is often held up as an example of British generosity to refugees, a shining light in the darkness that befell European Jewry under Nazi rule. It is commemorated by statues at Liverpool Street Station and at the port of Harwich, where most of the children arrived, as well as a plaque in the Central Lobby of Parliament. Every life saved from the Holocaust ought to be cherished, children especially, and there were between 60,000 and 70,000 Jewish refugees in Britain during the Second World War who would otherwise almost certainly have perished. But the brutal truth of the Kindertransport is that for every Jewish child rescued from the Nazis via this route, there were Jewish parents who were left behind, unable to escape the tightening Nazi grip. As the historian Louise London put it, 'Admission saved the children's lives. Exclusion sealed the fate of many of their parents ... The organisers of this exodus knew they were separating families in circumstances where parents abandoned to Nazi persecution had little prospect of survival.'[3]

The justification, such as it was, for limiting the number of adult Jewish refugees was that the influx of too many Jews risked inflaming antisemitism, which the British authorities feared could, in turn, increase support for Nazism within the UK. There was also a concern that adult immigrants would affect the labour market, depressing wages and competing against existing British workers, a notion endorsed and even encouraged at the time by British trade unions.[4] Britain's attitude to refugees, and to immigration more generally, has always contained this ambivalence, where natural human sympathy rubs up against anxiety over numbers. You can see it in the discrepancy between public expressions of support for Afghans and Ukrainians trying to escape the crises in their countries in 2022 and the reality of the bureaucratic obstacles placed in the way of so many refugees trying to reach safety in Britain. In the 1960s, legislation limiting immigration ran in parallel to laws against racial discrimination, because it was assumed that immigration restrictions were a necessary tool to prevent a racist backlash as immigrants from Britain's former colonies began to establish substantial communities in the United Kingdom. There was even a single Parliamentary Select Committee on Race Relations and Immigration, created in 1968 – as if you cannot have one without needing to take care of the other.

Partly, this exposes a dim view of the British people amongst our leaders. It suggests we are so inhospitable and incapable of embracing difference that 'too many' immigrants – with 'too many' meaning different things to different people – are bound to cause strife. It suggests a view of immigrants as too different, too foreign and potentially too disloyal – or that they are considered that way by sufficient others – to risk allowing too many in. Jews are far from the only immigrant or minority group to be treated this way, but the notion that Jews don't belong – that they can't be trusted and have a 'dual loyalty' – has stuck, because it connects so easily to conspiracist fears about what Jews are up to.

It may seem odd that people would feel sorry for refugees while also fearing them, but this contradiction explains why Britain extended safe haven to thousands of German and Austrian Jews fleeing Nazism, only to intern thousands of those same Jewish refugees as 'enemy aliens' in 1940. One of these internees was a relative whose name I share: my grandpa's uncle, David Bier, who was born in Lemberg, Austria, in 1895 and came to Britain in 1912.* He hadn't been naturalised as a British national by the outbreak of the Second World War, so he was interned in June 1940 along with 27,000 other 'enemy aliens' who were put in camps or shipped overseas. Since the 'vast majority' of these so-called enemy aliens were Jews, most of whom had arrived as refugees from Nazism in the 1930s, they were unlikely – to put it mildly – to be Nazi sympathisers, but there were many within the War Office and MI5 who had a 'long-held distrust of Jews as a whole' and 'had never trusted German or Austrian Jewish refugees'. There was an atmosphere of panic about Nazi spies and saboteurs whipped up by xenophobic newspapers after the defeat of France in May 1940, and the government, having initially ignored calls for mass internment both from within Whitehall and from the right-wing press, found the clamour impossible to resist.[5]

The policy of interning Jewish refugees from Nazism led to the surreal situation whereby even some Jews who had come to Britain on the Kindertransport in 1938 were then interned by the British authorities in July 1940. Public opinion swung both ways, supporting mass internment during Spring 1940 and then receding as the

---

* The Austrian city of Lemberg became the Polish city of Lwów after the First World War, then it became the Soviet city of Lvov, and it is now the Ukrainian city of Lviv.

year went on. The policy didn't last long: by the end of 1940 thousands of internees had been released and numbers steadily reduced over the next couple of years until hardly any remained. This was a temporary scare about suspected Jewish disloyalty, heated up at a moment of crisis and enforced as a form of collective discrimination against 'alien' Jews.[6] As for my great-great-uncle, he was released from internment after a year thanks to lobbying by his two nephews – my grandpa Louis and his brother – who were both serving in the British armed forces at the time. After he died I inherited his silver *kiddush* cup, which I use to say the blessing over wine before our Sabbath meal every Friday evening. It was a wedding gift to him from his Workers' Circle Friendly Society branch in Manchester, back in the days when British Jews were mainly working-class immigrants.

David's internment would have felt intensely personal to my grandpa Louis, whose own father Harry had been interned during the First World War. Louis was around six or seven years old at that time and the distress of seeing his dad hauled away from the family home in Strangeways, north Manchester, stayed with him for ever. In later life my grandpa told us that it had all been a ridiculous mistake following a row over his parents' piano playing. According to my grandpa, when HMS *Hampshire* sank in 1916 while carrying Lord Kitchener – of the famous 'Your Country Needs You!' recruitment posters – their neighbours, who always complained about the piano, called the police and claimed my great-grandparents had been playing extra loud in celebration. It's a funny story, but it almost certainly isn't true, and not just because my grandpa rarely let the facts get in the way of an amusing tale. The simple truth is that my great-grandparents were far too poor to own a piano. More likely is that my grandpa made it up, because the reality – that his father was rounded up just like all the other Austrian Jews (and like his uncle would be during the next war) – was either too painful or too humiliating for him to recount. Being treated as an 'enemy alien' ran in the family for a lot of British Jews during the twentieth century.

SPYING ON COMMUNISTS, SPYING ON JEWS

I only discovered just how much this was the case while researching for my PhD in the National Archives. One afternoon I decided to break the monotony by looking for my other grandpa's application to become a naturalised British citizen. I knew that my maternal grandpa Max had come to this country as a young child – the only one of my grandparents not to be born here – and I also knew, from the stories told by my mum, that he had never been able to get British citizenship. So I typed his name into the search bar and that's when I got my first surprise: his naturalisation file had been sealed for 100 years. Even after a Freedom of Information request I only received a redacted copy. When I finally read it – or the parts of it I was allowed to see – I realised that the reason my grandpa Max never held a British passport was because he had fallen victim to this same official mistrust of his loyalty to his adopted home.

Max had come to this country at the age of four, brought here with his brother and sister from Radom (now in Poland, then in Russia) by my great-grandparents shortly before the First World War. Twice as an adult, in the late 1940s and 1950s, he applied for citizenship and twice he was denied. When the Home Office made the usual internal enquiries they were told by MI5 that 'in 1945 this alien was reported to be an active Communist' who had been seen visiting the party's local headquarters (it was these MI5 reports that were partly redacted in the copy of the file I received). Special Branch concurred, having visited his home and found his bookshelves 'teeming with Communist literature'. I know this part is true, because I inherited his library of Lenin, Marx and other writers after he passed away and often dipped into his books for reference when studying for my degree. The file also noted that his work as an upholsterer did not bring in much income, but admits that poverty alone was insufficient grounds to deny citizenship. It was his politics that were the problem.

I always knew that my grandpa had been in the Communist Party, as well as being a lifelong trade unionist. I have a black and white photo of him striding proudly at the head of a group of marchers under the banner of the Amalgamated Union of Upholsterers. 'Workers of the World Unite,' it reads. He marched in the General Strike of 1926 and was at Cable Street a decade later, when most of the East End of London turned out to prevent a march by Oswald Mosley's Blackshirts. These are both celebrated events in British history now, but back then I expect the authorities saw them in a different light. Max was not very senior in the Communist Party – a minor local official at most, and possibly not even that – and he wasn't any kind of threat to national security. He shared the quiet patriotism of his generation, queueing with hundreds of thousands of others to pay his respects when King George VI lay in state before his funeral in 1952. However, he had organised at least one strike in support of fellow workers who had been made redundant, and there was another occasion when he was arrested while on a picket, although the case was dismissed at the Magistrates' Court. Combined with his political beliefs, this was enough to deny him citizenship.

The final refusal in Max's file concluded that 'his loyalty is still in doubt'.[7]

Max marching with his trade union comrades

Nowhere in his file does it mention that Max was Jewish, but Jews and Communists were often conflated. There had been Jews in prominent positions in the Soviet Union and other Communist states, and the Communist Party of Great Britain attracted Jewish support, but most Communists were not Jews and most Jews were not Communists. As ever with stereotypes the image was not a true reflection of reality, but the idea of 'Judeo-Bolshevism' joined the ranks of antisemitic mythology. At the same time, British officialdom retained a generalised suspicion of Jewish political activism. The authorities were monitoring a growing domestic Jewish anti-fascist movement, made up largely of Jewish soldiers who had returned from defeating Hitler only to find that Britain's far-right leaders, interned for much of the war, were now back on the streets.

These Jewish street fighters were known as the 43 Group, and 'the police, fascists and journalists frequently saw them as indistinguishable from Communists' – a link that the 43 Group, officially apolitical, adamantly denied.[8]

More revealing is the fact that Special Branch and MI5 also monitored the distinctly non-violent, and definitely not Communist, Association of Jewish Ex-Servicemen and Women (AJEX). AJEX held public meetings in the years after the Second World War in Hyde Park, Hampstead Heath, Hackney and other places at which Jewish speakers would denounce fascist antisemitism. Special Branch officers in the crowd carefully noted everything that was said and sent detailed reports of each speech to MI5, who feared that AJEX had been infiltrated by the Communist Party. The premise for this groundless fear was AJEX's public opposition to West German rearmament at the beginning of the 1950s, which MI5 thought might indicate sympathy for Communism (because the Soviet Union was also opposed to German re-armament) rather than a predictable Jewish fear of German militarism so soon after the Holocaust. Reports were sought from police forces in cities with AJEX branches, most of which came back with little evidence. MI5 knew from its own surveillance that the Communist Party was encouraging its Jewish members to join AJEX in the hope of gaining influence, but AJEX comprised the most conservative, patriotic parts of the Jewish establishment – literally British Jews who had risked their lives for this country just a few years previously – and the idea they might be Communist stooges was ludicrous. As Communist Party official Wolf Arnold lamented to comrades at a planning meeting in 1952, 'AJEX was completely controlled by Zionists.'[9]

MI5's fears betrayed a gross ignorance of the contours of the

Jewish community, but this came at a time when MI5's own employment policy was to not recruit any Jewish staff. There was growing violence in Palestine in the period following the Second World War, where Zionist forces were waging an increasingly bitter and deadly insurgency against Britain's colonial presence, and at its most extreme fringes this brought the threat of Zionist terrorism to British shores. The conclusion MI5 drew was that they couldn't trust any British Jews to be loyal enough to work for them, a policy that endured in one form or another into the 1970s. It is not inconceivable that this institutionalised suspicion would have coloured their views on the naturalisation of Jewish immigrants whose applications they were asked to assess.

The permanent rebuff bitterly hurt my grandpa. He knew no other home and spoke no other language but was left stateless throughout his entire life. It was a private humiliation that cut even deeper as his older siblings got their British passports. The absurdity is that his work as an upholsterer took Max into places that nobody who was genuinely a threat to national security should have been allowed anywhere near. During the war he worked at the Handley Page factory in Cricklewood, helping to make planes for the RAF. In later years he was taken on by a company that won contracts at the Houses of Parliament and Buckingham Palace, and he worked in both buildings (the red benches in the House of Lords and some of the Buckingham Palace curtains were partly his handiwork, according to my aunt). He was never a threat to anybody, just a working-class Jew from the East End of London like tens of thousands of others of his generation, but to the Home Office officials who pored over his life and decided his future he was an 'alien' and therefore a threat. It was more upsetting than I expected, when I finally read his file, to see him referred to in this way. 'The alien and his family are living in poor circumstances,' the file notes at one point. 'The alien has correctly completed his application form', says another entry. 'The alien and his wife possess Post Office Savings Books.' And on it went.

It hangs around, this thing about Jews and aliens, and I don't mean the Mel Brooks sketch about 'Jews in Space'.* One of the most damaging episodes of antisemitism in the Labour Party under Jeremy Corbyn's leadership involved a Facebook post by a party member from Liverpool, that showed an alien creature marked with a Jewish Star of David gripping the face of the Statue of Liberty. It was an image inspired directly by the movie *Alien*, in which a monster from another planet implants its egg in the stomach of its living human prey. In the movie, the egg hatches, killing its host as a new alien is born. The message of this Facebook post was clear: Jews are literally enemy aliens, planting their seed to destroy American liberty from within. 'The most accurate photo I've seen all year!' was the comment by this Labour Party member, who took the image from a far-right website. The party judged the image to be anti-Israel rather than antisemitic (even though it made no mention of Israel) and initially let her off with a warning, before some Labour MPs kicked up a fuss and she was suspended.[10]

Fifty years after my grandpa's last, failed, effort to become a British citizen, his daughter – my aunt – was awarded an MBE for a lifetime spent working at Great Ormond Street children's hospital. A family of immigrant heritage advancing in one generation from being considered a threat to national security to becoming a Member of

---

* It's typical Mel Brooks: Orthodox Jewish astronauts flying around the galaxy in Star of David-shaped spaceships, singing, 'We're Jews out in space / we're zooming along protecting the Hebrew race'.

the Order of the British Empire is, you might argue, a compelling example of successful integration. There is nothing more British than working for the NHS and meeting the Queen, and it is true that this country is now much more at ease with, and embracing of, diversity. But then the Windrush scandal happened, in which hundreds of Black Britons who had legally migrated to Britain decades earlier were treated as illegal trespassers, denied their rights and in some cases deported, often to a place they barely remembered. And I thought to myself: that could have been my grandpa.

WHO IS A RACE?

Referring to people who aspire to become British as 'aliens' is not reserved only for Jews, but it was for Jews that this language was first turned into legislation. The very first UK law designed to limit immigration was the Aliens Act 1905, and it was introduced specifically with Jews in mind. As large-scale Jewish immigration into Britain began to pick up speed in the 1880s, there was widespread alarm at the concentrations of impoverished, foreign-sounding Jewish immigrants in the East End of London and parts of other British cities where they settled. Scares about disease, crime, depressed wages and extremist politics that are familiar in present-day debates about immigration were all heard at that time. In 1902 a Royal Commission on Alien Immigration was set up to investigate, hearing ample evidence from various officials and experts about the numbers, origin, behaviour and character of 'Alien Jews'. This was all expressed in highly racialised terms that give the lie to the idea that antisemitism is not, or can never be, a form of racism. The 'average Jew' displays 'poverty of muscle' and a 'highly-nervous temperament', advised one witness giving evidence to the commission, but at the same time has a 'high moral tone' and 'an astounding capacity to extend exertion for a lengthy period of time'. In a comment that demonstrates the direct line between racialist thinking and assumptions of disloyalty, this witness said there is an aloofness to Jews because 'the racial tie between the Jews of different countries is greater than the tie between immigrants who arrive in London and the English by whom they are surrounded'.[11]

Alien Jews will not assimilate, said another witness, and when Jewish landlords give preferential rates to Jewish tenants 'the position becomes so intolerable considering the habits and customs, and the ways of the aliens – that the British go'.[12] Eye surgeons from London hospitals disagreed with each other over whether certain eye infections were 'a disease of race', brought in by 'aliens ... [who] spread it among English children'.[13] Several witnesses gave more sympathetic evidence, including leading members of the Jewish community, but disparaging views of 'Alien Jews' were widespread. Controls on Jewish immigration had support across the political spectrum: they were proposed by a Conservative government (although opposed by Winston Churchill, who was a Tory MP at that time), but supported by large parts of the trade union movement who saw Jewish immigrants as taking jobs away from British workers. The Royal Commission published its report in 1903, and two years later the Aliens Act became law.[14]

This was a time when racialist thinking was everywhere. Long-standing assumptions about the inherent superiority of European civilisation over other cultures and peoples translated into highly theorised, 'scientific' notions of superior and inferior races. The science was of course bogus, but the idea that a person's racial heritage shaped their inherent characteristics, their value to society and, crucially, their propensity to disloyalty was widespread. Jews, along with pretty much everyone else, were racialised through this process and a new language emerged through which Jews were predominantly spoken and thought about as a race, rather than exclusively or primarily as a religious group. This could have a positive or negative purpose. Winston Churchill wrote in 1920 that Jews 'are beyond all question the most formidable and the most remarkable race which has ever appeared in the world', which is quite the compliment, while Adolf Hitler in 1919 wrote that 'the Jews are definitely a race and not a religious community ... [their] activities produce a racial tuberculosis among nations', which is rather more insulting.[15] Hitler and Churchill didn't agree on much when it came to the Jews,* but their assumption that Jews were a race was shared by just about everyone. The phrase 'Jewish race' first appeared in *The Times* in 1803; it was first used in Parliament in 1826 (the first parliamentary usage was a report on the corn trade in Poland, which observed that 'the merchants, bankers, and traders, are nearly as exclusively of the Jewish race');[16] and first appeared in the *Jewish Chronicle* newspaper in 1842. As well as becoming a standard way of referring to Jews, this also became the primary language of antisemitism.

The idea that Jews are a race might jar with the modern reader. In today's identity politics, race is largely determined by skin colour, and Jews are largely perceived as white. This appears to be what Whoopi Goldberg was getting at when she said on American TV in February 2022 that 'the Holocaust isn't about race ... it's not about

---

* Churchill thought and wrote in highly racialised terms, but his understanding of race was still very different to Hitler's. Churchill, for example, argued, 'There are all sorts of men – good, bad and, for the most part, indifferent – in every country, and in every race. Nothing is more wrong than to deny to an individual, on account of race or origin, his right to be judged on his personal merits and conduct.' Hitler, on the other hand, saw racial characteristics as entirely immutable, calling Jews 'a non-German, foreign race, unwilling and unable to sacrifice its racial characteristics'.

race, it's about man's inhumanity to man ... These are two groups of white people.' She then clarified that in her view the Nazis 'had issues with ethnicity, not with race. Because most of the Nazis were white people and most of the people they were attacking were white people.'[17] Goldberg got it wrong, and not only because some Jews are not white: Nazi persecution of Jews was very much about race. Nazi ideology divided people into a whole range of different racial groups, with the Aryan race at the top of the pile and the Jews at the bottom. The 1935 Nuremberg Race Laws denied German citizenship to Jews (and others) on racial grounds and banned marriage or sexual relations between Germans and those deemed to be racially non-German – primarily Jews.* In contrast to the Nazi approach, in today's racial politics racism is seen as the domination of people of colour by white people with power, and most Jews are lumped in with all other people who present as white. Goldberg was projecting her understanding of race in modern-day America back through time onto a period when a totally different understanding of race was in play and ended up being widely criticised and temporarily dropped from TV as a result. Her misfortune was to unwittingly miss the way that consensus over race and racial categories follows shifting political and social attitudes of time and place rather than any meaningful biological reality, and therefore it can easily change.

You can see this evolution in the changing attitudes to one of the great politicians of the Victorian era, Benjamin Disraeli, who faced incessant antisemitic invective when he was Prime Minister due to his Jewish origins. Disraeli was born to a Jewish family and baptised into the Church of England by his father at the age of twelve, but

---

* The official names of these laws were the Reich Citizenship Law and The Law for the Protection of German Blood and German Honour.

his baptism did not deter his antisemitic critics. He was variously condemned as a 'traitorous Jew', a 'haughty Jew', and an 'abominable Jew' defined by his 'craftiness of race'. His childhood conversion to Christianity was treated as an irrelevance that could not erase the racial qualities he was born with. When Russia declared war on Turkey in 1877 and Disraeli argued for Britain to take Turkey's side, he was accused of backing a Muslim power against a Christian one because Jews are an 'Asiatic' and 'oriental' people, no matter how long they have lived in England, and his motives were supposedly 'to avenge the real or fancied injuries of the Jewish race' in Russia.[18] It may sound odd that anyone thought Disraeli's Jewish heritage would make him inclined to support a Muslim power rather than a Christian one. In today's global politics, you are more likely to come across talk of a 'Judeo-Christian civilisation' of shared values that is in conflict with Islam, rather than Jews and Muslims ganging up on Christian nations. Just as the supposedly unalterable characteristics of races often change to reflect broader prejudices rather than any coherent science, so the politics that they are deployed to justify can change with them.

British officialdom likes to define people by ethnicity or religion, but it is somewhat confused when it comes to Jews. The UK government website's official biography of Disraeli describes him as 'Britain's first, and so far only, Jewish Prime Minister', despite the fact that he converted out of the Jewish faith well before embarking on his political career.[19] This desire to celebrate Disraeli as a Jewish Prime Minister is a welcome nod to Britain's diverse past, but it throws up some awkward questions about whether Jews are a religion or an ethnicity in the eyes of the British state. If the government's official biography is correct and Disraeli was still Jewish when he took high office, despite having converted to Christianity in childhood, then Jewishness cannot be solely a religious identity. It is not possible to be simultaneously Jewish and Anglican if we are only talking about religious affiliation. Rather, if Disraeli was Britain's first Jewish Prime Minister then it must also be Disraeli, not Rishi Sunak, who was Britain's first ethnic minority Prime Minister, with Judaism being his racial identity.

However, elsewhere in the official record Disraeli is disregarded when it comes to ethnic minority parliamentarians. A publication from the House of Commons Library listing ethnic minority MPs elected between 1767 and 1922 makes no mention of Disraeli or any other Jewish MPs, and nor does a much longer report by the House of Commons Library on ethnic diversity in public life.[20] According to Diversity UK, 'an equality charity that aims to research, advocate and promote ideas for improving diversity and inclusion in Britain', the Conservative government in July 2019 presented Britain's 'most ethnically diverse Cabinet ever', with six ministers of black or Asian backgrounds. Even more striking, according to Diversity UK, there had only been five previous ministers of ethnic minority backgrounds in the whole history of British governments up to that point: Paul Boateng, Valerie Amos, Sayeeda Warsi, Sajid Javid and Priti Patel.[21] In keeping with many other organisations and commentators who track ethnic representation in public life, Diversity UK disregarded the numerous Jewish ministers who have served in Conservative and Labour governments when they recounted the history of ethnic minority Cabinet ministers.

It gets even more complicated when you look at how Jews are treated in British law. The Equality Act and other anti-discrimination laws have treated Jews as a race or ethnicity since the first Race Relations Act was drawn up in the 1960s. However when new legislation was introduced in the 2000s outlawing religious hatred, Jews were included in this too. If you attack a Jewish person in the street and are arrested for it, you might be prosecuted for a religious hate crime, a racial one, or both together. Jews are listed as a religion rather than an ethnic group in the UK census; except the 2021 census for Northern Ireland and the 2022 Scottish census also listed Jews as an example of 'other ethnic group', but the forms in England and Wales didn't.[22]

Confused? You aren't alone. When the British government passed the first Race Relations Act in 1965, the then Home Secretary, Sir Frank Soskice, tied himself in knots when an MP asked him whether it would include 'those British citizens who are of the Jewish faith, because it is widely held by many authorities that Jewish citizens are of British race'. Soskice was sure that his new law would protect Jews from discrimination, but he wasn't very clear why:

> It is certainly the intention of the Government that people of Jewish faith should be covered ... I would have thought a person of Jewish faith, if not regarded as caught by the word 'racial' would undoubtedly be caught by the word 'ethnic', but if not caught by the word 'ethnic' would certainly be caught by the scope of the word 'national', as certainly having a national origin. He would certainly have an origin which many people would describe as an ethnic if not a racial origin.

His suggestion that Jewishness constitutes a 'national origin' all of its own drew a howl of outrage from some MPs, who felt that it sailed uncomfortably close to the antisemitic notion that British

Jews are not really British. Soskice – who, remember, was trying to ensure that Jews would be protected by his new law banning racial discrimination – tried to explain himself but only dug his hole even deeper:

> Whatever the religion a person professes, whether the Jewish religion or any other religion, that person also has some origin. It may be purely a national origin. It may be that he has an English origin, many centuries back. He may be a person of foreign origin. But the word 'national' would cover him. Or he might be of an origin which ordinary people in ordinary English parlance might describe as of a particular ethnic origin. Whatever his religion may be, he must also have some blood origin ... that the words we have chosen ... are clearly wide enough to cover persons from whatever origin they may derive.[23]

What Sir Frank Soskice had stumbled upon, if only he had realised, is that Jews do not fit neatly into any of the identity categories that Western societies have come up with. For example, Judaism is a monotheistic religion that invented the idea of a single God, and much of the Jewish culture, tradition, calendar and diet revolve around religious laws and festivals. Like most religions, if you aren't born into Judaism you can join by converting. However, it is perfectly feasible, and more common than you might think, to be a Jewish atheist without any contradictions or complications. Being Jewish is something you inherit from your mother, like recipes for chicken soup and *kneidlach*, and a person who is born Jewish can dispense with every religious practice, custom and tradition, lose all belief in God and reject the entirety of Jewish religious law and practice and still be as Jewish as the Chief Rabbi. We take it for granted now that Christians, Jews, Muslims, Hindus and Jedis all belong in the category we call 'religion' and therefore share the same basic characteristics of faith and belief, but this is very much rooted in the Christian idea of what a religion is.

Just as being Jewish doesn't fit the common idea of what it means to be part of a religion, it also doesn't match ordinary notions of race or ethnicity, because the Jewish people comprise an ethnic or racial group in which you will find Jews of every skin colour and ethnic appearance (which further confounds the assumption that all Jews are white). This is most apparent if you go to Israel, which has absorbed Jewish immigrants from every continent during its short history. When you reach the front of the long and always frustratingly slow passport queue at Ben Gurion Airport, if the young, uniformed official who greets you in the booth is Jewish (approximately 25 per cent of Israel's population is not) then they are as likely to be of black or Middle Eastern appearance as they are to be white. Jews around the world share genetic similarities with each other, but they also, unsurprisingly, share genetic similarities with other populations in the countries where Jewish communities have lived over the past 2,000 years. There is no single way to 'look Jewish'.

Then there is the idea of Jewish peoplehood itself, a nationality bound by a common history, culture, religion and, in the distant past and once again in modern times, a common homeland – albeit one that most Jews don't live in. It is rooted in a story of dispersal from the ancient Jewish homeland in Judea in AD 70, only to return after 2,000 years of exile with the creation of the State of Israel. Whether or not this is an accurate or complete account of Jewish history, it is a narrative that drives a powerful sense of Jewish peoplehood. Zionism as a political movement relied on the idea that Jews form a nation of their own that has the right to a nation state, just like all others. It was a controversial idea at first because some took it to imply that Jews are not loyal citizens of their own countries, but that wasn't what this idea of Jewish nationhood was about at all. Rather, it appealed to Jews partly because it reflected the connection that Jewish people always felt with each other, wherever they were from around the world.*

What this all amounts to is the difficulty of pinning down Jewish identity within the standard terminology and categories that usually identify and distinguish different groups in British society. Religion, race, ethnicity, culture, ancestry, history, tradition and peoplehood all play a role in constructing what amounts, for want of a better word, to Jewishness. Most Jews define themselves more than one way: in a 2018 poll of 4,000 Jews across Europe, three-quarters defined their Jewish identity in multiple ways, with the most popular options being a combination of religion, parentage, culture, heritage and ethnicity.[24] And different parts of Jewishness will matter more to each Jew you'll meet. It's a mess, but no more than the rest of humanity.

With all this confusion, perhaps it is no wonder that we are still having to talk about what antisemitism actually is. It can be a form of racism, a type of religious prejudice, a conspiracy theory, a method of scapegoating and even, at times, an entire belief system. It allows you to look down on Jews as an inferior race or to imagine yourself a heroic fighter standing up for the oppressed against the hidden

---

* My great-grandfather Harry wrote 'Jews' in the nationality column for his entire family in the 1911 UK census, although that may have been a hangover from the system of categorising all ethnic groups as nationalities in Tsarist Russia, rather than a conscious expression of identity on his part.

hand of Jewish power. Just as Jews do not neatly fit into the non-Jewish shaped holes of race, religion, ethnicity or nation but straddle all of them in different ways, so antisemitism also crosses these categories without fitting any of them perfectly. It overlaps with racism and with religious discrimination but also has distinct features of its own. The different elements of antisemitism support each other like scaffolding: try thinking of it as something that shares aspects with other types of prejudice and bigotry, while having characteristics all of its own. But if anyone tells you that antisemitism is not racism because Jews are not a race – with the implication that if it isn't racism then it doesn't matter as much – they really have missed the point. Jews have been *treated* in racist ways enough times in the past for it not to *matter* whether antisemitism meets today's definition of what racism is. Once you've been given the alien label, it is hard to shake off.

NOTICING AND NAMING
The antisemitic charge of dual loyalty relies on the sense of alienness to imply that British Jews cannot be as British as others whose family roots reach deeper into British soil. They can never be truly and solely British and therefore can never really be trusted. It connects racist prejudice that Jews don't belong here to broader antisemitic conspiracy theories about what they are up to. While the overtly racist language might have receded, the idea that Jews can never be truly and wholly loyal to the country of their birth reappears with unnerving frequency.

In 2011, Labour MP Paul Flynn questioned whether Britain's then ambassador to Israel, Matthew Gould, could be trusted to do his job properly because Gould was Jewish. According to Flynn, it would have been preferable to appoint 'someone with roots in the UK [who] can't be accused of having Jewish loyalty'. Flynn told the *Jewish Chronicle*, 'In the past there hasn't been a Jewish ambassador to Israel and I think that is a good decision – to avoid the accusation that they have gone native.'[25] Flynn later apologised. In 2009, veteran British diplomat Oliver Miles objected to the fact that two of the five members of the Chilcot Inquiry, appointed to investigate the causes, conduct and aftermath of the Iraq War, were Jewish. Writing in *The Independent*, Miles pointed out that Sir Lawrence Freedman and Sir Martin Gilbert, two historians on the inquiry panel, were Jewish, 'and Gilbert at least has a record of active support for Zionism'. In Miles's view, this meant that 'if and when the inquiry is accused of a whitewash, such handy ammunition will be available. Membership should not only be balanced; it should be seen to be balanced.'[26] At best, Miles was pandering to prejudice by conceding that having Jewish panellists might invoke an antisemitic reaction in others; at worst, he was guilty of it himself. He was supported by Richard Ingrams, the former editor of *Private Eye*, who called it 'a perfectly respectable point to raise'.[27]

The implication is that Jews can only be trusted so far and certainly not with anything that involves Britain's national interests in the Middle East, because they can't be wholly loyal to those interests to the same extent as a person of pure British stock. It takes us right back to the idea of Jews as aliens, a potential enemy within. Ingrams came up with a simple solution, which was to ignore the opinion of any Jew writing about Israel. He explained how this works in his *Observer* column in 2003:

> I have developed a habit when confronted by letters to the editor in

support of the Israeli government to look at the signature to see if the writer has a Jewish name. If so, I tend not to read it. Too few people in this modern world are prepared to declare an interest when it comes to this kind of thing.[28]

The sheer perniciousness of his suggestion reveals itself if you follow his logic a little further. The challenge for Ingrams and others who are so-minded is that some Jews are more difficult to identify than others: because what, after all, counts as a 'Jewish name'?

Former BBC Middle East correspondent Tim Llewellyn was vexed by exactly this quandary, which was made worse by the habit of Jewish families to anglicise foreign-sounding surnames. This is very common: my family name was Reich until sometime in the late 1920s or 1930s, when official documents show that my relatives started to use Rich instead. Pretty much every famous American Jewish actor, musician or composer in the twentieth century changed their name to fit in, but Llewellyn thought this mundane practice had more devious motives. Speaking about US Middle East envoy Dennis Ross at a Glasgow book launch in 2004, Llewellyn said, 'What a lovely Anglo-Saxon name! But Dennis Ross is not just a Jew, he is a Zionist, a long-time Zionist … and now directs an Israeli-funded think tank in Washington. He is a Zionist propagandist.' Not only that, but Israelis, Llewellyn said, have 'learned all sorts of tricks. They are wizards at communication; they speak ten different sorts of English, from American to South African to Canadian.'[29] Cunning Jews, hiding their true loyalties behind English-sounding surnames and American accents.

Jewish-sounding names were also considered troublesome by the Foreign and Commonwealth Office in the 1970s. At the time the FCO ran a diplomatic school in the hills above Beirut called the Middle East Centre for Arab Studies (MECAS), where staff posted to the Middle East were sent to learn the Arabic language and culture. This centre also offered courses to external students from the diplomatic services of friendly countries and from private companies operating in Arab countries, and from the late 1960s these commercial courses were increasingly popular. This created a problem, because some of these commercial applicants, according to the then director of the centre, were Jewish or had 'names that sounded Jewish'. The FCO was already sensitive to local conspiracy theories in Lebanon that MECAS was a base for British espionage; having Jewish students on site could, they feared, bring the whole thing down. One of MECAS's former directors and probably the FCO's greatest post-war Arabist, Sir James Craig, put the dilemma in these terms: 'Which was the correct course: to knuckle under to prejudice or to risk the life of an important institution, damage the interests of British diplomacy and hinder the careers of generations of British officials, businessmen and students?' The FCO's solution was indeed to 'knuckle under to prejudice'. Acting with clearance from the department's legal adviser, they resolved to inform any applicant that people 'of the Jewish faith or of Jewish descent' would be unlikely to get a Lebanese visa (even though their Beirut embassy advised this was not the case), and therefore could not study at MECAS. This followed a precedent set in 1968 when Saudi Arabia rejected the nominated British Ambassador, Horace Phillips, upon discovering that he was Jewish. Phillips never served in an Arab post again. Tellingly, in his recounting of this episode Craig distinguished between 'British' applicants and 'Jewish' ones, even though the latter were often British themselves.[30]

Similar thinking got Jeremy Corbyn in trouble when it emerged that he had said, in a 2013 speech, that 'Zionists ... have two problems. One is that they don't want to study history, and secondly, having lived in this country for a very long time, probably all their lives, they don't understand English irony either.'[31] He didn't specify, but 'Zionists' who have lived in the UK for most or all of their lives is a form of words that only makes sense as a reference to supporters of Israel with immigrant heritage – and that generally means Jews. The assertion that Jews who were born in Britain have failed to acquire that most English of qualities – a sense of irony – is a reminder that this xenophobia-tinged antisemitism is not limited to the political right.

Sometimes the idea that Jews cannot be loyal to their own country becomes a national scandal. One of the most famous antisemitic episodes in modern European history happened in France in the 1890s, when a Jewish army officer, Captain Alfred Dreyfus, was arrested and accused of spying for Germany. Dreyfus was found guilty, publicly humiliated in a ceremony stripping him of his military rank and insignia and imprisoned on Devil's Island, a French prison colony off the coast of South America. It soon became apparent that he was innocent and the real spy was another officer, Major Ferdinand Esterhazy, but at this point the army closed ranks and covered up the truth. Pressure from Dreyfus's supporters led to a retrial six years after the original verdict, but Dreyfus was yet again found guilty. Better to allow a Jew to be considered a traitor than to sully the honour of the French military, so the thinking went. The affair was the single most explosive dividing line in French politics and society for much of the 1890s: liberalism and republican values on one side, tradition and military honour on the other. The most famous authors, artists and intellectuals in France lined up on either side of the argument while antisemitic mobs rioted in the streets, and all over the question of whether loyalty or treachery was the true nature of the Jews. Dreyfus was eventually cleared and, astonishingly, after all he had been through, went on to serve in the French Army in the First World War. The affair caused shockwaves precisely because France had been the first country in Europe to extend full citizenship to its Jews following the Revolution. This had not been a smooth path to integration: there had been anti-Jewish riots in Alsace a decade earlier by farmers and peasants who were indebted to Jewish moneylenders, and the National Assembly only granted full citizenship to Jews in 1791 after a debate over whether Jews were commanded by religious law to charge interest on loans. In 1808 Napoleon Bonaparte, despite liberating those Jews across Europe who lived in the territories he conquered for France, introduced a charter limiting where in France Jews could settle and restricting Jewish involvement in moneylending. Antisemitism was already prevalent in French society by the 1890s, and the Dreyfus Affair unleashed its full potential. It remains an example of how antisemitism can become a force that shapes an entire nation.

It is an insult felt painfully by anyone of recent immigrant heritage, this idea that however hard you try, even if you are yourself born here, you can never truly be one of them. It is something that has been experienced by Jews throughout the ages, and even though British Jews are much more integrated today, it still operates in different ways. I suspect most people don't even think of this kind of racism as affecting Jews, but it does. Sometimes these reminders that we are not full members of the British club are more clumsy than malicious. I was once invited by a national sporting body to the launch of a taskforce to investigate antisemitism and Islamophobia, only to be served sausage rolls for lunch. Every year I am invited to meetings with the police to discuss hate crime or community relations that have been arranged on a Jewish holiday, when orthodox Jews cannot attend. I'm sure these are innocent mistakes (although it really isn't that hard to google for a religious holidays calendar), but they rub it in nonetheless.

At other times it is much nastier. The dual loyalty charge cuts so deep because, as with Dreyfus, it has been the cause of so much Jewish suffering throughout history. For Jews to be treated as a people apart, who have weird rules about not eating pork and who pray on the wrong days, is insulting but not necessarily threatening. It is the idea that this tiny group of people pose a mortal danger, either by conspiring with each other or through hidden loyalties to enemy states, that brings calamity. There is a long tradition of Jewish communities doing their best to fit in and prove their loyalty, and there remains within living memory the ultimate example of what can happen when Jews are turned back into aliens on a whim. The Holocaust was the greatest crime ever committed on European soil, and it could only have been inflicted on the Jews in the time, place and way that it was, because it was only in relation to Jews that this murderous mix of religious intolerance, bogus science, conspiracy theory, myth, libel, fear and contempt had such a hold on the European imagination. The Holocaust instilled a permanent sense of precariousness to Jewish life that is often invisible to others but lies unarticulated beneath the surface of all diaspora communities. You can only understand the impact that antisemitism still has by tracing the shadow that the Holocaust casts over Jewish life – no, over all of Europe – today.

CHAPTER SIX

NEVER AGAIN

Dubno is a small town in western Ukraine, about sixty miles from the village where my great-grandfather was born. It is best known for its castle, one of Ukraine's oldest, beneath whose walls the River Ikva winds its way through the town. There is a disused Russian fort from the days of Tsar Alexander II, all ghostly ruins overgrown by the encroaching forest, a cathedral, a smattering of domed churches and, like many places in Ukraine, a statue of the poet Taras Shevchenko. There is a forlorn old synagogue, too; a reminder that Dubno used to be home to a substantial Jewish community, until the German SS and their Ukrainian accomplices murdered the last of them – 5,000 Jewish men, women and children – at an old airfield just outside town in October 1942.

There had been Jews in Dubno since at least the 1500s. In different times the town had several synagogues and Jewish schools, a Jewish printing press and hospital, youth movements and summer camps. By the time German forces arrived in June 1941 there were 12,000 Jews living there, over half the population of the town. They were forced into a ghetto in April 1942 and murdered in a series of SS *Aktions** over the course of the year, until October when the last few thousand were packed into trucks and driven out to the airfield by Ukrainian militiamen. On arrival they were greeted by German officers, whips in hand, who forced them to undress until completely naked. Clothes were carefully sorted and left in separate piles, hundreds of items deep. Families stood together, parents comforting weeping children in a final embrace. An old woman held a baby in her arms, singing softly while the child's parents stood by, awaiting their final moments. Then, in groups of twenty, they were herded to the side of a large ditch where thousands of corpses already lay bleeding. An SS machine-gunner sitting by the ditch, feet dangling over the edge and cigarette in mouth, instructed them to lie facedown on top of the previous victims, and then shot them all, one by one, in the back of the neck. On and on it went, truck after truck, group after group, for three days, until all 5,000 were dead.

This was not the first time the Jews of Dubno had been victims of an atrocity. Over a thousand were slaughtered during a national Cossack uprising led by Bohdan Khmelnytsky in 1648 and 1649, in which tens of thousands of Jews were murdered across Ukraine, and there was a smaller pogrom in 1918 that killed more than a dozen. But this was the last time Jews were ever murdered in such numbers in Dubno, because by the end of 1942 there were no more Jews left to kill.

5,000 people: slightly less than the capacity of the Royal Albert Hall, give or take. When we look at the Holocaust as a whole, with its hundreds of camps and killing sites strung across the European

---

* An *Aktion* was the name for an operation where a large number of Jews were assembled, transported to a killing site and then massacred.

continent, connected by thousands of miles of railway lines, all planned, managed and run by countless SS officers, camp guards, bureaucrats and scientists serving an unprecedented industry of death, the 5,000 Jews murdered on those autumn days in Dubno are easy to miss. They make up less than 0.01 per cent of the 6 million Jewish victims of the Nazi genocide; a rounding error numerically speaking, if I can be so crass. The equivalent of half a day's work for the gas chambers of Auschwitz when they were running at full pelt, processing live Jews into dead ones at maximum efficiency. Sometimes you can lose yourself in the mind-boggling scale of the killing, the sheer vastness of the numbers involved, and forget that each one represents an individual human life, each with its own unique blend of talents and skills, likes and dislikes, worries and flaws, memories of the past and hopes for the future. All murdered for the same, simple reason: they were a Jew.

This is a book about antisemitism today: the kind of antisemitism that affects Jews in Britain and around the world, right now. It is about why this antisemitism still happens and what you can do about it. This isn't a history book (although as you will have noticed by now, how we got here is very much part of the story), so in theory it shouldn't need a chapter dedicated to the Holocaust, because that was all a long time ago and, however bad antisemitism is today, it isn't a genocide. Except the Holocaust is a cloud that hangs over all conversations about antisemitism today, perhaps more so than ever before. The Shoah (the Hebrew name for the Holocaust) was antisemitism's most extreme expression, and its memory is the most powerful, urgent warning against the resurgence of this – or indeed, any – deadly hatred. It shapes our reactions to antisemitism and informs our efforts to educate about broader prejudice and discrimination. This means that a book about antisemitism in the twenty-first century cannot avoid looking up at the Holocaust-shaped cloud that overshadows this entire subject. The events of the Holocaust may be in the past, but the questions they demand of us are as vivid as ever.

In a way it feels superfluous, disrespectful even, to explain why I want you to read about the Holocaust. As the Soviet Jewish writer Vasily Grossman wrote in his account of Treblinka death camp, shortly after its liberation:

> It is the writer's duty to tell this terrible truth, and it is the civilian duty of the reader to learn it. Everyone who would turn away, who would shut his eyes and walk past would insult the memory of the dead. Everyone who does not know the truth about this would never be able to understand.[1]

You could read only books about the Holocaust for the rest of your life and still not know every detail or grasp the depth of its inhumanity. But I don't want you to learn about the Holocaust just for the sake of it. I want to think about what it means, both for people who are Jewish and those who are not. When we say 'never again', what is it that we are committing to? Opposing genocide, for sure. But given that genocide is not an everyday occurrence in our society (although, appallingly, post-war genocides have still happened), there must be more to it than that. The philosopher Theodor Adorno declared that humanity is compelled 'to arrange their thoughts and actions so that Auschwitz will not repeat itself, so that nothing similar will happen'.[2] What, then, ought those thoughts and actions to look like?

Sometimes using the Holocaust as a reference point can be misleading. Not every antisemite is a Nazi, but the Holocaust encourages the misconception that antisemitism is exclusively a far-right pursuit. This especially means that antisemitic attitudes and stereotypes on the political left or from within other minority communities, amongst those who define themselves as anti-fascist or anti-racist, are missed. Similarly, not every antisemitic comment is the first step to genocide: most people who make a caustic remark about Jews being stingy or who mull conspiracy theories about the Rothschilds would never physically harm anyone, much less endorse the extermination of 6 million people. However, the knowledge that the Holocaust began with anti-Jewish rhetoric and propaganda, escalating through different stages before ending with murder, means it feels complacent to dismiss racist insults as just words. It urges us to treat every manifestation of anti-Jewish prejudice as potentially the first step on that long, twisted road to the gas chamber. Meanwhile for Jewish people the Shoah is a warning of the fragility and uncertainty of our existence, even in democratic states. Jews were set upon by their neighbours, rounded up by their own police forces, deported by their own governments and murdered by their fellow Europeans. Every legal, cultural and behavioural taboo that might have prevented such atrocities was swept away in a crime of unprecedented barbarism.

I asserted at the end of the previous chapter that the Holocaust could only have happened to Jews. I do not mean that only Jews can be victims of genocide or that Fascism persecuted nobody else, neither of which would be true. There have been genocides before and since the attempt to eradicate the Jewish people. Nazi Germany targeted many different groups for elimination, including gay people,

Jehovah's Witnesses and those with disabilities or mental illness, mainly because the Nazis considered their lives to be worthless. They hoped that, through eugenics, these supposed 'weaknesses' could be bred out of society. The genocidal murder of between 200,000 and 500,000 Roma and Sinti people ran in parallel with the Holocaust of Jews, while Germany also planned for the death of millions of Slavs through starvation and slave labour. Humanity's lamentable capacity for hatred and violence on a monstrous scale is a depressing part of our history and did not end in 1945, but the Jewish Holocaust was nonetheless unique.

Unlike other genocides, the Nazis did not murder 6 million Jews because they wanted to occupy their land or steal their possessions or as a spasm of violent hatred (although all of those happened). It occurred during wartime, but the Jews were not an active combatant in the Second World War, whatever the Nazis thought. It was not territorially limited: the goal was to kill every single Jew, everywhere they lived, including in neutral and yet-to-be conquered countries far from any warzone (the planners of the Final Solution drew up a list that totalled 11 million potential Jewish victims, including 330,000 Jews in the UK and 4,000 in Ireland). There was no escape through religious conversion, displays of political loyalty or any other route: if you were considered part of the Jewish race, you were marked for death.*

---

* The Nazis went to extreme, and at times bizarre, lengths to determine who counted as a Jew. When German forces occupied the Caucasus in the southern Soviet Union in 1942, they came across small communities of 'Mountain Jews', who had adopted many of the customs of the surrounding Muslim population. This confused Nazi racial theorists, who spent several months pondering whether these Mountain Jews were racially Jewish enough to be killed. The matter was referred to the highest racial authorities in Berlin, while 'German officers visited Mountain Jews' homes, attended ceremonies such as weddings, and interviewed witnesses about their customs'. Despite this extensive research the Nazi authorities never resolved the question of whether the Mountain Jews were racially Jewish or merely followed some Jewish religious practices and, while hundreds were massacred, most Mountain Jews survived Nazi occupation. (Kiril Feferman, 'Nazi Germany and the Mountain Jews: Was There a Policy?', *Holocaust and Genocide Studies*, vol. 21, no. 1 (Spring 2007), pp. 96–114)

The goal was not just to kill Jewish people: it was to erase Jewish culture, both religious and secular, from history. During the 1930s Nazi Germany organised public bonfires of Jewish religious books and works by Jewish authors. In Nazi-occupied Poland, special German squads were assigned the task of burning synagogues and *Torah* (Old Testament) scrolls, as part of the systematic plunder and destruction of synagogues, libraries and Jewish collections. In Lublin, a German military band played as the contents of the Talmudic Academy, one of the greatest institutions of Jewish religious learning anywhere in the world, were burned.* 'The destruction was highly organised and a central part of the overall plan of annihilation.'[3] It wasn't enough that Jews had to die. The very *idea* of a Jewish people had to be killed off for ever.†

Nazi policy always envisaged a Europe empty of Jews, but it was only with the German invasion, first of Poland in 1939 and especially Russia in 1941, that the method for achieving this definitively shifted from forced emigration to annihilation. The 6 million Jews murdered in the Holocaust were mostly killed in Poland, Belarus, Ukraine, the Baltic States and Russia: all lands to the east of Germany that had been earmarked as *lebensraum* by the Nazi regime that coveted them as essential for the growth, prosperity and sustenance of the German Reich. This was a war of territorial expansion for a German racial empire in Europe, but it would be a mistake to assume that the extermination of the Jews was just an accident of circumstance, one of several racial groups targeted for elimination

---

* This was not the first time this had happened in Europe. In 1240 the Talmud was put on trial in Paris, found to be blasphemous and copies were later seized and publicly burned.

† The Nazis did keep some looted Jewish books, artefacts and archival documents, which they planned to display in a 'Museum of an Extinct Race' in Prague after they had finished off all the Jews. This collection is now held in the Prague Jewish Museum.

or removal because they were in the way of Germany's territorial ambitions. The Nazi desire to clear millions of non-Germans out of their newly conquered territories in the East cannot explain why Jews from Paris, Antwerp or Amsterdam were transported hundreds of miles eastwards into these same lands, before being killed. Nor, if the goal was to build a German Empire on Russian, Polish or Ukrainian soil, was it necessary to kill French, Belgian or Dutch Jews at all. The Holocaust cannot be explained by the usual military, economic or territorial factors that underpin other genocides.

If you think of the Holocaust as an aspect of the Second World War rather than as part of Europe's long tradition of antisemitism, you'll miss this. The driving force that propelled this multi-year, international campaign of extermination was the obsessive Nazi belief that the Jewish race posed a mortal threat to Germany, and thereby to the world. The Nazis viewed Jews as sub-human *untermenschen* like Slavs and other non-Aryans, but they also feared them as rivals for global dominance. It was because they were utterly convinced that the Jews were the secret force behind every other world power, driving them all into another war to benefit so-called International Jewry, that the Nazis concluded they had to eradicate Jews from the earth. The belief that Germany had lost the First World War because it was 'stabbed in the back' by Jews, socialists and other traitors was widely held on the nationalist right in Germany, and Hitler was determined that lightning would not strike twice. In an infamous speech in the Reichstag on 30 January 1939, the Führer made this chilling promise:

> Today I will once more be a prophet: if the international Jewish financiers in and outside Europe should succeed in plunging the

nations once more into a world war, then the result will not be the Bolshevisation of the earth, and thus the victory of Jewry, but the annihilation of the Jewish race in Europe!'[4]

Of course, 'international Jewish financiers' were doing no such thing. Jews were not responsible for either of the world wars. Nor did Jewish bankers have greater sympathy for Communism than any other bankers did, but in Hitler's mind Judaism and Bolshevism were effectively synonymous. When Hitler uttered his threat in January 1939 Nazi policy was still to try to deport Jews from Germany rather than kill them, but once war began and the doors of the world, already barely open to Jewish refugees, slammed shut, this prophecy became reality. The Holocaust is the only genocide predicated on such a fantastical conspiracist belief about a cosmic struggle for the future of humanity.

This was the culmination of all the myths, libels and conspiracy theories that Europe had nurtured about its Jews for centuries, given a thoroughly modern, pseudo-scientific twist. The Nazis used the blood libel, the *Protocols* and many other, older antisemitic tropes in their anti-Jewish propaganda. The Holocaust was not an inevitable outcome of this antisemitic history, and in many ways it was different from the persecutions that had gone before. Medieval antisemitism, for all its occasional murderousness, held to Christian doctrine that Jews should be left alive as witnesses to their own sinfulness and offered salvation through conversion. Neither was true of Nazism, but the Holocaust nevertheless 'was inconceivable and is unexplainable without that deep history of thought.'[5]

The Holocaust, therefore, is not only a Jewish story: it is also part of Europe's past, a genocide imagined and orchestrated by the most culturally and scientifically advanced nation in the heart of Europe and a warning of where antisemitism can lead. Jews never amounted to more than 1 per cent of Germany's population, yet a political movement that promised to save Germany by ridding it of its Jews managed to take hold of the entire nation and, ultimately, led it to ruin. We usually think of antisemitism as a danger to Jews, which primarily it is, but it is also an existential threat to any society that falls under its spell. The combination of irrationality, cruelty and injustice makes antisemitism an act of wanton self-harm. Nazism set out to annihilate Europe's Jews and it led to the destruction of Nazi Germany itself, and the same fate awaits any society that allows antisemitism to evolve from a fringe fanaticism into a normal way of viewing the world or, worse, a governing ideology.

LOOKING FOR LESSONS

Discussion of the Holocaust usually comes with a promise, or an instruction, to learn its lessons, and the amount of time, money and effort that goes into Holocaust education in the United Kingdom is exemplary. It is the only compulsory part of Britain's secondary school history curriculum. The Holocaust Education Trust runs a government-funded programme called Lessons from Auschwitz that takes sixth-formers from schools across the country to Auschwitz. Holocaust Memorial Day has become a national event, attended by political and religious leaders and marked by special programming on television and radio each year. There is a National Holocaust Centre and Museum in Nottinghamshire and dedicated Holocaust galleries at the Imperial War Museum, both of which will be eclipsed by the UK's planned Holocaust Memorial and Learning Centre. According to a survey in 2021, 89 per cent of British people have heard of the Holocaust, most of whom first heard about it at school, and 63 per cent have heard of Auschwitz. There is still much to do to embed detailed knowledge of the Nazi genocide,* but awareness of the Holocaust is now relatively widespread.

This is all a far cry from the post-war decades. Back then, knowledge of the Holocaust ought to have been much stronger than it is now, given how recent it was, but public awareness was actually much lower. This has its origins in the reluctance of British officialdom, before, during and after the war, to publicly recognise the specifically anti-Jewish aspects of Nazi ideology. Whitehall didn't want to give the impression that Britain was fighting the war for Jewish interests or to acknowledge that the pre-war refugee problem in Europe almost entirely consisted of Jewish refugees. Awareness of the Holocaust was galvanised in the 1960s when Israel captured Adolf Eichmann, one of the architects of the Final Solution who was hiding under a false name in Argentina, and flew him to Israel to stand trial. The 1978 American TV series *Holocaust* and films like *Sophie's Choice* dramatised it for a mass audience for the first time, but it was only in the early 1990s that Britain introduced retrospective laws to prosecute Nazi war criminals and put Holocaust education on the school history curriculum, while films like *Schindler's List* and *Life Is Beautiful* presented the Holocaust on the screen for a new generation.

Since then, the Holocaust has moved towards the centre of our national consciousness at all levels of culture,† and Holocaust

---

* The other death camps are much less well known. Single-figure percentages in that 2021 survey had heard of Treblinka, where around 900,000 Jews were killed, and Sobibor, where at least 167,000 died. Belzec – death toll over 400,000 – didn't even register. The full results are available at https://www.claimscon.org/wp-content/uploads/2021/11/UK-Exec-Summary-final.pdf

† In the week I am writing this, the Holocaust has featured in episodes of the TV shows *DNA Family Secrets*, *The Repair Shop* and *Gogglebox*. At the other end of the cultural scale, portraits of seven Holocaust survivors went on display in the Queen's Gallery in January 2022, having been commissioned by the then Prince of Wales, now King Charles III.

commemoration has become a much more prominent part of our national life. This seems to have a much broader purpose than education about the Holocaust itself. A few years ago I was at a Holocaust Memorial Day event at City Hall in London, hosted by the Mayor, and marvelled at the eloquence with which two sixth-formers from a school in the capital spoke about meeting Holocaust survivors and visiting Auschwitz. Neither of these students were Jewish and, judging by their ethnicities and surnames, I doubt their families even lived in Europe during the Holocaust, but you could tell that they had immersed themselves in its collective memory as Londoners, British citizens and Europeans and that it had deeply affected their own understanding of the world they were growing up in. It was genuinely moving and touched on a deeper truth about official Holocaust commemoration. The content may speak of antisemitism and its Jewish victims, but the purpose is something quite different, which is to embed the values of a new, modern Europe where (in theory) liberal democracy and diversity are cherished and militarist nationalism is consigned to the dark corners of our history.

It may be the case that as events recede into the past – as they pass from memory to history – it becomes easier for them to be shaped and filtered into a teachable message. But the questions of how to raise awareness about the Holocaust and what its abiding lessons ought to be are not so straightforward. Mostly we are encouraged to think about the way that prejudice combined with untrammelled power and murderous propaganda can fuel a mechanism of mass murder. Hateful words lead to violence, or, as the German–Jewish writer Heinrich Heine warned with chilling prescience over a century before the Nazis, 'Wherever they burn books, they will also, in the end, burn human beings.'[6] Dig a little beneath the surface, though, and you soon find that the Holocaust is a troubled and contested history for every occupied country, and the moral choices and contemporary lessons people derive from it start to diverge depending on whether they see themselves as standing in the footprints of its perpetrators, as bystanders or as victims.

This brings us back to Dubno, where those 5,000 Jews were killed in October 1942. We know about these shootings because of a remarkable man called Hermann Friedrich Graebe, and it is through him that we start to see what the different lessons of the Holocaust might look like. Graebe was an engineer who worked for the Josef Jung construction company in Germany from the late 1930s onwards. During the war they had various contracts to build and maintain essential infrastructure in occupied Ukraine, and in 1941 Graebe was sent to Lwów (today called Lviv) to supervise some of their construction jobs. One of these was to build grain warehouses on the old Dubno airfield, which is how Graebe came to witness the shootings there in October 1942. Those killings were part of what has come to be known as the 'Holocaust by Bullets', an early phase in the Nazi genocide that sometimes gets overshadowed by the focus on Auschwitz-Birkenau and the other death camps. This focus is understandable: over 1 million people were murdered in Auschwitz-Birkenau, and most of the sprawling complex was liberated intact (unlike other death camps where the Nazis efficiently destroyed evidence of their crimes). There are survivors – sadly fewer with each passing year – who have devoted their lives to bearing witness to what they and others endured there, and huge numbers visit every year. It has come to be seen as the epicentre of evil and the greatest affront to our sense of shared humanity. Mass shootings and executions of civilians are tragically common in wartime, but there has never been anything like Auschwitz, a conveyor-belt factory of death.

Yet by the time the main, purpose-built gas chambers of Birkenau started their work in spring 1943, most of the victims of the Holocaust were already dead.* When Germany invaded the Soviet Union in June 1941, frontline troops were followed by SS *Einsatzgruppen*, whose role was to round up Jews, Communist Party officials, partisans and others deemed either undesirable or a threat, and shoot them *en masse*. This quickly developed into a programme whose overwhelming purpose was the mass killing of Jewish men, women and children. These *Einsatzgruppen*, supplemented by German police battalions of reservists and local collaborators from the newly conquered territories, murdered at least 1.5 million Jews, the vast majority of whom were shot. This was an intimate form of murder, in which killer and victim often found themselves face to face in their last moments, and yet one that played out at an unimaginable scale. There is a project called Yahad-In Unum that catalogues *Einsatzgruppen* execution sites (including the one at Dubno), interviewing witnesses and painstakingly gathering evidence. At the time of writing they have documented over 3,200 locations of mass shootings of Jews and Roma, from the Gulf of Finland to the shores of the Black Sea, and they are still going.[7]

What kind of person would take part in such a gruesome atrocity? It is comforting to assume that the *Einsatzgruppen* were made up of monsters, criminals and psychopaths, but this would be quite

---

* The first, somewhat improvised, gas chamber at Auschwitz was created in late 1941, around the same time that gas vans started to be used at Chełmno. Belzec, the first death camp designed and built solely for systematic murder through purpose-built gas chambers, became operational in March 1942. Treblinka and Sobibor soon followed. In total 3.8 million Jews had been killed by the end of 1942, either in these camps, by the *Einsatzgruppen* or in ghettos and other locations. (Laurence Rees, *The Holocaust: A New History* (Penguin, 2017), p. 329)

wrong. American historian Christopher Browning's book *Ordinary Men* reconstructs the activities of Reserve Police Battalion 101, which was involved in several round-ups and mass shootings of Jews in Poland. He found that the personnel of this battalion were not unusually violent or criminally minded people. If anything, these 'middle-aged, working class' men from Hamburg were 'by age, geographical origin, and social background ... least likely to be considered apt material out of which to mould future mass killers'. Most did not start out as monsters: they were ordinary people who did monstrous things, which is perhaps much more alarming.[8]

Nor were they forced to kill. The abiding myth that German soldiers, SS men, police reservists and the others who made up the *Einsatzgruppen* risked their own lives if they refused the order to murder Jews is a post-war excuse made up by the killers themselves, for which there is no evidence. Writing in the early 1990s, Browning noted that 'in the past forty-five years no defense attorney or defendant in any of the hundreds of postwar trials [for war crimes] has been able to document a single case in which refusal to obey an order to kill unarmed civilians resulted in the allegedly inevitable dire punishment'.[9] On the contrary, there are many examples of people asking to be excused and being put on guard duty or given other tasks with no meaningful punishment at all. Browning found that between 10 and 20 per cent of Reserve Police Battalion 101 refused to take direct part in the shootings and suffered no significant negative consequences as a result. The reason the men of the *Einsatzgruppen* became mass killers is because it was easier to do so than it was to refuse. Jews had been completely dehumanised in the minds of their killers, who like all in Nazi Germany 'were immersed in a deluge of racist and anti-Semitic propaganda'. And even without the threat of formal punishment, social pressure to stay in with your peer group or follow authority is always a powerful inducement to follow the crowd rather than step out of line.¹⁰

This was especially the case for people who were far from any actual killing. The Holocaust was a machine with millions of cogs, large and small, from the senior officials who planned the whole thing to the people who did the killing, the minor functionaries who sat in an office somewhere helping the whole system to operate smoothly and the people who passively benefited in different ways, turning a blind eye without ever taking part. This most wicked of acts was the product of complex organisation and resource distribution and extraction, designed by an advanced nation using all its industrial, scientific, bureaucratic and technological know-how in pursuit of 'The mass-production and cost-cutting of death'.¹¹ It developed piecemeal at first, but following the Wannsee Conference in January 1942 the Final Solution was meticulously planned by some of the Nazi regime's leading minds. The scale and complexity of the Holocaust means it could only have been carried out by the machinery of a modern, developed state.

Jews were rounded up where they lived, whether that was Brussels, Warsaw, Thessaloniki or anywhere else under Nazi rule. In western Europe they were put into holding camps like Drancy in France or Westerbork in Holland before being transported eastwards by train to meet their fate. These arrests, round-ups and deportations were usually done by local police forces rather than by German soldiers.* In eastern Europe they were forced into ghettos where the living conditions were appalling. In the Warsaw Ghetto, the largest of all,

---

* The organisation I work for, CST, used to take British police officers on trips to Auschwitz organised by the Holocaust Educational Trust. They were always shocked to learn that it was local police officers just like them, not German soldiers or SS guards, who conducted the initial arrests of Jews in many countries.

over 400,000 Jews were walled into just 1.3 square miles of the city. Immense overcrowding and a lack of food meant that 80,000 Jews died from starvation and disease within the ghetto itself; the rest were deported to Treblinka and other death camps to be gassed. In addition to the transit camps where Jews were held before deportation and the death camps where they were gassed, there were hundreds of forced-labour camps and factories often run by (or for) German companies exploiting the free slave labour on offer.

All these camps had to be designed, built and staffed. Camp guards included Ukrainian, Latvian or other pro-Nazi sympathisers from occupied countries: the Holocaust was a German crime abetted by large numbers of non-Germans. Train wagons and drivers had to be allocated and transport schedules drawn up and coordinated. The latest technology – punch card machines from the US firm IBM – was used to keep track of the number of Jews in each ghetto, camp and transport. Victims were stripped of their clothes, money and other belongings, their hair was shaved and gold teeth removed: all that bounty needed to be allocated back into the system for others to exploit further. All this, under wartime conditions, in hundreds of towns, cities and districts across Europe. In the popular imagination, 6 million Jews were murdered either by one man – Adolf Hitler – or by a gang of Nazi psychopaths. In reality, it involved an enormous number of people across Europe who participated in, or benefited from, the mass murder of millions of their fellow citizens, many without killing anyone themselves or witnessing a single death.

HEROES AND VILLAINS (AND EVERYONE IN BETWEEN)
When Hermann Graebe saw the shootings at Dubno he didn't go along with the crowd. Instead, he did a remarkable and courageous

thing: he secretly used his position to save the lives of the Jewish slave labourers who provided the manpower for his building projects. Graebe deliberately accepted many more construction contracts than he could fulfil, exaggerated the number of workers he needed for them, invented fake branches in other towns and requested even more workers to staff them, and at times personally intervened as his workers were due to be deported to the death camps – all to save as many Jews as possible.* He took immense personal risks. After the war he was the only German who gave evidence for the prosecution at the Nuremberg Trials, where senior Nazi leaders were tried for war crimes and crimes against humanity, and it is from his affidavit for those trials that we know the details of the Dubno shootings.

Like so many who lived under Nazi rule, Graebe inhabited what Primo Levi dubbed 'the grey zone' that straddled a porous boundary between cooperation and resistance.[12] Graebe had joined the Nazi Party in Germany in 1931 but spent a few months in prison in 1934 after criticising their anti-Jewish campaign at a party meeting. He is rightly feted as a hero now, but he cooperated with the Nazi machine at the same time as subverting it, benefiting personally while also endangering himself. He personifies the moral ambiguities that confronted everyone who the Holocaust touched, however directly or remotely. Jews were not exempt from these pressures: the Nazis' cruellest trick was to induce Jewish leaders to cooperate in the deportations of their own people or the running of ghettos, in the (usually futile) hope of saving at least some Jewish lives. The

---

* Graebe used similar methods to the more famous Oskar Schindler, who saved over 1,000 Jewish workers at his factory and was the subject of Thomas Keneally's book *Schindler's Ark* and Steven Spielberg's film *Schindler's List*.

facts of the Holocaust take a lifetime to learn, but the meaning of the Holocaust is often reduced to this simple question: what would you have done?

Before you answer, it's worth bearing in mind that the risks for civilians who actively helped Jews were enormous. If you were an ordinary civilian who agreed to hide your Jewish neighbour or you were caught passing a loaf of bread to a starving child in a ghetto, you would be arrested and probably executed. In October 1941 Germany issued a decree that any Pole helping Jews in hiding would be killed. Many took the risk anyway: according to one estimate, between 7 and 9 per cent of the non-Jewish population of Warsaw helped Jews during the Nazi occupation.[13] The Holocaust presents us with extremes of what humanity is capable of and we rightly cherish and celebrate stories of astonishing courage and moral clarity amongst the horror. It is much easier and more reassuring to focus on these heroes rather than on the tens of thousands of Nazis and their collaborators who later stood trial for war crimes and the many others who never faced justice.

Israel's Holocaust Remembrance Center at Yad Vashem, just outside Jerusalem, honours those who risked their own safety or their position to save Jews during the Shoah. It has investigated and verified almost 28,000 instances of what it calls the 'Righteous Among the Nations', Hermann Graebe amongst them, and their stories, detailed on the Yad Vashem website, are as inspiring as they come.* Leopold Socha and Stefan Wróblewski were two Polish sewage workers who hid several Jews in the sewers beneath Lwów

---

* By definition, the cases verified by Yad Vashem are mostly ones where either the Jews involved, or their protectors, survived to tell the tale. There will be many others where people tried to help, were caught and have been lost for ever.

for over a year, ten of whom survived the war. The Latvian docker Jan Lipke and his wife Johana helped around forty Jews escape from camps near Riga and found hiding places for all of them.* A group of British prisoners of war found a starving, emaciated Jewish girl hiding in a barn, nursed her back to health and hid her in a hayloft in their POW camp near the Baltic coast. The French village of Le Chambon-sur-Lignon, led by Pastor André Trocmé and his family, gave refuge to around 5,000 people, mostly Jews, and helped them across the Swiss border to safety. The people of Denmark spirited away almost the entire Danish Jewish community on small boats to neutral Sweden. The diplomats of several countries, including Britain's Frank Foley, issued visas to thousands of Jews seeking refuge in any place in the world that would take them. There is even Princess Alice of Battenberg, mother of the late Duke of Edinburgh and grandmother of King Charles III, who hid a Jewish family in her residence in Athens and was honoured by Yad Vashem as a Righteous Among the Nations in 1993. The penalty for these acts of heroism would have been certain arrest and probable death, either through execution or being deported to a camp themselves. But they all took the risk.

It's worth going on YouTube to watch an old episode from 1988 of Esther Rantzen's BBC programme *That's Life*, that featured Nicholas Winton, one of the organisers of a Kindertransport from Czechoslovakia that saved over 600 Jewish children.† Winton is seated in the front row of a middle-aged studio audience, and Rantzen gradually reveals that many of the people sitting around him are the children he

---

* Approximately 200 Jews survived in Latvia out of a 1941 Jewish population of 70,000. Jan and Johana Lipke saved 20 per cent of them.
† In 1993 Czechoslovakia split into two countries: the Czech Republic (or Czechia) and Slovakia.

had saved fifty years earlier, now with their own families who would never have been born were it not for Winton's efforts. You will struggle to watch this life-affirming clip without sharing the tears that Winton sheds as he realises who he is surrounded by. It is a visual expression of the Jewish saying that is inscribed on the medal that Yad Vashem awards to the Righteous: 'Whosoever saves a single life, saves an entire universe.'[14] Winton is not recognised by Yad Vashem as a Righteous Among the Nations, presumably because, as a British diplomat acting in the 1930s, his rescue efforts did not carry the threat of Nazi retribution, so his life was not at risk. Instead, he showed a bravery that is just as rare: the courage to act when the moment comes, rather than just sitting back and watching.

The prosaic truth is that most people, when confronted with such a situation, do nothing. A small minority throw themselves into active, committed roles either as collaborators or resisters, but the most common human response is to keep your head down, go with the flow and hope to survive. For most people living under Nazi rule this involved myriad small acts of both cooperation and resistance, just to get by. I am reluctant to condemn this: who is to say which of us would behave differently? But it has left a complicated legacy in every country occupied by Nazi Germany. In eastern Europe in particular, where some of those who collaborated are heralded as nationalist leaders in their own right, the question of local responsibility for the Holocaust is fiercely contested. And let's not kid ourselves: if the RAF had not kept the Luftwaffe at bay in the summer of 1940, this country would have had its fair share of collaborators too. In the one part of the British Isles that was occupied by Nazi Germany – the Channel Islands – local authorities assisted in the registration and deportation of Jews, while there are two Channel

Islanders, Albert Bedane and Dorothea Weber, who have been recognised as Righteous Among the Nations at Yad Vashem.

'Never Again' cannot only mean that we commit not to be the person who pulls the trigger or who operates a gas chamber: those scenarios are hardly relevant to our daily lives. Rather, it must challenge us to pre-empt, and hopefully prevent, emerging persecution and hatred before it becomes truly dangerous. Nazi assaults on Jews began with street violence before Hitler took power. Once Nazi rule was established there were boycotts of Jewish-owned shops and restrictions on professions and other areas of society from which Jews were gradually forced out, racial laws limiting Jewish interactions with non-Jews and, running throughout, a vicious campaign of anti-Jewish propaganda. We all make our own choices about the point at which it would be necessary to intercede or how large a part you have to play to share the responsibility for what happens. If you take one thing away from this book, it should be the willingness to speak up, to act, when your moment comes.

WHOSE HOLOCAUST IS IT?
The memory of the Holocaust, and of the Second World War in general, has become so powerful in the European imagination that it gets exploited by everyone, from the well-meaning and frivolous to the most scurrilous and cynical. An example of the latter is Russian President Putin's claim that the invasion of Ukraine in February 2022 was an operation to 'denazify Ukraine', which he claimed had been captured by 'far-right nationalists and neo-Nazis'.[15] This idea of 'de-Nazification' became a fixture in Russian justifications for the war, repeated in speeches at the United Nations and elsewhere. The Russian Ministry of Foreign Affairs has published material about

alleged antisemitic desecrations and other hate crimes in Ukraine to paint a picture of a country gripped by Nazi antisemitism. However, this narrative keeps running up against one problem: the Ukrainian President, Volodymyr Zelenskyy, is Jewish, as is former Ukrainian Prime Minister Volodymyr Groysman. In fact, for a period when Groysman and Zelenskyy's terms in office overlapped (the Ukrainian constitution divides power between a President and Prime Minister), Ukraine was the only country in the world other than Israel to have a Jewish President and a Jewish Prime Minister. There are other prominent Ukrainian politicians with Jewish roots, which does not seem to have been an impediment to their political careers.

When Russian Foreign Minister Sergey Lavrov was asked how Ukraine can be run by Nazis when Zelenskyy is Jewish, he replied:

> So what if Zelenskyy is Jewish? The fact does not negate the Nazi elements in Ukraine. I believe that Hitler also had Jewish blood. It means absolutely nothing. The wise Jewish people said that the most ardent antisemites are usually Jews. Every family has its black sheep, as we say.[16]

The rumour that Hitler had Jewish ancestry has been debunked countless times. It stems from the fact his paternal grandfather is unknown. Mischievous gossip that this mystery grandparent was Jewish began to circulate in Germany right from the start of Hitler's political career, but numerous investigations into his family have failed to turn up any evidence. It's just another false tale, and an especially revolting one at that. As for Lavrov's assertion that 'the most ardent antisemites are usually Jews', there are examples of Jewish people absorbing antisemitic stereotypes about their fellow Jews and even supporting antisemitic movements, but to suggest that these are 'the most ardent antisemites' of all is scandalous. In any event, President Zelenskyy has never exhibited any antisemitic tendencies or expressed any views that might accord with anti-Jewish stereotypes. If anything, he seems wholly at ease with his Jewish and Ukrainian identities.

The consequence of trying to justify their claim that Ukraine is run by Nazis was that the Russian leadership resorted to its own antisemitic libels to justify their stance. It's a vicious cycle that only the most cynical would engage in. In truth, the apparent pro-Jewish atmosphere in modern Ukraine does take some getting used to. Historically, Ukrainian nationalism has been associated with some of the worst massacres in Jewish history, and like many British Jews part of my family tree has its roots in that blood-soaked land. Icons of Ukrainian nationalism who are now lauded with statues and street names, like Bohdan Khmelnytsky, whose followers slaughtered Jews in their thousands in 1648 and 1649, or his twentieth-century counterparts Semyon Petliura and Stepan Bandera, are also the ones with the most Jewish blood on their hands. Ukrainian Jewry has produced some of the most enduring and celebrated Jewish writers, thinkers and leaders, so the history is not all melancholic; but when the pogroms raged between the two world wars 'Ukraine was the epicentre of antisemitism'.[17] And of course, as at Dubno, some of the worst shooting atrocities in the Holocaust were on Ukrainian soil, aided by Ukrainian collaborators. It is discombobulating to now see a modern Ukrainian nationalism that appears for all the world to wrap up its Jews in a warm embrace. But one thing we don't need – and I am yet to meet a Jewish person who welcomes it – is Russia, of all countries, claiming to be on a mission to save Ukraine from Nazism. The hypocrisy is nauseating.

This Russian propaganda follows a scurrilous Soviet tradition of accusing Israel of behaving like Nazi Germany. This groundless comparison, now so common across the British anti-Israel left, is the legacy of decades of Soviet propaganda. 'However monstrous this may appear, especially for Jews, the present policy of the Zionists towards the Arabs is almost a copy of the policy of the German fascists', according to a booklet about Israel published by the Soviet Novosti publishing house.[18] 'The actions of the Israeli occupationists remind us of the grim years of war against Hitlerism,' read an article in *Pravda*.[19] It is not such a conceptual leap from equating Israel with Nazism to claiming that the Jewish politicians leading Ukraine today are also Nazis. Even before the 2022 invasion, Russian politicians were exploiting Zelenskyy's Jewishness in distinctly antisemitic tones. In October 2021 former Russian President and Putin ally Dmitry Medvedev described Zelenskyy as 'a man with certain ethnic roots' who has betrayed Russia in the manner of a Jew working for the Nazi SS. He accused Zelenskyy of being controlled by overseas governments and motivated only by money. 'Ukraine is headed by weak people who only strive to line their pockets ... They will sell at any moment for a five-kopeck piece.'[20] Remind you of anything?

Russia, and before it the Soviet Union, have form when it comes to exploiting the trauma of the Nazi period as a tool to destabilise democratic countries. In 1959 a worldwide campaign of swastika graffiti on synagogues and Jewish cemeteries was orchestrated by a new disinformation department of the KGB, the Soviet Union's external intelligence agency. The aim was to demonstrate that

West Germany was still riddled with Nazi sympathisers fourteen years after the end of the Second World War, thereby tarnishing its image in the eyes of its allies. Starting with graffiti on a synagogue in Cologne in December 1959, the antisemitic daubings became an epidemic, reaching thirty-four countries within a month. Some of these will have been copycat incidents by genuine neo-Nazis who saw what was happening and got swept along in the excitement, but the campaign was instigated and spread internationally by Soviet intelligence. In Germany some of the graffiti was even done by neo-Nazis who had been recruited by the KGB. In the United States alone, 637 antisemitic incidents were recorded in 236 cities by the beginning of March 1960.[21] In the UK, three swastikas and the Nazi slogan *'Juden Raus'* (Jews Out) were daubed on a synagogue in Notting Hill, West London, on New Year's Eve 1959; by the end of the first week of January 1960 there had been similar desecrations in Bolton, Manchester, Liverpool, Leeds, Bournemouth, Bristol, York, Axminster, Newcastle, Lowestoft, Bognor Regis, Sheffield, Dagenham and Kingston, plus additional anti-Jewish graffiti in Scotland and Ireland. In London, swastikas were painted on the offices of the *Jewish Chronicle*, the Chief Rabbi and the Board of Deputies of British Jews. Significantly, the perpetrators phoned the Press Association to tell them what they had done. The aim was publicity rather than purely damage, because only with publicity could the political goal of smearing the Soviet Union's enemies as Nazis be achieved.[22]

It had the desired impact. Governments held emergency sessions to debate the outbreak of anti-Jewish hate, 50,000 people marched in protest to the German Embassy in London and the United Nations held an investigation. 'Nazi Infection Persists' in Germany, ran one headline in the *Jewish Chronicle*. 'The ugly spirit of Nazism is still abroad in the country of its origin,' was the assertion of an outraged Board of Deputies of British Jews.[23] An encrypted Soviet cable, intercepted by British intelligence, revealed the purpose behind this seditious operation:

> Undercover comrades have proved to the world that a potential Nazi threat exists not only in Germany but in the whole Western world ... [the] argument that West Germany is a potential bastion of Nazism and that consequently West Germany must under no circumstances be fully re-armed has been considerably strengthened.

You could swap 'Ukraine' for 'West Germany' in that extract and it would perfectly describe what Putin – himself a former KGB officer – is trying to achieve when he says he aims to 'denazify Ukraine'.[24] It is a deliberate effort to weaponise the memory of the Holocaust and Nazi atrocities for a modern campaign of territorial conquest and destruction, and it is abhorrent.

Other examples of the misuse of Holocaust memory are more banal but can nonetheless still be offensive, and it shouldn't be so difficult to commit not to dilute or distort the lessons of the Holocaust beyond meaning. Some comparisons are obscene, like when anti-vaccine campaigners wear yellow stars, mimicking the Nazi treatment of Jews, and claim that Covid health measures are analogous to the Holocaust.* Some are boorish, such as Alastair Campbell's repeated comparisons of the *Daily Mail* to the Nazi newspaper *Der Stürmer*, which was notorious for publishing abhorrent anti-Jewish

---

* One of Britain's best-known anti-vaccine campaigners, Piers Corbyn, was arrested in February 2021 for distributing leaflets with a picture of the entrance to Auschwitz, in which the infamous 'Arbeit Macht Frei' sign over the camp gates had been replaced with the slogan, 'Vaccines are safe path to freedom.'

material.²⁵ Some are ridiculous, as when Bristol Rovers manager Joey Barton said one of his players had 'a Holocaust, a nightmare, an absolute disaster' after an especially poor performance.²⁶ There is a well-known rule of the internet called Godwin's Law, which states that the longer any online discussion grows, the more inevitable it is that someone, or something, will be compared to the Nazis or Hitler. My favourite parody of this cultural tic is in *The Young Ones*, when Lenny Henry turns up as a German-speaking postman and Rik Mayall's character exclaims: 'Bloody hell! Give them a uniform and they think they're Hitler.'²⁷ Whether it is politics, comedy or just angry people online, Hitler and the Nazis have become dominant cultural figures, a byword for ultimate evil, authoritarianism, banal cruelty and many other things besides in ways that have nothing to do with antisemitism.

This may be unavoidable, but it comes with peril. The Holocaust was a crime against the Jewish people, and it was also a crime against all of humanity (the phrase 'crimes against humanity' was invented for the Nuremberg Trials as a way to describe the Holocaust).²⁸ While both readings are legitimate and necessary, there is a danger of over-universalising our understanding of why the Holocaust happened. Some scholars have tried to insert the Holocaust into the sordid history of genocides perpetrated by Western colonialism on other continents. Others, especially on the left, have argued that it was the logical endpoint of Fascism or even of capitalism and imperialism. This is a problem if it deters people from thinking in more depth about why the Nazis tried to eliminate Jews specifically. If a theory of why the Holocaust happened treats antisemitism as irrelevant, or at least incidental, to why the Nazis and their accomplices acted as they did, then it has taken the wrong path. It wasn't pure chance that it was the Jews, amongst all non-Aryan peoples, who were earmarked for total destruction.²⁹

EVERYONE WANTS TO BE ANNE FRANK

You see the implications of this in some of the attempts to appropriate the Holocaust for other causes. Probably the best-known, and most widely read, Holocaust memoir is *The Diary of Anne Frank*, written by the eponymous Dutch teenager while she and her family hid from the Nazis in a secret annex behind an Amsterdam house. Its fame remains unmatched amongst Holocaust literature decades after it was first published in 1947, to the extent that Anne Frank 'may be the most famous child of the twentieth century'.³⁰ Her face has become a global symbol of hope under intolerable suffering, and everyone, it seems, wants a piece. In March 2022 the Italian street artist aleXsandro Palombo painted Anne Frank wearing Ukrainian colours and burning a flag of Russian militarism to stand against the Russian invasion of Ukraine.³¹ In 2014, an anti-Israel campaign group in Holland adopted an image of Anne Frank wearing a Palestinian *keffiyeh*.*³² The Bosnian–Irish author Zlata Filipović, who wrote her own diary as a child during the 1990s Balkan Wars, was dubbed 'the Anne Frank of Sarajevo'.³³ In 2019, American author and activist L. R. Knost used the example of Anne Frank to campaign against immigrant detention centres in the United States.³⁴ In 2021, Fox News presenter Mark Levin did the same to condemn US President Biden's handling of the withdrawal from Afghanistan, asking, 'How many Anne Franks are there tonight in Afghanistan? How many Anne Franks are hiding in cellars all across the country

---

* Comparing Israeli policies towards the Palestinians with Nazi treatment of Jews is one of the despicable, and commonplace, aspects of anti-Israel campaigning. But we'll get to that in the next chapter.

today?'[35] You may sympathise with some or all of these causes, but even so, it feels grubbily exploitative to put Anne Frank to work in their name. It's not as if anybody can ask her for permission.

The pandemic seemed to open up a whole new world of inappropriate appropriation. A gym owner in Harlow used Instagram to compare themself to Anne Frank because they had to close their gym for a month during a Covid lockdown.[36] American anti-vaccine campaigner Robert F. Kennedy Jr invoked Anne Frank's name to condemn US Covid regulations, saying 'even in Hitler's Germany you could cross the Alps into Switzerland, you could hide in an attic like Anne Frank did' (Kennedy later apologised).[37] The Canadian newspaper the *Globe and Mail* also apologised after publishing an article comparing living through Covid lockdowns to Anne Frank's wartime experiences.[38] A school in Aberdeenshire used Anne Frank's diary, 'kept whilst she and her family hid during the Second World War to avoid being sent to a concentration camp', as a teaching aid that 'inspired the pupils to write their own journals of life during the Coronavirus pandemic'.[39]

These all seem particularly distasteful because of Anne Frank's youthful innocence and they sting because they universalise her story to the exclusion of its central component: that she was hounded and killed because she was a Jew. It leaves you with a hollowed-out version of Anne Frank's life that suits the purposes of everyone except Jews. Those schoolchildren in Aberdeenshire probably came up with some moving accounts of life under lockdown, which I don't doubt was difficult for them, but – how shall I put this? – Aberdeen was not crawling with Nazi soldiers trying to deport them to Auschwitz.

Sometimes it feels like an awful lot of people want to imagine themselves or their favoured cause as Anne Frank; all except Jews, who want to not be like Anne Frank, because we can never overlook her ultimate fate and we don't want to play that role again. I apologise if this sounds brutal, but the story of Anne Frank is, for Jews, a story of antisemitism and the betrayal and murder of a Dutch family who were stripped of all their rights and their possessions, and ultimately of their lives, because they were Jewish and had nowhere else to go. There is nothing inspiring in that. Her diary has been an amazing tool of Holocaust education, but, like all the best books, it doesn't work if you miss out the ending. Nathan Englander's short story 'What We Talk About When We Talk About Anne Frank' depicts an American–Jewish couple who induce their friends to play a game called 'Who Will Hide Me', otherwise known to them as 'the Righteous Gentile game'. In the event of an American Holocaust, one of them explains, we sometimes talk about which of our Christian friends would hide us.[40] It's an amusing take on Jewish post-Holocaust angst, and I won't ruin it by telling you what happens: but it drills right into one the most sensitive points of Jewish insecurity when it comes to antisemitism.*

NEVER AGAIN, AGAIN

When we read the inspirational stories of the Righteous Among the Nations, we all hope that we would show the same courage in their position. Yet that is not the full story, because when I read those accounts, as well as looking at the heroic rescuers I mainly think about the Jew who is being hidden. I ask myself not only whether I would have helped others, but, in a much more personal way, I wonder: would I, a Jew, have survived?

---

* I'll admit that I've had the same thought myself, and I know who I'm going to call if I need to hide one day.

For all the individual acts of selfless courage, collectively the Jews were on their own before and after the war. One of the most dishonourable episodes in the path to the Shoah, which has come to rank alongside Auschwitz, the Warsaw Ghetto and the *Einsatzgruppen* in the lesson it taught subsequent generations of Jews, was not a death camp, deportation or a mass shooting: it was a diplomatic gathering in Évian-les-Bains, France, in July 1938, well before the first shot was fired. This was an international conference to discuss the urgent refugee problem in Europe, which consisted entirely of hundreds of thousands of German and Austrian Jews trying to escape Nazi persecution. One by one, with callous self-interest, each country gave its reason not to help, some revealing an ingrained antisemitism in the process. The Canadian Prime Minister William Lyon Mackenzie King wrote in his diaries that 'nothing is to be gained by creating an internal problem in an effort to meet an international one' and noted his desire to keep Canada free from 'too great an intermixture of foreign strains of blood'. The Australian delegate to the conference said that 'as we have no real racial problem, we are not desirous of importing one'.* As for Britain, there would be no further space for Jewish immigration beyond the Kindertransport (which was in any event a privately funded and organised enterprise only for child refugees). British policy applied equally to Palestine, where Britain was the colonial power, and Jewish immigration was heavily restricted into Palestine from 1936 onwards. 'If we must offend one side' in that conflict, Prime Minister Neville Chamberlain said in April 1939 when discussing the refugee question, 'let us offend the Jews rather than the Arabs'.[41]

---

* Another example of Jews being viewed as a race by all concerned.

The Holocaust did not just obliterate the great Jewish civilisation in eastern Europe and with it the religious, political and cultural heart of the Jewish world. For many Jews, it shattered the idea that a secure Jewish existence in Europe was even tenable. The countries of the world mostly turned their backs on Jewish refugees before the Holocaust, and after the war hundreds of thousands of Jewish survivors were stuck in displaced persons camps, unable or unwilling to return to what used to be home. It was an irrevocable blow to all those Jews who had argued that their safety would be guaranteed by loyal service to their countries or by discarding their distinctive Jewishness and assimilating into wider society. One hundred thousand German Jews served in the German armed forces in the First World War, 12,000 of whom were killed in the war, and the German and Austrian Jewish communities were amongst the most assimilated in Europe, but this did not protect them. The lesson many Jews took from the Holocaust – rightly or wrongly, fairly or not – is that the countries they considered home could turn them back into aliens in the blink of an eye.

Even in Britain, it quickly became apparent that the Holocaust had not put an end to antisemitism. The hope that the shock of Auschwitz would stun the world's Jew-haters into shameful silence was understandable but naive. It became taboo in polite society, and antisemites developed new coded language to express the same old ideas. But the worst anti-Jewish riots in Britain in modern times happened in August 1947, just two years after the end of the Second World War, when mobs smashed the windows of hundreds of Jewish shops and other premises up and down the country. This outburst of violence was a reaction to the growing Zionist insurgency in Palestine in the years between the end of the war and Israel's independence in 1948. British soldiers and colonial officials were getting killed, and a minority of people in Britain – including those with fascist sympathies – took their anger out on British Jews. Barely had the doors of the last gas chambers closed and here we were, needing to defend ourselves once more against fascist antisemitism.

It isn't true that Jews were completely abandoned during the Holocaust. Many survivors are only with us because other people risked their lives to help them. But many others didn't, and often their neighbours were only too pleased to see the back of them. In some places, locals started killing Jews as soon as the German army arrived in June and July 1941, without needing any encouragement. In Kaunas, Lithuania, around fifty Jews were murdered by nationalist vigilantes while a crowd stood and cheered. In Romania, upwards of 4,000 Jews were killed by local forces in a pogrom in the city of Iași. Thousands were similarly murdered by Ukrainians in Lwów. After the war, Jewish survivors returning home found this hostility had not abated. Most notoriously in Kielce, Poland, forty-two Jews were murdered and forty injured in July 1946 when they were attacked by Polish soldiers, police and civilians. The ostensible spark was an allegation that Jews had kidnapped a Polish child, making this yet another blood libel-induced pogrom, but the underlying message was clear: Jews were not welcome any more.*

This is where 'Never Again' acquires an additional, very Jewish,

---

* In a shameful postscript, Jewish Holocaust survivors who left Poland for Allied-occupied Germany in 1945 and 1946 were treated by the British authorities in Germany as 'infiltrators' who were acting for political or economic reasons. While the British troops who liberated Belsen acted with great compassion, the British government was much more suspicious and hostile towards Jewish refugees in the years immediately following the Holocaust. Even after the Kielce pogrom, Prime Minister Clement Attlee insisted – against the advice of his own diplomats in Warsaw – that the desire of Jews to leave Poland was artificially engineered 'with a view to forcing our hands over Palestine'. It was even British policy to deny food rations to any Jewish refugees who arrived in the British-controlled zone in Germany after 1 July 1946. (Arieh J. Kochavi, 'Britain's Image Campaign against the Zionists', *Journal of Contemporary History*, vol. 36, no. 2 (2001), pp. 297–307 (p. 302)) meaning. Every Jewish family in Britain is either descended directly from Holocaust survivors; has parts of its family missing, branches of the family tree that were cut off and never regrew; or shares the collective loss of a global Jewish population that still, in 2022, has not fully recovered to the numbers of 1939. All my immediate family members were safely in Britain before the Nazis came to power, but they had cousins and siblings in Lwów with whom contact abruptly stopped in 1942. I have no idea what happened to them: they and their non-existent descendants are the unacknowledged ghosts at every family celebration, every wedding or *Bat Mitzvah*. And all British Jews know that had Nazi Germany successfully invaded this country, we may never have been born at all.

During the Jewish festival of Passover, Jews are instructed to remember the biblical Exodus from Egypt as if we were there in person. We recite the epic account of slavery, the ten plagues, the parting of the Red Sea and the giving of the ten commandments as if they are our own memories. We eat indigestible *matzah* (big square crackers) instead of bread, because in the story our ancestors didn't have time to bake bread to take with them on their journey. It's a massive annual role-play in which we imagine ourselves walking where our ancestors stepped. In a similar (if much less fun) way, when Jews study the Shoah today we know that each of us would have been in those camps, on those trains or standing on the edge of those pits of death. This feels much closer than the bible stories we tell at Passover. In a 2018 survey of over 16,000 Jews in twelve different European countries, 78 per cent ranked 'Remembering the Holocaust' as the most important aspect of modern Jewish identity – more than religious belief, supporting Israel or enjoying Jewish festivals.[42] The trauma of the Shoah is a collective memory seared into the global Jewish consciousness, and it reaches everywhere. 'You don't say "gassed" to Jews if you can help it,' Howard Jacobson wrote in his 2006 novel *Kalooki Nights*. It is one of those words that 'should be struck out of the human vocabulary for a while, while we regroup, not for ever, just for a thousand years or so – gassed, camp, extermination, concentration, experiment, march, train, rally, German. Words made unholy just as ground is made unholy.'[43]

The legacy of all of this is an internalised Jewish version of 'Never Again' that goes as follows: never again will we allow that to happen to us. Never again will we be so defenceless, relying on others for our safety who will not come when we need them. Never again will we fail to heed the warning signs. Been there, done that, never going back. If the antisemitism that has always been part of our world refuses to disappear – if the world we live in is incapable of leaving it behind – then Jews will find our own ways to protect ourselves against it. This is partly where the metaphor of Jews keeping a packed suitcase under the bed comes from. If the Nazis return, we want to be the Jews with foresight who left Germany in 1933, not the ones trapped there in 1940. It has also inspired a more muscular, proactive approach to tackling antisemitism. There is a proud history of Jewish anti-Fascism in post-war Britain that began with the 43 Group that was mentioned in the previous chapter and ran through the 62 Group of Jewish streetfighters that was fictionalised in the BBC series *Ridley Road*. Jews who fought back, physically in some cases, politically in others.

You can see this in the different days on which the Holocaust is commemorated. The UK's Holocaust Memorial Day is on 27 January, the anniversary of the liberation of Auschwitz, and the same date is marked globally. But in Israel and across the Jewish world the

Holocaust is remembered on a different day. *Yom HaShoah* marks the anniversary of the Warsaw Ghetto Uprising, when a rudimentary Jewish resistance network, knowing they were doomed, fought back when the Germans came to liquidate the ghetto. They held up the German army for three weeks before finally succumbing, and in doing so left behind a shaft of light in the darkness that enveloped European Jewry. There is meaning in these different choices about what to commemorate.

When I was learning about the Holocaust in my Jewish youth movement Habonim-Dror, we spoke about Abba Kovner as much as, if not more than, Anne Frank. Kovner was a youth leader in Lithuania who commanded the Jewish resistance in the Vilna ghetto. He was one of the first to comprehend that the Germans were set on annihilation and wrote a manifesto on New Year's Eve 1941 that became a rallying cry to resistance:

> Jewish youth! Do not trust those who are trying to deceive you. Hitler plans to destroy all the Jews of Europe ... We will not be led like sheep to the slaughter! True, we are weak and defenseless, but the only reply to the murderer is revolt! Brothers! Better to fall as free fighters than to live by the mercy of the murderers. Arise! Arise with your last breath![44]

Kovner and his friends escaped from the ghetto and formed a formidable partisan unit responsible for dozens of successful operations against German forces in Lithuania, while also saving many other Jews. Wartime photos of Kovner show a thin-faced man with wild hair, very much the intellectual except that he and the people around him are invariably holding sub-machine guns. Like many survivors, he chose Israel as the place to build his new home, fighting in Israel's War of Independence before becoming a renowned poet. Unlike Anne Frank you won't find anybody else trying to co-opt this Jewish hero for their non-Jewish cause, but if you want to understand how the Shoah has affected Jews' sense of their place in the world and the importance that Israel's existence now has for them, Kovner's story is a more reliable guide.

In the final scenes of Steven Spielberg's Oscar-winning film *Schindler's List*, which tells the story of more than 1,000 Jews saved by the Czech-German industrialist Oskar Schindler, the survivors are shown asking a Russian officer where they should go now that they had been liberated. 'Don't go east, that's for sure,' he tells them. 'They hate you there. I wouldn't go west either, if I were you.' We then see these lost Jews, with no homes, no food and no friends in the world, walking proudly over the crest of a hill as the Hebrew song *Yerushalayim Shel Zahav* (Jerusalem of Gold) swells in volume. The black and white film of the actors in their Holocaust-era clothing morphs into footage of the real-life Schindler Jews in full colour, each laying a stone on Schindler's grave in Jerusalem.* It is an unashamedly Zionist ending.[45]

The determination that Jews should never have to rely on others for their safety is fundamental to Israel's sense of itself. On *Yom HaShoah* 2022, the Israeli Defense Forces tweeted a video with the slogan: 'Israel and the IDF means Never Again.' In this telling, Israel is the phoenix that rose from the ashes of Auschwitz, redeeming Jewish life that was all but extinguished, the protector of Jewish existence in the future. A strong Israel means Jews will never again

---

* It is Jewish custom to put a stone on someone's grave rather than flowers.

be victims of another Shoah, is how the message goes. It is more complicated than that, of course. Reality is never as simplistic as the narratives that sustain national or collective identities. But just as the Shoah devastated the Jewish world, so the creation of the State of Israel a few years later provided renewed hope of survival. The Holocaust isn't the only reason why Israel exists, nor its only justification for existing, but the link is clear enough.

This has brought its own problems. The lesson that European governments and elites drew from the Nazi period, and especially the Holocaust, was that nationalism, military power and ethnic pride were too dangerous to be allowed to roam free ever again. Much of western Europe's post-war politics have involved a project to constrain these ideas for good. Meanwhile Jews drew the opposite conclusion from the Shoah, seeking safety via their own national movement, Zionism, the reassuring strength of the Israeli army, and Israel's promise that Jews will never again have to rely on others for their own protection. Typical, in this long history of antisemitism, for Jews to again refuse to fall neatly into the categories set by others and stubbornly insist on following their own path. And as Israel, the world's only Jewish state and its first expression of sovereign Jewish power in nearly 2,000 years, has blossomed, so antisemitism found itself a whole new focus.

CHAPTER SEVEN

JERUSALEM

In 2012, as part of a national festival of culture to mark the London Olympics, Shakespeare's Globe theatre had a brilliant idea: to stage all thirty-seven of Shakespeare's plays in just seven weeks, each one performed by a different theatre company from around the world in their own language. Nigeria's Renegade Theatre performed *The Winter's Tale* in Yoruba. *Henry IV, Part One* and *Henry IV, Part Two* were both done in Spanish by companies from Mexico and Argentina respectively. *King Lear* was performed by the Belarus Free Theatre, which had been banned by the dictatorship in their own country. There was a hip hop *Othello* from Chicago, a British Sign Language *Love's Labour's Lost*, and a Dari *Comedy of Errors* from Iran. In what you might think a laudable gesture of peace, this global melange included a Palestinian company performing *Richard II* in Arabic and a Hebrew version of *The Merchant of Venice* by Israel's Habima National Theatre. And of all these eclectic and innovative interpretations of Britain's greatest theatrical export, it was, somewhat inevitably, the Israeli one that was seen as controversial.

Three dozen well-known British actors, directors and playwrights wrote a public letter to *The Guardian* calling for the invitation to Habima to be revoked. Their grievance was not that their Israeli counterparts intended to perform as notoriously antisemitic a play as *The Merchant of Venice*; that did not appear to trouble them at all. Rather, for Mark Rylance, Emma Thompson, Richard Wilson and the rest, it was that Habima 'has a shameful record of involvement with illegal Israeli settlements in Occupied Palestinian Territory', and by inviting them 'the Globe is associating itself with policies of exclusion practised by the Israeli state and endorsed by its national theatre company'.[1] Their call for Habima to be disinvited was contentious, even within the world of theatre. The actor Simon Callow denounced

> any attempt to ban the work of any artist, especially artists with the distinguished record for challenging and fearlessly exploratory work of the Habima company ... If there is to be confrontation, it must be done through the agreed channels of discussion and debate. Let us see what Habima has to tell us about human life, before we try to silence them.

Sir Arnold Wesker went further, comparing the boycott call to 'Nazis burning the books of the finest minds and talents of Europe'.[2]

The play went ahead, with supporters and opponents of Israel in the audience, and the charge of hypocrisy lingered long afterwards for those who signed that letter. Of all the invited theatre companies from around the world, Habima was the only one subjected to a boycott campaign. There was no comparable call for the National Theatre of China to be disinvited or for Moscow's state-funded

Vakhtangov Theatre to be shunned. There was no protest about the participation of an American theatre company, despite the then ongoing occupation of Iraq and Afghanistan. It does not seem that any of the other participants were scrutinised for alleged association with the human rights abuses of their governments: only the Israelis were put to a political test and found wanting. The Globe alluded to this singling out of Israel in their response to the Habima boycott call:

> We came to the conclusion that active exclusion was a profoundly problematic stance to take – because the question of which nations deserve inclusion or exclusion is necessarily subjective. Where does one start in such an endeavour? Clearly for you with Israel, but for many others, it would be with a host of different states. And more pertinently, where does one stop?[3]

Where it stops is usually the same place that it starts: Israel. The signatories of that letter calling for only Israelis to be excluded from a global celebration of Shakespeare were following a well-trodden path. People who boycott Israel rarely boycott any other country, just as those who will march in the streets for Palestine would be much less likely to do so for Yemenis, Kurds, Tibetans, Uighurs, Yazidis or, most recently, Ukrainians. Bestselling author Sally Rooney announced in October 2021 that she would not sell translation rights to her most recent novel, *Beautiful World, Where Are You*, to an Israeli publisher. She had the grace to acknowledge that 'many states other than Israel are guilty of grievous human rights abuses', but did not give any indication that her concern for human rights would be similarly applied to publishers from those other countries.[4] Professor Stephen Hawking pulled out of a conference in Israel in 2013, having been asked to boycott it by Palestinian academics. Again, it seems it was only Israel that troubled Hawking's conscience: he had been to academic gatherings in Iran and China in the years prior to his decision not to do the same in Israel.

Academia is where this double standard is most glaring. In 2015, over 300 academics at seventy-two different British universities and other institutions signed a commitment to boycott Israeli universities. This would mean not attending conferences in Israel, sharing research projects or peer-reviewing papers from Israeli institutions. If fully implemented, it would amount to shutting Israeli universities (and only Israeli universities) out of the intellectual collaboration that sustains the global academic community. This was not unprecedented: in 2007 the newly formed University and College Union (UCU), the main trade union for British academics, passed a policy supporting the boycott of Israel universities. They did this at a time when the American-led occupation of Iraq was at its peak, but there was no suggestion from these British academics that American universities – or those of the many other countries that contributed troops to the occupation of Iraq, including, of course, Britain itself – might be worth boycotting. Just Israeli ones.

Then there are the demonstrations. Whenever Israel is at war (and sometimes when it isn't), huge numbers of people will gather in towns and cities across Britain to march, chant and wave their placards, all furious about whatever Israel has done (or is accused of doing) that week. These gatherings can be enormous. On 15 May 2021, as conflict escalated in Israel and Palestine, 100,000 people marched through central London.[5] The following week, 180,000 people demonstrated for Palestine, and there were smaller protests around the country.⁶ Similar-sized marches happened during the previous flare up in fighting in 2014 and the one before that in 2009.

Not only are these demonstrations bigger than anything seen in Britain for any other foreign conflict, they are also much angrier. During the war in Gaza in 2009 there were several nights of rioting outside the Israeli Embassy in London; over fifty police officers were injured, over 100 alleged rioters were arrested and around two dozen were imprisoned. In 2021, thirteen people were arrested towards the end of the march on 15 May, after a large group went to the Israeli embassy and started throwing missiles at police.⁷ One group on that protest was filmed chanting the Arabic battle cry *Khaybar Khaybar Ya Yahud, Jaish Muhammad Sauf Ya'ud*, which translates as 'Khaybar Khaybar Oh Jews, the army of Mohammed is returning'. It refers to a seventh-century battle in the Arabian Peninsula in which Muslim armies defeated a Jewish tribe and the contemporary meaning is: watch out Jews, we're coming to get you.⁸ The next day, a convoy of cars from across the north gathered in Bradford before heading down the M1 to London on a 'Drive for Palestine'. The cars were emblazoned with large Palestinian flags stuck to their bonnets or waved out of the windows. As the convoy stood at traffic lights on Finchley Road in north London, somebody in one of the cars decided to say what he really thought. 'Fuck the Jews,' he shouted through his megaphone. 'Fuck their mothers, fuck their daughters and show your support for Palestine ... we have to send a message.'⁹

This is not normal. There is no other foreign conflict that generates this scale of reaction, this rage, amongst sections of the British population. The war in Yemen is estimated by the United Nations to have cost an astonishing 377,000 lives from 2014 to the end of 2021,¹⁰ several times more than the casualties in the entire history of the Arab–Israeli conflict. One of the main protagonists in that war, Saudi Arabia, is the world's largest purchaser of British arms – but you will never see hundreds of thousands of people marching through British towns and cities in protest. Demonstrations against arms sales to Saudi Arabia do happen from time to time, but they are just not as exciting as protests against Israel. The Russian invasion of Ukraine in February 2022 caused outrage across society, but this was expressed in a very different way by the British public: through sympathy for Ukrainians, donations to charity and offers of hospitality to Ukrainian refugees. It did not manifest in widespread expressions of hatred for Russians. Thankfully the police did not record a spike in hate crimes against Russian people or property in Britain in 2022, just as there hadn't been one after Russia invaded Crimea and shot down a Malaysian passenger airplane in 2014. But in May 2021, during the conflict in Israel and Gaza, hate crimes targeting Jews in London more than trebled.[11] The previous time Israel and Hamas fought a war, in the summer of 2014, anti-Jewish hate crimes doubled nationally.[12] It's a pattern that repeats whenever Israel is at war, but it isn't one that happens for any other overseas conflict.

Despite these hate crimes, the discourse that animates Britain's anti-Israel movement is, on the whole, not expressed in explicitly anti-Jewish terms. Taken separately, much of it is unremarkable: criticism of human rights abuses, complaints about the occupation of Palestinian land, objections to the building of Israeli settlements. Collectively, though, it looks like an obsession. It is this fixation with Israel, different in quantity and quality from any other foreign issue, that is unnerving, and it isn't immediately obvious why it happens. Israel, after all, is the size of Wales, with a population similar to that of Greater London. It has few natural resources and its once-significant strategic position as a land bridge between Africa, Asia and Europe has little relevance in a modern world of air travel and satellite communications. The conflicts that have consumed Syria, Libya, Yemen and other parts of the Middle East and north Africa over the past decade have exposed the inanity of the old idea that settling the Israel–Palestinian dispute is the key to regional peace. Yet there are a lot of people in Britain who treat this conflict as if it is the most important on earth. Understanding why this happens is an essential part of cracking the code of how antisemitism and anti-Israel sentiment are connected.

SINGLING OUT

Why does Israel get all this attention and not, say, Turkey? As a NATO member Turkey is in a formal military alliance with Britain, which means if Turkey is attacked then Britain is, in theory at least, obliged to go to war to defend it. We export almost nine times as much military hardware to Turkey as we do to Israel, and Turkish forces participated in NATO's military operations in Afghanistan, Libya and Kosovo. Turkey also does plenty of things that you might expect anti-war, pro-human rights campaigners to abhor. For much of the past century Turkey has severely repressed Kurdish nationalism, banning Kurdish political parties, newspapers and cultural associations, and even placed legal restrictions on the use of the Kurdish language. Military conflict between Turkish forces and the Kurdish PKK has cost up to 40,000 lives since 1984 and displaced hundreds of thousands of people.* Turkey has repeatedly invaded

---

* For comparison, the Israeli–Palestinian conflict is estimated to have cost around 14,000 lives from December 1987 to mid-May 2021 ('The Israel–Palestine conflict has claimed 14,000 lives since 1987', *The Economist* (18 May 2021))

neighbouring countries in its relentless effort to obstruct Kurdish national aspirations in the region. Turkey has also occupied Greek territory in northern Cyprus for almost as long as Israel has occupied the West Bank and, unlike Israel, has never looked like giving any of it back. Unlike Israel, a free press is something of a dream in Turkey: according to the Stockholm Center for Freedom, there are, at the time of writing, seventy-two journalists in prison in Turkey, another eighty-nine awaiting trial, and 167 who are either in exile or in hiding.[13]

I don't mean to pick on Turkey. My closest friend at university was from a Turkish Cypriot family and whenever our Students' Union debated either Israel or Cyprus I felt like we shared an understanding of how it felt, at a human level, to be in the eye of the storm, while political hacks argued back-and-forth over places that mattered deeply to us in a way they never appreciated. I learned enough to know that the background to conflict in Cyprus, like so many other places, is never as clear cut as some would claim. But still, I do wonder why nobody of note boycotts Turkey, if boycotting a country that occupies somebody else's land is the done thing for artists with a conscience. There are no online lists of famous authors, musicians and actors pledging not to perform in Istanbul or sell their books there. Protesters are rarely called out onto British streets when Turkish tanks roll into Kurdish territory; on the few occasions when they are, those demonstrators do not turn up in anything like the same numbers as when Israeli forces enter Gaza. Nor do people in Britain seek out Turkish people to shout racist abuse at when Turkey goes to war – but they do seek out Jews when Israeli bombs begin to fall. It leaves me wondering why Israel always seems to get singled out, and what this unique treatment says about our own country.

I know what answer Israel's opponents would give, because I've heard it so many times. It is that Israel deserves unique treatment because it is a unique case. Israel's occupation of Palestinian land has gone on since 1967 and shows no sign of ending. Human rights abuses are a regular occurrence in the occupied Palestinian territories, with daily humiliations rooted in a framework of racist laws, policies and behaviour. When open conflict breaks out between Israel and Palestinian militias, the stark disparity in power is always reflected in heavy casualties amongst Palestinians, and few in Israel. Palestinians want us to boycott Israel, so the argument goes, and that is the least we can do to help. Some more radical critiques argue that the treatment of Palestinians by Israel is comparable to the horrors of apartheid South Africa or, worse, Nazi Germany. Increasingly it is said that Israel is a remnant of European colonialism in the Middle East, a settler-colonial state on stolen land that should never have been created and ought to be consigned to history.

These claims about the politics and history of the conflict can be argued on the facts. Even the argument that Palestinians want us to boycott Israel is not as straightforward as it sounds. It is true that there is a wide-ranging coalition of Palestinian civil society groups who campaign in support of a boycott. However, it is also true that the Palestinian National Authority does not support a full boycott of Israel but only of Israeli settlements in the West Bank. 'We do not support the boycott of Israel. But we ask everyone to boycott the products of the settlements,' said Palestinian President Mahmoud Abbas in 2013.[14] And that's before you get to the moral quandary of whether the ability of Palestinian civil society to organise a campaign for a boycott of Israel means that, by definition, Israel is not as repressive as other states where no such civil society could operate.

Still, there are clearly human rights abuses worth protesting and Palestinian life under occupation seems pretty grim. Israeli settlements are built on land that is generally regarded, outside Israel at least, as Palestinian, and a viable Palestinian state feels further away than ever. You'll find that a lot of Jewish people who want to talk about whether excessive or gratuitous criticisms of Israel are antisemitic will feel the need to acknowledge Palestinian suffering when they do so. They will declare their own unhappiness at Israel's political direction or the policies of the current government. It is a kind of tax you have to pay to get a hearing on this subject, an entry ticket to the debate. I tend to keep my views about Israel's politics to myself, mainly because it shouldn't matter what I think. My right not to have antisemitic abuse shouted at me in my own country should not depend on whether I support a two-state solution to the Israeli–Palestinian conflict. It's another example of singling out, the pressure that Jews – especially liberal, left-wing Jews – feel to fit in.

Anyway, this is not about whether complaints of Israeli human rights abuses, the misery of Palestinian daily life or the longevity of the occupation and the depth of Western complicity are well-founded. Even if they are completely accurate and fair, it still doesn't answer the question why Israel alone gets this treatment. If anything it makes that question even more pertinent. Some of the explanations merely serve to highlight the double standard at play. The journalist and broadcaster Mehdi Hasan, for example, argued that because Israel is a Western ally that enjoys arms sales and political support from our own government, we are 'complicit in its crimes' and therefore compelled to act.[15] If he is right, that would also apply to Saudi Arabia, Turkey and others, but while Hasan personally is scathing about Saudi's war in Yemen, there are no mass protests of comparable size to the ones against Israel's wars in Gaza, no equivalent of the BDS movement that seeks to isolate Israel from the international community.* My intention in querying this double standard is not to persuade people to stop criticising Israel when it deserves to be criticised. I'm not asking Israel's critics to look away from what Israel does; I'm asking them to look at themselves and the choices they make, and to wonder why that choice always lands on Israel.

It would be easy to put it down to straightforward antisemitism, in which British Jews get attacked as proxies for Israel because Israel is a Jewish state, and that does play a role. The people shouting 'Fuck the Jews' from that car on Finchley Road clearly went beyond legitimate political commentary, as did the person who daubed a swastika and 'Free Palestine' on the door of a synagogue in Norwich. They may have been espousing the language of pro-Palestinian activism, but they did so to threaten and harass British Jews who have no involvement in, or responsibility for, conflict in the Middle East. More worryingly, as outrageous as these incidents were, there is evidence to suggest they reflect a broader trend. The largest ever opinion poll into British attitudes towards both Jews and Israel found that, when you correlate how someone thinks about Jews with how they think about Israel, 'the stronger a person's anti-Israel views, the more likely they are to hold antisemitic attitudes'. This poll found that the same works in the opposite direction: 'Most of

---

* 'BDS' stands for Boycott, Divestment and Sanctions, and it is the main organisation and slogan promoting a boycott of Israel.

those holding antisemitic attitudes also hold anti-Israel attitudes.'[16] Hostility to Jews and hostility to Israel are not automatically tied together – you can have one without the other – but they tend to come as a package.

The same research suggests this also applies to people who support a boycott of Israel. If a non-Jewish person advocates the boycott of Israel, the polling evidence shows 'It is ... scientifically reasonable to conclude' that this person 'is also predisposed towards anti-Jewish feeling, thereby indicating antisemitic feeling, motive or intent.'[17] This happens at governmental level too. A different piece of research found that 'a government which votes more often than average against Israel in the UN General Assembly' is also more likely to discriminate against Jews in its own country.[18]

For some of Israel's supporters this is all they need to know. There's a temptation to assume that every opponent of Israel is using a very real, and tragic, conflict as a cloak to mask their anti-Jewish prejudice. They don't want to admit they hate Jews – perhaps they can't even admit it to themselves – so Israel becomes the proxy instead. A socially acceptable way to hate something Jewish in our modern, liberal world. Ben & Jerry's were accused of stoking Jew-hatred when they banned sale of their ice cream in Israeli settlements on the West Bank, just as the actor Emma Watson was called an antisemite when she posted a pro-Palestinian message on Instagram. I can't go along with that. It's too simplistic, unfair and it doesn't help us get to the crux of the problem. Antisemitism alone cannot explain why so many people gravitate towards Israel and Palestine as their chosen cause, to the exclusion of so many others. There must be space for people to support the Palestinians, or to oppose Israel, in the way of normal politics. But I do wish some of them would ask themselves the same question I'm asking now: why always Israel, and why only Israel?

Take Brian Eno. The 1970s glam-rock star and ambient music wizard is now president of the Stop the War Coalition, whose stated purpose is to oppose 'foreign policy based on Washington's global ambitions or on a junior imperial role for Britain'.[19] As such, it is far from obvious why the Stop the War Coalition should spend as much time and energy as it does on Israel. They help to organise countless anti-Israel demonstrations, and Israel/Palestine is the only overseas conflict not directly involving British forces that is namechecked on the 'About' page of their website. In 2003 the coalition even put its name to a statement endorsing 'military struggle' against Israel, which is an odd thing for an anti-war group to do.[20] The rest of their website includes well-balanced, thoughtful articles with headlines such as 'Israel Is The Jimmy Savile Of Nation States Abusing Gaza's Children' and 'Why ISIS Is Israel's Key Ally In Stopping The Creation Of A Palestinian State'.

These are all pretty extreme, but it was a personal piece by Eno, written in 2014, that caught my eye. Writing during that summer's conflict in Israel and Gaza, Eno explained that singling out Israel for protests, campaigns and boycotts is the right thing to do, because Israel 'claims to be like us, part of the Western First World, part of the same set of moral assumptions'. This gets to the heart of the answer. Most people in Britain do not care about Israel or Palestine, if they think about the issue at all. However, for those who really do care, they treat Israel differently because they do not see it as foreign but as part of our world, an extension of who we are, in Britain and in the West. The real driver of this anti-Israel exceptionalism is the notion of a shared culture, rather than any political, financial or material links. This is why Eno justifies his stance by saying that Israel 'claims to be like us' with the same 'moral assumptions'. Israel and Britain share the same culture and are part of the same civilisation, in a way that Turkey and Saudi Arabia are not, and therefore Israel's actions reflect on the West's own sense of who we are. That is why what Israel does – or is accused of doing – matters so much to so many people who act as if they have a personal investment in a conflict to which they have no individual connection.

Eno claims his campaigning against Israel is about 'what my government is doing in my name. The money we pay in taxes is helping to support this situation,' but when it comes to Saudi Arabia – a much more consistent and substantial military client of Britain's than Israel has ever been – he isn't interested. What does Saudi Arabia 'have to do with me?', he asks dismissively. 'I don't understand them, and I don't know that my government has any particular role within them.'[21] The reason Eno thinks he understands Israel but not Saudi Arabia is that he sees Arabs as culturally different and Jews as culturally aligned. This is primarily about a sense of shared values rather than military alliances or other material factors, and Eno isn't alone in thinking this way. 'Israel is legitimately singled out,' according to an article in the left-wing magazine *Red Pepper*, because it claims to be 'defending western values and presents itself as an outpost of these values'. It sees itself as a democracy whose Declaration of Independence stresses 'the precepts of liberty, justice and peace' and whose army follows a moral code. These are arguments based on common values rather than an objective comparison of human rights abuses. Furthermore, *Red Pepper* notes, 'Israel is special in that it controls a number of religious sites that are of special significance to three world religions.' We'll come back to that point.[22]

This might make sense – it is natural to care more about people and places with which you feel an affinity – but it comes with a twist. Israel is, one way or another, Jewish. It defines itself as a Jewish state and a homeland for all the world's Jews. Most of its population are Jewish, it has Jewish symbols on its national flag and it has made the ancient Jewish voice of prayer, Hebrew, its primary daily language. Israeli governments repeatedly and proudly declare the state's essential Jewish character and assert its place in global Jewish life. If Israel is targeted for boycotts and protests because it is part of the West, part of 'us', then logically this will be informed by the ways that Jews have been viewed and treated in the social mores and cultural values of the West. Because Israel is so distinctly Jewish, attitudes towards it – positive and negative – will be influenced by the ways in which people have related to Jews in the past. It's unavoidable that the history and contemporary reality of how people think about, and treat, Jews, will influence how they think about and relate to Israel – and vice versa. And here's the catch: for most of Europe's history, Jews have not been fully, uncomplicatedly, 'like us' or carriers of 'western values'. Brian Eno alluded to this, probably unwittingly, when he said that Israel *'claims to be* like us' (emphasis added). When Israel's opponents justify singling it out because Israel is part of the West, it's always going to be more complicated than that.

Jews have long played an ambivalent role in Europe's sense of itself: often present but for much of it not on an equal footing. At times the contributions of Jews to European societies have been valued and cherished, but they have also been expelled from different countries, persecuted and blamed for all sorts of social problems and crises. Until relatively recently, across most of Europe and for much of its history, rights for Jews were limited and strictly conditional. Normal rules did not apply. Some would like it to be that way for Israel too.

TWO JERUSALEMS

The imprint of Jews and their history on our own culture is so common that it often passes unnoticed or forgotten. Whenever someone proposes that England ought to have its own national anthem, similar to 'Flower of Scotland' or Wales's 'Land of my Fathers', the most popular option is always 'Jerusalem'. Chosen by BBC *Songs of Praise* viewers as Britain's favourite hymn in 2019, it is sung before every England cricket match and – thanks to a public vote – played when England wins a gold medal at the Commonwealth Games. Based on a poem written by William Blake in the early 1800s and first put to music by Sir Hubert Parry in 1916, 'Jerusalem' takes the ancient vision of a 'new Jerusalem', a utopian ideal of a world free from all suffering and oppression, and infuses it with the essence of Englishness. Everyone from the Labour Party to King George V, the suffragettes to Last Night of the Proms, has tried to claim 'Jerusalem' as representing their own version of what England means, or what it could be. One of the most celebrated plays of modern times, Jez Butterworth's *Jerusalem*, draws on the same mythology for its own elegy to a lost England. When David Cameron was Prime Minister he backed its use by English sport teams as an alternative to 'God Save The Queen'. I agree with him: partly because it was my old school hymn, sung on the final day of summer term each year, and partly because it would avoid the embarrassment of England having the dreariest anthem at every international football tournament. But nobody ever seems to notice how strange it is that such an English song, the most popular choice for an alternative national anthem, is named after the capital city of a foreign country thousands of miles from these shores.

Not just any capital city, but one laden with symbolic meaning. When England's Barmy Army belt out 'Jerusalem' before the first ball is bowled at Lord's, they are probably unaware that they are invoking thousands of years of Jewish and Christian apocalyptic yearning. The metaphor of a 'new Jerusalem' first appeared in Jewish messianic writings in the centuries before Christ's birth, at a time when the actual Jerusalem was still a thriving Jewish city. Its most influential account comes in the Book of Revelations, which tells of a new Jerusalem descending from the heavens on judgement day to usher in a messianic age lasting a thousand years. This image has, for centuries, wielded extraordinary metaphorical power. During the First Crusade in 1095, when thousands of volunteers journeyed to the Holy Land to free the actual Jerusalem from Muslim rule, 'the Jerusalem which obsessed their imagination was no mere earthly city but rather the symbol of a prodigious hope'.[23]

The opening lines of Blake's verse –

> And did those feet in ancient time
> Walk upon England's mountains green
> And was the holy Lamb of God
> On England's pleasant pastures seen!

– allude to an apocryphal story that Jesus once visited the town of Glastonbury. The play *Jerusalem* is, likewise, set in England's south west. Taken literally, 'Glastonbury' – traditionally a centre for English spiritualism and mythology – ought to have been a more fitting title for both than 'Jerusalem', but, despite its annual music festival, Glastonbury does not matter to billions of people like Jerusalem does.* Symbolism usually outdoes reality, and there are few symbols more potent than Jerusalem, with its holy places, its religious gravity, its myths and fables. 'The history of Jerusalem is the history of the world,' wrote the city's biographer, Simon Sebag Montefiore: 'She is the only city to exist twice – in heaven and on earth.'[24]

Except as well as the ethereal Jerusalem of apocalyptic fantasy, there is a real Jerusalem, where just shy of a million Jews, Muslims and Christians live, work, pray, complain about the trams, take their bins out and deal with the ebb and flow of daily life – while also fighting for control over holy places of immense importance to billions of people, as they have for thousands of years. In May 2021 the latest flashpoint† was a long-running legal dispute between Palestinian tenants and their Jewish landlords over unpaid rent for six homes in Sheikh Jarrah, a predominantly Arab neighbourhood a little over a mile north of Jerusalem's Old City. Violence broke out between Israeli police and Palestinians protesting against the impending eviction of the tenants, and the situation threatened to spiral out of control. In Britain there were demonstrations around the country. Forty-five thousand people wrote letters to their MPs, and an Early Day Motion was lodged in Parliament calling on Israel to end 'the continued evictions of Palestinian families from Sheikh Jarrah'.[25] Mick Lynch, the general secretary of the National Union of Rail, Maritime and Transport Workers (RMT) wrote to

---

* I've been to the Glastonbury Festival and to Jerusalem several times each, so I'm well placed to compare them. Perhaps surprisingly, it was at Glastonbury rather than in Jerusalem that I was exhorted to 'put your hands in the air if you love Jesus'. The Christian preacher leading this prayer was the Rev. Al Green, and of course I joined in. It was a memorable gig and definitely worth the mild blasphemy on my part.

† Latest at the time of writing; depending on when you are reading this, there are likely to have been others since.

every branch of his union, urging them to support a 'National Day of Action for Palestine' because 'Palestinian families are currently being forcibly evicted from their homes in Sheikh Jarrah, occupied Jerusalem'.[26]

You can try to follow the twists and turns of the Sheikh Jarrah controversy if you want. Depending on your point of view, it was either 'an ordinary property dispute between private parties' that ought to be of no wider consequence, or part of 'a continuum of dispossession', another step in a long-term Israeli project to ethnically cleanse Palestinians from Arab East Jerusalem.[27] It's complicated: while Sheikh Jarrah is mostly an Arab neighbourhood, the six properties at the heart of this dispute have been owned by Jews since the 1800s and, to confuse things further, have had Arab and Jewish residents at different times depending on who held Sheikh Jarrah following the various Arab–Israeli wars. My point is not to try to sort out who is right and wrong – I'll leave that to the Israeli courts to decide – but to wonder at the ability of a dispute over a property contract in a suburb of Jerusalem to generate such a reaction in Britain. Because it turned out – who knew? – that an awful lot of people in this country care very deeply about the fate of six homes in Sheikh Jarrah. There aren't many tenancy hearings in corners of foreign cities that can persuade tens of thousands of people to march on the streets of the United Kingdom or write to their MP. But the Sheikh Jarrah legal case did, for the same reason that Mark Rylance and his fellow actors called for Shakespeare's Globe to boycott only the Israeli theatre company and no other.*

---

* There is some irony in the fact that Mark Rylance, who assiduously boycotts the real Israel, cemented his reputation as Britain's greatest living stage actor with his performance of the lead role in the play *Jerusalem*, which draws so heavily on the tradition of an allegorical Israel.

Almost twenty years before the Sheikh Jarrah court case, in March 2002, violence was raging in Israel, the West Bank and Gaza. Repeated Palestinian suicide bombings caused havoc in Israel, and Israeli forces repeatedly struck at Palestinian targets. Many had died on both sides, and the Israeli government tried to break the cycle by sending thousands of troops into Palestinian towns and cities where most of the suicide bombers emanated from. In Bethlehem, dozens of Palestinian fighters, including some from a group called the Al-Aqsa Martyrs' Brigade – named after the Al-Aqsa Mosque in Jerusalem – took refuge in the Church of the Nativity, which was surrounded by Israeli forces. A five-week siege ensued, with British and American mediators eventually brokering a deal. Imagine this: one of Christianity's most sacred sites, the birthplace of Jesus himself, at the centre of a standoff between fighters named after one of Islam's holiest mosques and soldiers from the first Jewish sovereign military force since Jesus walked on that same land. There is nowhere else on earth that anything remotely as culturally, religiously or politically resonant could happen.

It is simply improbable that Israel's fiercest critics are able to detach themselves entirely from their own cultural moorings when deciding who to boycott, which march to go on or where to lodge their moral protests. When activists in Britain weigh up which cause to give their limited time and energy to and choose Israel on the basis that it is 'like us', they do not only put measurable things like arms sales or political support on their mental and emotional scales. The option of Israel is weighted with all this historical and cultural baggage; less tangible but potentially decisive. Turkey cannot compete. There is no comparable history of thinking about Turks to match Europe's long and troubled grappling with the status and significance of Jews. There is no discourse about Turks embedded in our language and literature that compares in scale and breadth to the antisemitic narratives, characters and images that exist. No Turkish Fagin or Shylock in our popular culture, no blood libels or *Protocols of the Elders of Zion* to propel anti-Turkish sentiment through the generations. When Turkey was the focus of Europe's 'Eastern Question' in the nineteenth century, this was seen as an external problem regarding the future of the Ottoman Empire; in contrast, the contemporaneous 'Jewish Question' was treated as an internal challenge about the place of Jews within European societies. Turks are simply not deemed as relevant to our own lives, or to how we explain our world, as Jews have been.

DISPLACING SHAME

For centuries Europe's political, religious and intellectual thinkers tied themselves in knots over what to do about Jews. It was considered an essential question that said something important about the country, religion or political movement that was doing this Jew-thinking. Sometimes it worked out well: since the seventeenth century at least there has long been a strain of philosemitism, which has at times encouraged a sympathetic and welcoming disposition. When Jews were permitted by Oliver Cromwell to return to England in 1656, over 350 years after their expulsion by Edward I, it was in part because 'the self-identification of Puritans as the new Israel had fostered a boom in the study of Hebrew, [which] might on occasion shade almost into admiration'.[28] After the French Revolution in 1789, the new Republic devoted considerable time and debate to the question of what to do about French Jews. They decided, in the end, to grant them full citizenship – the first in Europe to do so – albeit with conditions. 'Jews should be denied everything as a nation; granted everything as individuals,' was the mantra by which Jews were accepted as French citizens.[29] This philosemitism is obviously preferable to the discrimination suffered in other times and places, but there is always a nagging sense that they share a common root, which is the idea that the way a country treats its Jews is thought to have some special significance.

This is partly reflected today in the inflated importance Israel is accorded. 'Now Europeans see Israel as a threat to their existence,' ran the headline over an article by *Guardian* correspondent Martin Woollacott in 2003.[30] Woollacott, an experienced observer of the way the Middle East is reported, felt that 'the European media' had adopted a collective line that was not just critical of Israeli policies but that 'call[ed] out to save the world from Israel'.[31] There is no rational basis on which this tiny country threatens the existence of Europe, unless you count their occasional victory in the Eurovision Song Contest. And the notion that the world needs saving from Israel, just a strip of land a few miles wide at the edge of the Mediterranean Sea, is mindboggling. Former Labour minister Clare Short claimed that Israeli policies, and American backing for them, are 'the major cause of bitter division and violence in the world'.[32] This claim that cannot possibly be true unless you discount any conflict outside the Middle East, and even there, the devastating civil wars in Syria, Yemen and Libya over the past decade have nothing at all to do with Israel.

Today the pendulum has swung towards the philosemitic pole when compared to centuries past. In January 2015, after four French Jews were murdered in a kosher supermarket in Paris, French Prime Minister Manuel Valls declared that 'without its Jews France would not be France', a sentiment that would have seemed absurd for much of French history (Jews were expelled from France in 1306, again in 1394, and did not return in significant numbers until the eighteenth century).[33] According to Roberta Metsola, President of the European Parliament, 'To be antisemitic is to be anti-European.' Life is obviously much better for Jews in Europe today than it was in medieval times or during the long centuries when Jews' rights were severely restricted and persecution was common. But while these practices have largely ended in Europe, the traditional patterns of thought that sustained them have not eroded completely. Explicit anti-Jewish language may be less respectable, but ways of thinking about Jews and Jewish things established over centuries can still have a magnetic pull – in either direction. Whether seen as laudable or iniquitous, Jews have been given an unwanted and unwarranted role in society's hang-ups.

The negative side of this phenomenon is found in people who, in every phase of Europe's intellectual and political development, singled out Jews as the example of how not to be: the opposite of what is considered good, moral and just. The demonic representation of Jews for much of the Middle Ages performed this role. More recent variants include the right-wing myth of Judeo-Communism and the left's imaginings about Jewish capitalism. Jews have long been Europe's traditional 'Other', but this doesn't only mean they have been an unwanted minority: it incorporates a more profound imagining of Jews as a representation of the evils that need to be purged to make the world pure.

This is why it is so striking that Israel, the most visible global expression of Jewish life today, is held up as the archetype of a human rights transgressor in a world in which human rights are the highest measure of moral good. It matches the role accorded to Jews in the past too closely to be a coincidence. Israel does things that are deserving of censure, but not uniquely, nor to such an outlandish extent that would justify why Israel alone is the focus of all these boycotts, protests and hate crimes, out of all proportion to its size and material importance, while others are ignored. If it really is because Israel is perceived as being part of the West, then that strongly suggests Israel has inherited the role that the West accorded to Jews in centuries past: a screen onto which people have projected the worst things in our own societies. This would explain why anti-Israel marches are so emotionally charged, berating the Jewish state as the carrier of all of the West's most egregious sins. Racism, colonialism, militaristic nationalism, even apartheid and Nazism: Israel's critics paint it as the embodiment of what they consider to be their – our – most shameful aspects. By making Israel the totem of all the worst things in our world, we make ourselves look, and feel, better by comparison.

When the actor Maxine Peake falsely claimed that 'the tactics used by the police in America, kneeling on George Floyd's neck, that was learnt from seminars with Israeli secret services',[34] she was indulging in exactly this kind of displacement. This calumny, transferring some of the blame for George Floyd's murder away from the Minneapolis police officers who killed him and onto Israeli police, spread widely and rapidly as violent protests shook American cities in 2020. Peake probably read it in Britain's Communist-aligned *Morning Star* newspaper, which put it on their front page. The allegation was quickly debunked. There are exchange programmes between US and Israeli police officers, but they don't involve instruction in how to kneel on people's necks. Plus, the implication that American police would not mistreat Black Americans were it not for the advice of Israel is ignorant and insulting. However, shifting responsibility onto Israel for an event as traumatic, politically fraught and socially destabilising as the murder of George Floyd diverts all that pain and division safely onto an external actor. It is classic scapegoating. Antisemitism is largely about blaming Jews for things that go wrong, but this isn't quite that: it is using Jews as a vehicle to cast out what is considered evil or harmful. You might argue that Peake blamed Israel rather than Jews, so it isn't antisemitic. Except that this happens to Israel repeatedly, it happened historically to Jews and it is improbable that it would happen so much, using this language and way of thinking, if Israel wasn't Jewish.

Since the murder of George Floyd and the rise of the Black Lives Matter movement, there has been a transparent attempt to reclassify the Israeli–Palestinian conflict not as a clash of two rival national movements – Jewish/Israeli and Arab Palestinian – who both have a legitimate claim to the same land but instead as a case of a white colonial oppressor and a colonised people of colour: foreign settlers versus indigenous natives. This is not a new argument, but it has gathered steam at a time when many in Britain are rethinking the history and legacy of our own empire.* A common refrain heard on rallies and in protest speeches during the conflict in Israel and Gaza in May 2021 was that 'this is not a conflict'. 'To frame this as a war between two equal sides is false and misleading,' declared a letter

---

* Britain was the imperial power in Palestine in the three decades before Israel's independence in 1948, under a United Nations mandate following the First World War. At times Britain favoured the Zionist movement; at others it gave primacy to Arab concerns. Supporters of Palestine consider the 1917 Balfour Declaration, in which the British government pledged its support for 'the establishment in Palestine of a national home for the Jewish people', an act of historic betrayal. Supporters of Israel look with similar disgust at the British policy of severely restricting Jewish immigration to Palestine from 1936 onwards, just when Jews living under Nazi rule in Europe most needed a refuge. You can take your pick of examples to argue either that Britain was the midwife of the Jewish State or that it did everything in its power to obstruct its birth.

signed by thousands of artists, writers and musicians in 2021. 'Israel is the colonising power. Palestine is colonised. This is not a conflict: this is apartheid.'[35] The implied meaning of this letter is that Israel was never a legitimate nation but is an artificial Western transplant into the Middle East. Rather than Zionism being a genuine national movement, it 'was simply one of the many settler colonialist movements that grew out of the late-Victorian imperialist zeitgeist'.[36] As for the Jews who migrated to Palestine dreaming of a Jewish homeland from the nineteenth century onwards – initially under Ottoman rule, then during British control after the First World War – they would be comparable to French settlers in Algeria or European settlers in north America, 'supplanting, dominating, driving out or massacring already-existing societies'.[37] It's as if all Israelis are settlers from Poland or Brooklyn and all Palestinians have lived in the land of Israel since the days of Jesus.

In 2018, after the United States announced it would move its embassy from Tel Aviv to Jerusalem, Palestinian Authority President Mahmoud Abbas said in a speech that 'Europeans wanted to bring the Jews here to preserve their interests in the region ... Israel is a colonial project that has nothing to do with Jews.'[38] Abbas may have had strong grounds to be angry with America's decision given that the status of Jerusalem remains disputed between the parties, but his statement was something else: it relied on the idea that Israel was nothing other than a creation of Western colonialism to erase the role of Jews in building their own state, treating them instead as pawns or accomplices in the West's drive to conquest. As Abbas showed, this argument necessitates the denial of any legitimacy to the Jewish desire for a national home in the land that was, historically, the only place on earth where there had previously been Jewish sovereignty. It paints Israelis as European interlopers, even though around half of Israel's population are Mizrahi Jews who originate in Jewish communities that had lived in the Middle East and north Africa for, in some cases, thousands of years, before being driven out of those Arab countries in the twentieth century. Around 850,000 Jews were ethnically cleansed from Muslim-majority countries in the middle decades of that century, an aspect of the Israeli–Palestinian conflict, and of modern antisemitism, that is often overlooked.

This version of history rejects the idea that the Jews are an authentic people deserving of self-determination at all, much less a persecuted people who need to hold power in their own hands. Yet the early Jewish settlers in Palestine were hardly sent on a mission by their home countries. Far from being colonialists who settled Palestine as part of Europe's imperial domination, they were refugees, the persecuted and downtrodden, escaping a Europe that 'began to vomit up its Jews' well before the Holocaust.[39] And not just Europe: in 1941, Jews were not only being massacred in Ukraine, Belarus and the Baltic States, but also in Baghdad, where between 150 and 180 Jews were murdered, hundreds more raped or injured and 1,500 Jewish shops and homes looted and damaged, in a two-day pogrom instigated by pro-Nazi elements in Iraq.[40] This is the best-known example of twentieth-century anti-Jewish violence in Arab countries, but it is far from the only one.

The purpose of this chapter is not an attempt to tell the history of the Israeli–Palestinian conflict: that isn't the focus of this book, and the moment you start trying to explain the conflict you get sucked into a quagmire of competing claims and narratives. I intend to do it as little as I can get away with in this chapter and I'm already anxious about what I've included or left out. But I'll just say this: the reason that Jews started migrating to the part of the Turkish Ottoman Empire known as Palestine in the late nineteenth and early twentieth centuries, with the aim of establishing a Jewish national home on that land, is not because some Victorian imperialists dreamt it up in a back room in Whitehall. It is because the Jewish connection to the land is authentic, ancient and enduring.

The land of Israel is intrinsic to the traditional Jewish account of the birth of the Jewish people and their religion. This includes familiar Old Testament stories like the Garden of Eden, Noah's Ark, the Tower of Babel, the slavery of Jews in Egypt, the ten plagues, Moses leading his people to freedom across the divinely parted Red Sea, the burning bush, the ten commandments, forty years of wandering around the desert and, eventually, the establishment of a Jewish kingdom in the land of Israel as originally promised to Abraham by God around 4,000 years ago. How much of this actually happened, and how much is either allegory or the kind of foundational myth-making that all nations rely on, is for bible scholars, archaeologists and historians of the ancient world to debate (and they do, endlessly). The further back you go in history the less archaeological or documentary evidence there is to confirm or contradict any of it, but even if you put all the bible stories to one side, there is enough evidence to suggest that the earliest Jewish (or rather, Judean) kingdom had taken form in the area around Jerusalem, with the Temple at its physical and spiritual heart, by the ninth century BCE.

Over subsequent centuries, this Judean kingdom endured invasion, conquest, exile and return, its Temple destroyed and rebuilt, until AD 70 when the Temple was destroyed for the second time, this time by the Roman Army, and Jewish sovereignty effectively came to an end. This transformed the nature of Judaism, which until that point had revolved around the Temple as the locus of its religious rites and festivals, but it could not sever the Jewish connection to its heartland, even if that attachment became more spiritual than physical.* Instead, Jerusalem took its place as a reference point in the daily prayers of Judaism's emerging liturgy, and remains the direction of prayer for Jews around the world up to the present day.

In the 1,878 years between the fall of the Second Temple and the foundation of the State of Israel, individual Jews still travelled to Jerusalem and there were times when whole Jewish communities fell for false messiahs who promised redemption. Largely, though, dreams of a return to the land of Israel remained in the realm of messianic fantasy until modern nationalism came along and offered a political alternative. Zionism arose in the nineteenth century to offer a revolutionary solution to the problem of endemic anti-semitism in Europe. The granting of civil rights in the Enlightenment and assimilation into wider society had failed to dissipate the old hatreds, and Europe's Jews were searching for a new idea. Socialism promised liberation alongside the rest of humanity, but Marxist theory expected Judaism to wither away in the process and that wasn't what most Jews were after. Zionism suggested an alternative to Jews: liberation in their own homeland, Jewish self-determination in line with the nationalism that was swelling across

---

* This shift from sovereignty to exile was never binary. By the time of the Roman conquest of Judea there were already more Jews living outside its borders than within, and even after the fall of the Temple the Jewish presence, though much reduced, never entirely ended.

Europe. The Zionist movement held out the utopian dream of self-empowerment, control over their own destiny and the normalising of Jewish life.

When Zionism began gaining momentum in the late nineteenth and early twentieth centuries the territory that is now Israel, Gaza and the West Bank was all part of the Turkish Ottoman Empire, with a mainly Arab population and a growing Jewish minority. Like many modern nationalisms, the Zionist movement did not pay much attention to the claims of others to the same land, the consequences of which are glaringly obvious today. It sought the support of governments in the Christian West, but its success depended on its ability to win the hearts of the downtrodden Jewish masses, propelled by each new surge of pogroms and persecutions, rather than because of some imperialist conspiracy.

I'm the first to argue that religious belief is not a sound basis on which to make policy, and ancient history rarely provides a usable template for political arrangements in the modern world. That's not my argument, and the reason I've outlined the historic Jewish connection to the land of Israel isn't to try to convince you of the Israeli case. Rather, it is to emphasise that the Jewish link to Israel is not a modern invention, nor is it something that Western colonialists or political Zionists have artificially grafted onto Judaism. It has always been there, and today it is found in the many familial, cultural and religious ties that Jews around the world have to Israel – well before you get to the question of whether anyone supports this or that political position on the conflict.

I know that similar paragraphs could be written about the Palestinian connection to the same land and about the history of the

Palestinian national movement.* My argument that the Jewish connection is authentic is not intended – does not need – to exclude the idea that Palestinians also feel such a connection. For what it's worth, I think it's pointless to try to persuade a people that they don't really exist or that the things they believe about their origins and their identity aren't true. There are people who try to do this on both sides. Zionists who argue that Palestinian national identity is a relatively modern construct and therefore artificial; anti-Zionists who spend their time tracing Jewish genetics to try to prove that most Jews today do not have biological linkage to the Jews of the Old Testament. To which I can only say: so what? It's an unavoidable truth that Israelis and Palestinians are now two peoples with strong national identities. Whatever the political outcome of the conflict, that isn't going to change.

The story of Israel's creation is a complex one, and like any episode in history there will be different interpretations of the roles played by the various actors. Historians research the role of colonial powers in supporting the creation of the State of Israel, just as modern analysts of the Middle East debate the extent to which Israel uses colonial methods today in the way it treats the Palestinians under its control. Israel itself uses the language of settlement when talking about the West Bank. Discussing whether, and how, Israeli practices compare to, and differ from, other cases of land being settled and colonised is the normal business of both academia and politics. That isn't what I'm talking about here. The problem

---

* I haven't written a parallel passage about Palestinian history because – as I keep trying to remind myself – this book is about Jews and antisemitism, and this chapter is about the relationship between attitudes towards Jews and towards Israel.

comes when all this is reduced to a simplistic political narrative that flattens all complexity and converts Palestinians and Israelis into morally one-dimensional characters, in which Israeli Jews are made symbols of Western conquest and Palestinians are used to represent the virtue of the oppressed. A narrative that makes this all about the West and Europe's guilt for its own colonial past. It's a version of history that de-centres Jews from their own story.

If Israel really is nothing other than a creation of Western imperialism, the implications are stark. It would suggest that the Jews are not a real people with any claim to statehood or any historic link to the land on which Israel now sits. This will be news to the millions of Jews around the world who feel themselves to be part of a Jewish whole. There are so few of us that it always feels weirdly thrilling to spot another Jew in a strange part of the world. They are usually an Israeli tourist: there may not be many of them, but boy do they travel. I've rarely been anywhere in the world, or in the UK for that matter, without overhearing Hebrew from a passer-by, a stranger on a train or (often) a fan at Old Trafford. You can come up with lots of sociological and anthropological definitions of what makes a 'people', but for me, it has to include this feeling of connection with a complete stranger and with all other Jews throughout history.

Today Israel stands at the heart of the Jewish world. It is the location of the world's largest Jewish community and, for most Jews, plays a central role in their Jewish identity.* This might sound like a

---

* A 2010 survey by the Institute for Jewish Policy Research found 95 per cent of British Jews said Israel plays some role in their Jewish identity, 82 per cent said it plays a central or important role and 90 per cent said they see Israel as the ancestral homeland of the Jewish people. A 2015 survey by City University London found 90 per cent of British Jews support Israel's right to exist as a Jewish state and 93 per cent said it plays a role in their Jewish identity. This doesn't necessarily translate into political support for Israeli government policies: both surveys found strong support for a two-state solution and opposition to expansion of Jewish settlements in the West Bank.

controversial statement to some, but within the Jewish world the involvement of Israeli culture, learning and people in daily Jewish life is utterly normal. Given that Israel is now the world's largest Jewish community and its most powerful and creative generator of new ideas, inventions, cuisine, scholarship and pretty much everything else – its TV shows are even turning up on Netflix in increasing numbers – it could hardly happen any other way.

I've felt this myself. It is a strange experience for a British Jew to visit Israel, coming from a country where my fellow Jews are a tiny minority, barely visible in the contours and rhythms of public life, to a place where people you walk past on the street, the shopkeepers and bus drivers, waiters and police officers, are mostly Jewish. A country where you never have to explain to anyone that you are Jewish, or what that means, where public holidays are arranged around the Jewish calendar rather than the Christian one and kosher food is plentiful. The beauty of the land itself, its mountains and deserts, is infused with a history that even the most secular, atheist Jews find hard to resist. Hiking is big in Israel, and walking through river valleys, swimming in natural pools or tramping up mountains to see the sunrise just feels different from doing the same in other countries. It isn't about religion for me. I don't even believe in the God that supposedly promised that land to Abraham a very long time ago. It's about the here and now: a world in which Jews have suffered too much and been let down too often. A world where Jewish civilisations have risen and thrived in lands ruled by others, whether medieval Spain, early-modern Poland or twentieth-century Iraq, only to be utterly extirpated, leaving nothing other than ruined buildings and sorrowful memories. It's about our big world having room for one small space that is undeniably, ineradicably Jewish.

At least, that's the sentiment. I know the reality is much more complicated and that Jews are not the only people who feel a special connection and a legitimate right to that land. You can look at the promises of early Zionist pioneers and count the myriad ways in which the modern State of Israel has fallen short of those lofty ideals. You can outline the many flaws and fractures in Israeli society and politics and question whether the reality could ever live up to the ideal. But even here, the failings of the Jewish national project are intensely human. All nations, Israel included, tell stories about themselves that prefer to ignore ugly or inconvenient truths. And frankly, I'm relieved it's not my job to work out a peaceful solution between Israel and Palestine.* But you can't understand the way that anti-Israel activism affects how Jews around the world, and in Britain, feel about themselves if you aren't aware of this aspect.

JUST DON'T DO IT

If there is one thing you pledge never to do having read this book, please make it this: do not compare Israel to Nazi Germany. Just don't. Reducing Israel to an outcrop of Western colonialism is nothing compared to this pernicious comparison. Nazism has become the ultimate yardstick for evil but this is no generic use of the slur. It hijacks the greatest trauma in Jewish history, one that still causes pain for survivors and their descendants, and uses it as a moral club to bash the country founded out of the ashes of that very trauma.

---

* Tony Blair was made Middle East peace envoy in 2007 by the Quartet of United Nations, European Union, Russia and the United States, with the goal of working towards a peaceful solution to the Israeli–Palestinian conflict. On the day he was appointed I overheard two men discussing the announcement on the train home from work. 'You know why he took the position, don't you?' said one of them. 'It's a job for life.' Blair stuck it out until 2015, and even with the most generous view you couldn't say the Middle East was a more peaceful place by the time he'd finished.

The comparison is not justified by any factual evidence. Gaza is not the Warsaw Ghetto; Jenin is not Auschwitz; the Israeli army is not the SS.* However, the superficial utility is obvious. If you believe that Israel was created due to the world's post-Holocaust guilt then equating Jews with their persecutors does away with their moral claim. Maybe the Jews shouldn't have been given Israel after all, is how the thinking goes. In a world where victim status can be a powerful political currency, there are those who envy Jews for their supposedly privileged position as Holocaust victims. The perverse logic of competitive victimhood demands that Jews get taken down a peg, and how better to do this than to accuse them of learning only how to persecute others.

There is a subliminal appeal too, seen in all the placards bearing signs with a 'Swastika equals Star of David' motif. This is another way in which Israel is singled out: anti-Israel rallies have, for years, been the British political protests where you are most likely to find people brandishing swastikas. It is not a coincidence that this happens on protests against a Jewish state. It allows people who consider themselves left-wing to feel the thrill of transgressing the ultimate political taboo, protected by their status as progressives. Waving swastikas at Israel is how anti-racists get to play at being Nazis for a day.

---

* During the crisis of antisemitism in the Labour Party, Ken Livingstone encouraged a lot of people on the left of the party to believe that the Zionist movement in the 1930s and early 1940s collaborated with Nazi Germany. Historians have repeatedly debunked his claims, which take kernels of truth and distort them so much that they become completely misleading. In fact the Arab national movement in Palestine received financial and material support from Nazi Germany in the 1930s. From 1936 to 1939 an Arab revolt against the British was partly financed by Nazi Germany and led by Hajj Amin Al-Husseini, the dominant religious and political figure in the Palestinian national struggle during that period, who became notorious for his pro-Nazi sympathies during World War Two.

Anti-Israel demonstrators with a swastika placard, London, May 2021

This post-war libel has found its place in high culture. In 2009, after a three-week conflict between Israel and Hamas in Gaza, Caryl Churchill wrote a short play for the Royal Court Theatre in London called *Seven Jewish Children: A Play for Gaza*. The play revolved around imagined conversations between Jewish parents and their Jewish children over the course of a century or more, through pogroms, the Holocaust, emigration to Israel and subsequent conflicts in that country. It didn't explicitly mention Israel at all, but all the characters were Jewish: any Jewish families anywhere, was the inference, and it was developed and performed in London, so that means people like me. This was Churchill's attempt to get inside the heads of Jewish parents and work out why the 'chosen people', as she put it, kill Palestinian babies and apparently don't care ('Tell her we killed the babies by mistake ... tell her I look at one of their children covered in blood and what do I feel? tell her all I feel is happy it's not her,' is the exact wording).⁴¹* It was a particularly objectional example of the accusation that Jews have failed to learn the correct lessons from the Holocaust, with an echo of the blood libel thrown in for good measure through allusions to blood-soaked child murder.

I would never deny that the Holocaust, and antisemitism in general, has a profound impact on Jewish sensibilities, but Churchill asked the antisemitic version of this question: not how antisemitism makes Jews feel about our own safety and belonging, but why it makes Jews treat non-Jews so badly. Her greater crime, though, was her unmitigated failure as a playwright to find any understanding, much less empathy, for the people she was writing about. If she was trying to represent the challenge of raising Jewish children in a world where the Holocaust happened within living memory, where people go into synagogues with guns to shoot us dead, where people march through the streets of my home city chanting for Jews to be killed, and to do so without filling our children with fear or shame but only pride and self-confidence, she missed the mark entirely. But then, that parenting task is not made any easier when the response of a leading London theatre to war in Gaza is to put on a play asking why it is that Jewish parents screw up their kids so much that they turn them into killers.

Naturally Churchill denied her play was antisemitic, dismissing complaints as 'the usual tactic' of conflating criticism of Israel with antisemitism.⁴² It is comforting, but dangerous, to reject concerns over antisemitism as a bad-faith attempt to silence Israel's

---

* As explained in Chapter Two – but in case you missed it – the Jewish theological concept of the 'chosen people' has long been abused by antisemites to claim that it proves Jews have a sense of racial superiority. In fact it conveys something completely different, which is the biblical idea that the Jews were chosen by God to live by his commandments. In other words, it is more of a burden than a privilege, depending on how you look at it.

opponents. This is itself an antisemitic charge, as it presumes that her (mainly Jewish) critics are deliberately lying about something as serious and weighty as antisemitism to score a political point – which would be a grave offence if it were true.*

Calling Israel a colonial hangover or a revival of Nazism is not just a rhetorical device. In today's world it carries a demand for action, because colonialism and Nazism are both intolerable crimes that lead inexorably to only one conclusion: that Israel shouldn't exist, just as colonialism and Nazism both needed to be confronted and eradicated. There are more people than you might imagine who want to see this happen. Pro-Palestinian circles are replete with discussions about what might come after Israel is dismantled. 'From the River to the Sea, Palestine Will be Free,' the ubiquitous cry heard on every anti-Israel protest, is loaded with this eliminationist urge. It implies, for those who want to hear it, that all the land between the Jordan River and the Mediterranean Sea is Palestine; all of it is unfree; all of it must be liberated. This doesn't leave much room for Israel. In a way, I understand this. Nobody ever built a successful social movement to ask for compromise, and the psychology of protest tends towards absolute demands. But it is a discourse that links progressive protesters on the streets of the UK with violent, anti-Jewish forces in the Middle East that are actually trying to destroy Israel and don't care how they do it.

Again, people tend not to notice just how unusual this is. No serious observer of the Russian war in Ukraine has suggested that the solution would be to get rid of Russia. You don't hear thousands of people calling for Saudi Arabia to be wiped off the map

---

* Churchill was also a co-signatory of the letter to the Globe theatre calling for the Israeli Habima National Theatre to be boycotted.

as punishment for the suffering in Yemen. Turkey can do whatever it wants to the Kurds, and nobody concludes that it would be best to dismantle Turkey and replace it with a different country. The idea that Israel is intrinsically a 'guilty nation', devoid of legitimacy through both its behaviour and its innate character, is peculiar to this one country.[43] Singling out, contingent rights, double standards: they are everywhere in this obsession with Israel if you look closely enough.

This, frankly, is what terrifies many Jews. When rockets are flying into Israel, and people in Britain are chanting 'From the River to the Sea, Palestine Will be Free' or posting on social media that Israel is a fake country that shouldn't exist, what many Jews hear, rightly or wrongly, is the same old bloodlust for their destruction. Hamas declared in a 2017 statement of principles that 'no part of the land of Palestine shall be compromised or conceded, irrespective of the causes, the circumstances and the pressures and no matter how long the occupation lasts. Hamas rejects any alternative to the full and complete liberation of Palestine, from the river to the sea.'[44] Ayatollah Khamenei, the Supreme Leader of Iran, put it more succinctly: 'The Zionist regime is a deadly, cancerous growth and a detriment to this region. It will undoubtedly be uprooted and destroyed.'[45] Why would anyone in Britain want to be associated with that?

Perhaps it is because Jews are not the only people for whom this all feels personal. In 2012 an academic called Rusi Jaspal – now a professor at the University of Brighton – set out to interview British Pakistani Muslims about their views of Israel, Zionism and Jews. Unsurprisingly, he found strong support for Palestinians and a deep loathing for Israel and Zionism; crucially, for many of his interviewees this was rooted in their own Muslim identity. Jaspal observed that 'the perception that Zionism sought to position Jews as superior to Palestinians ... posed challenges to individuals' sense of self-esteem', because of the fear that Zionism posed 'an existential threat to Muslims and Islam'. They engage with the conflict 'as Muslims', and 'construe Zionism as posing a threat ... to their individual identity'. There it is again: just as with the Stop the War Coalition and other campaigners, Israel is not seen as another overseas conflict but as something much closer to home. These were British Pakistanis, not Palestinians. They were all under the age of thirty-five, and none appear to have visited Israel or Palestine. It was their self-identity as Muslims that created the powerful conviction that they had a personal stake in the conflict. Just like Brian Eno and all the Stop the War Coalition marchers who see Israel as a representation of 'us', these British Pakistani Muslims did not treat the Israeli–Palestinian conflict as a distant event in a foreign country but as something that affected their own sense of who they are, here in Britain, today.[46]

Antisemitism from within Muslim communities is a problem that is simultaneously ignored by some and exaggerated by others. Historically Islam has viewed Jews as a 'people of the book', a fellow, though inferior, monotheistic faith. Muslim-majority lands provided relative havens for Jews fleeing medieval Christian persecution, where Jews could practise their faith, work in most professions and not be confined to ghettos. Muslim rule in Spain was, for a while, a golden age for Jews, until it was conquered by a Christian king and queen who promptly expelled the Jews – many of whom found sanctuary at the other end of the Mediterranean under Ottoman rule. However, even at the best of times, Jews were never allowed to forget their lower status. They were forbidden from bearing arms or riding a horse. Synagogues could never be taller than mosques.

There was the annual *jizya* tax to pay in return for being allowed to practise the Jewish faith, which came with ritualistic and gratuitous humiliations. The idea that Jews should wear a badge to identify them in public was a Muslim invention, not a Christian one. And even here, there were occasional pogroms and massacres: Granada in 1066, for example, where most of the Jewish community was wiped out. Overall, the situation of Jews under Muslim rule was 'never as bad as in Christendom at its worst, nor ever as good as in Christendom at its best'. No Inquisition or Holocaust, but no Enlightenment or emancipation either.[47]

In the past century this has reversed. While most Western societies have, with varying degrees of sincerity and effectiveness, tried to move beyond their histories of anti-Jewish prejudice, many Muslim-majority countries have absorbed European-style antisemitism which has, in turn, accentuated the negative aspects of Islam's traditional attitude towards Jews. This process began under European colonisation, well before Israel entered the picture, but that conflict has acted as a potent accelerant. In some places hostility towards Jews has become completely normative. A 2010 survey by Pew Research Center found an astonishing 95 per cent of Egyptians, 97 per cent of Jordanians and 98 per cent of Lebanese said they had unfavourable opinions of Jews, as did 73 per cent of Turks, 74 per cent of Indonesians and 78 per cent of Pakistanis.[48]

In Britain, polling shows Muslims are 3.5 times as likely as the general population to 'hold hard-core antisemitic attitudes'.[49] Some of the individual polling results are staggering. According to a 2019 survey, 44 per cent of British Muslims believed 'Jews are responsible for most of the world's wars', 55 per cent believed 'Jews have too much control over the global media', and 56 per cent believed 'Jews have too much control over global affairs'.⁵⁰ However – and this is a considerable caveat – while successive polls show that British Muslims are more likely than others in the UK to subscribe to antisemitic stereotypes and beliefs, they also show that many British Muslims do not harbour any anti-Jewish views at all. Only 13 per cent hold the 'hard-core antisemitic attitudes' that would suggest a generalised and confirmed hostility. Importantly, their minority status means that they alone cannot account for most antisemitism across the country. In fact, their 'overall "responsibility" … for the total level of antisemitism in Great Britain is, in fact, rather small'.⁵¹ In other words, even if you discounted every British Muslim from the picture, the amount of antisemitism circulating in society would hardly reduce at all. Muslims are themselves sometimes a convenient scapegoat for people who would rather blame them for antisemitism than think about their own responsibility or that of wider society.

Jaspal's interviewees were at pains to stress that their hatred of Israel had nothing to do with antisemitism. 'I have nothing against Jews,' said one. 'I've got Jewish friends. I know Judaism and they are my cousins … It's Zionism and this fake state that they've created … I don't see why Jews should even have a state.'⁵² Despite this insistence that they bore no animosity towards Jews, it was apparent to Jaspal that it was '*Jewish* control of *Muslim* land [that] was perceived as abhorrent' by the participants, who frequently slipped into overtly antisemitic language.⁵³ 'Hating Jews is one thing and hating Israelis is another – they've got nothing to do with each other,' said another participant, before explaining herself in undeniably antisemitic terms:

Israelis are cruel, they're an evil group of people. They just want to get rich. Look all over the world and you can see them controlling it all, influencing people, manipulating governments for their own selfish needs ... Historically they have been involved in murdering kids and innocent people so it's nothing new now, is it?[54]

I've encountered this contradiction myself, when speaking at an interfaith meeting in London shortly after the war in Israel and Gaza in the summer of 2014. An official from one of the local mosques told me in strident terms that 'we love Jews, it's those fucking Nazi Zionists we hate'. He was friendly, but also angry, and clung to his determination not to think of himself as antisemitic while saying things that tended to point in the opposite direction.

Of course Israel is singled out: it is singled out whenever anyone tells the story of Christ's birth and crucifixion at Christmas and Easter, whenever a Muslim remembers Muhammad's night journey from Mecca to Jerusalem and his ascension to heaven from a spot on the Haram al-Sharif, and every day that Jews pray towards the Temple Mount in Jerusalem. It is singled out in the symbolism and cultural weight of Jerusalem, Nazareth, Bethlehem and the stories and places that infuse our culture. It carries just as much symbolic power for the secular doctrines of human rights, international law, peace and justice. Palestine is 'the great cause, the great international cause of our time', according to former *Guardian* columnist and Jeremy Corbyn aide Seumas Milne.[55] 'In our thousands, in our millions, we are all Palestinians,' exclaimed Corbyn himself.[56] This is where the true connection between criticism of Israel and antisemitism lies. Not in every anti-Israel activist being driven by animus for Jews, but in their inability to stand outside their own cultural inheritance.

For Israel's Jewishness to have no bearing on the emotions, thoughts and language that excite and energise the world of anti-Israel activism, for the unmatched pull of the protests and the assumed significance of the conflict to be entirely insulated from the singular role that Jews and their story have been bestowed in the intellectual and philosophical construction of our world, would mean Israel's fiercest opponents are truly people-blind. I find that hard to believe. There are assumptions about Jews and Jewishness hardwired into our civilisational culture. Jews touch a traditional nerve, especially when they wield power or are accused of using it to do terrible things like shedding children's blood, whether in medieval Norwich or in modern-day Gaza. These ingrained ideas and sentiments cannot help but play a role, however unrecognised, by influencing what gets people so worked up and why a protest against Israel should feel like it matters so much more than one about Turkey, Saudi Arabia or Myanmar. French philosopher Jean-Paul Sartre wrote that antisemitism is not an opinion; 'It is first of all a *passion*.'[57] So too is anti-Zionism.

The historic treatment of Jews is unique, the contemporary treatment of Israel is unique, and the fact that Israel is Jewish means it is stretching credulity to imagine that these two things are unrelated. Do campaigners single out Israel because they are antisemites? I'd like to think that this is unlikely to be the reason for most. But do they single out Israel because it is Jewish? This I find much harder to dismiss. Israel matters because Jews have always mattered. This singling out of Israel is not a coincidence but a continuation. In the history of Western thought, Jews do count.

CHAPTER EIGHT

THINGS CAN'T ONLY GET BETTER

What was Jack Reed thinking?

Growing up in New Brancepeth, a former mining village a few miles west of Durham, Reed was in his early teens when he began to take an unhealthy interest in extreme right-wing politics. At the age of fourteen he was calling himself a fascist. He immersed himself in the online propaganda of neo-Nazi organisations like National Action and even created a group of his own, which he named the Blutkrieg Division. By the time he was sixteen Reed was convinced that violence was the only way to spark the race war that he hoped would cleanse Britain of the alien influence of Jews and Muslims. He wrote a 'manual for practical and sensible guerrilla warfare against the kike system in the Durham city area'* and began looking up lists of synagogues to firebomb.[1] By the time police raided his home and arrested him, Reed had moved on to researching

---

* 'Kike' is a racist slur for Jews.

explosives and firearms. A month before his seventeenth birthday, in November 2019, Reed became the youngest person in Britain to be convicted of plotting a terrorist attack.

Images of Reed's journal released by the police after his trial make poignant reading, full of doodles and semi-coherent teenage defiance, pathetic and chilling in equal measure. As well as synagogues, his hit list included post offices, banks, schools, pubs, council buildings, telephone wires, a bus station and the passport office where his mother worked. However, there is one major difference between these potential targets and the synagogues that he wanted to bomb: all these other places existed in Reed's immediate environment. There are pubs, banks, council buildings and schools in New Brancepeth, or in neighbouring villages, or in Durham, just a ten-minute drive away. There is even a passport office, one of only seven in the whole of the United Kingdom. But there are no synagogues in New Brancepeth, or Durham, or anywhere close. The nearest are in Gateshead, around twenty miles to the north, or Darlington, a similar distance south. According to the 2021 census there were just three Jewish people living in the Brancepeth area and a few dozen at most in Durham. Yet Reed was convinced there was a 'kike system in the Durham city area' worthy of guerrilla war.

One of my earliest memories is of being taken round Durham Cathedral by my parents on a visit to the city. I have no idea why they thought a three-year-old would be interested in Norman ecclesiastical architecture, but dragging small children round old churches is a holiday habit we have taken up with our own family, so I guess it worked. I've been back since to have a proper look and it is a magnificent building, all high vaulted ceilings and immense stone pillars that look like they could stand for ever. I've stayed at Durham

University for work, and one of my nephews studied there. But on all my visits, it never struck me as a hotbed of neo-Nazism or as the epicentre of a secret Jewish system of nefarious power. Antisemitism truly can happen anywhere.

Reed is not the only teenager growing up in 21st-century Britain who became convinced that the Jews are their enemy. Thomas Leech, from Preston, was nineteen years old when he was found guilty of encouraging terrorism against Jews and Muslims. He had become convinced that Jews were planning to engineer the extinction of white people by encouraging Muslim immigration into the West: in other words, the Great Replacement Theory that is now widely accepted as truth in far-right circles. As in New Brancepeth, there are no synagogues in Preston (the last one closed in the 1980s) and not many Jews, but Leech, like Reed, became fixated with them nonetheless. In fact, there have been quite a few British teenagers in recent years who have set their minds to killing Jews and destroying their places of worship, like the sixteen-year-old from Liverpool who searched online for 'nearest synagogue to me' and posted the message: 'I am a domestic terror threat. I will bomb a synagogue.'[2]

These teenage would-be terrorists don't limit themselves to antisemitism. All minorities and symbols of officialdom, like politicians and senior police officers, are considered fair game. But underpinning this cornucopia of hate is the same old belief that there is a hidden Jewish hand pulling everyone else's strings. This is why antisemites can hate Jews so much when there are so few Jews around for them to hate. It is based on the fantasy of an imaginary Jewish conspiracy, the spectre of the demonic Jew that has been lurking in the shadows of Western culture for centuries, rather than the real-life behaviour of any actual Jewish people. The old 'Jewish

Question' that gripped nineteenth-century Europe has even been revived for this generation's cyberhate in the acronym JQ, found on message boards and social media channels across the far-right ecosphere. Amongst the far-right youth of today, even the most ardent racists and conspiracists are mistrusted if they don't trace it all back to the traditional enemy. 'If they don't name the Jew, their message isn't true.'³

It's hardly a startling revelation that neo-Nazis are antisemitic, and you don't need me to write a book to tell you that they want to kill Jews. But there is something new going on here: not just the unprecedented number of Hitler worshippers turning to terror, but the youthful age at which it is happening. Violent neo-Nazis are not usually so young, and far-right terrorists never used to be as common. When David Copeland planted three nail bombs in London in 1999, killing three people and wounding well over a hundred more, far-right terrorism was a relative rarity in Britain. At the time, one of my jobs for the Community Security Trust was to act as the contact for an informant called Arthur who had infiltrated the far right in London.* Arthur used to spend his evenings at British National Party meetings and rallies or go on election leafleting drives with the inevitable drink in the pub afterwards, and then meet me every week or two and tell me all about it. He often provided valuable intelligence about the far right's venomous plans, spreading hatred and division wherever they went. Arthur knew almost everyone on the far-right scene in and around London, and

---

* Arthur was not his real name, for obvious reasons. There is a long history of anti-fascists infiltrating far-right groups to gain intelligence about their activities. This particular operation was run jointly by CST and Searchlight, an anti-fascist organisation with a long and celebrated record of infiltrating and disrupting the British far right.

one of the people he had shared a drink with more than once was fellow BNP member David Copeland. When the police issued the first CCTV image of the London nail bomber, Arthur recognised him immediately and we were amongst the first to give Copeland's name to the police, along with details of his political affiliations and activities. But Copeland was an anomaly in the 1990s. While racist violence was shockingly frequent at that time – the black teenager Stephen Lawrence was murdered six years before Copeland's terror campaign – actual terrorist bombings were rare. The neo-Nazi world that Arthur immersed himself in with great bravery and intelligence was full of violent thugs, racists, wife-beaters and drunks, but there were thankfully few actual terrorists.

What we see today is radically different. In the twelve months to the end of March 2022, 15 per cent of all terrorism arrests in the UK were of under-eighteens, mostly linked to right-wing extremism, and the number is growing.[4] It is shocking, but even so, the temptation is to dismiss them as a handful of misguided youths: dangerous, yes, but indicative of nothing beyond themselves. Nazis will as Nazis do, many of these kids are troubled and vulnerable in different ways, and the best response is to shake our heads in despair. After all, only a vanishingly small proportion of Britain's youth would ever go this far. However, the danger is not that tens of thousands of teenagers will join the most violent fringes of Britain's far right: that is, thankfully, unlikely to happen. Instead, the question is whether Jack Reed, Thomas Leech and the rest are nothing more than a bunch of random outliers, or if they are the crest of an ominous wave of growing youthful intolerance and anti-Jewish hate. To answer that question, we need to look more generally at what young people think about Jews, and when you dig into the opinion polls and look the evidence in the eye, there is an unmistakeable and unnerving pattern.

Every generation likes to imagine that it is part of the most informed, rational age yet to live on this earth, that there's no way it would fall for the superstitions of its less educated and worldly predecessors. Today, we see myths about blood libels and well-poisonings as the product of a long-forgotten time and wonder at the ignorant fools who believed in them. Unfortunately when it comes to antisemitism this self-assurance appears to be misplaced. The history of antisemitism is not one of linear progress from the restrictions and persecutions of the Middle Ages to the relative freedom of today. Nor does it go in the other direction, a steady, ominous path to genocide that climaxed in Auschwitz. Instead, it waxes and wanes, coming to the fore at times of insecurity and uncertainty or when political leaders use it as a weapon of division within or between societies. My fear is that right now, with so much turbulence in the world, the rise of illiberal politics and the popularity of conspiracy theories, antisemitism is set to make hay. And it is doing so already in the place you might least expect it: young people.

None of this is conclusive – no poll can be – but it looks very much like antisemitism is starting to swell beneath the surface of Britain's younger generations far beyond neo-Nazis or the occasional lost boy. This may be counter-intuitive, but we shouldn't be too surprised. The popularity of conspiracy theories in that age group, spread via the social media apps that are fully integrated into teenage and millennial lives, combined with the breakdown of trust in established authority, create the perfect conditions for antisemitism to flourish and that is what appears to be happening. Within mainstream society, amongst people drawn to right-wing and left-wing politics and even those with no particular ideological bent, antisemitism is much more prevalent than it ought to be amongst younger people, and – most worryingly – more common than in their elders. That's right: millennials are more prone to anti-Jewish views than pensioners, and today's teenagers and young adults are much more likely to be taken in by antisemitic conspiracy theories than their parents ever were.

To take just one example: an opinion poll by the anti-fascist group Hope Not Hate in October 2020 found that 30 per cent of 25–34-year-olds, and 27 per cent of 18–24-year-olds, agreed that 'Jews have disproportionate control of powerful institutions, and use that power for their own benefit and against the good of the general population'. These figures, shocking in themselves, look even worse compared to the 6 per cent of 65–74-year-olds and 7 per cent of 55–64-year-olds who agreed with the same statement. In other words, adults under the age of thirty-four were up to five times more likely than people over the age of fifty-five to endorse a fairly standard antisemitic conspiracy theory, one that served Nazi propaganda to justify the Holocaust. In total, 17 per cent of people across all age groups said they agree with this anti-Jewish libel: but the fact that younger people were, by some distance, the age group most likely to back such a blatantly antisemitic belief is alarming.[5] Nor is this a lone finding that bucks the trend. Another poll by Hope Not Hate, this one in 2022, found that 34 per cent of 18–24-year-olds believe that 'Jewish people have an unhealthy control over the world's banking system', and again, they were the age group most likely to hold this antisemitic view.[6]

This goes against everything we think we know about a younger generation that is less racist, more at ease with diversity and less characterised by the prejudices that prevailed in their parents' and grandparents' generations. In Britain, adults under the age of thirty-four are the least likely age group to describe themselves as racially prejudiced.[7] They are the most likely to say they would be happy for their child to marry someone from another ethnic group and the most optimistic that Britain is becoming a more diverse and tolerant country.[8] Younger people were more likely to support the Black Lives Matter protests in 2020, irrespective of their colour or ethnic background, and are the most likely to think that immigration has been good for Britain.[9] Younger people in Britain are growing up in a country that is visibly both more diverse and more at ease with diversity. In greater numbers than ever before, people of different ethnicities, nationalities and religions go to school with each other, work alongside each other, live next door to each other, marry and have kids with each other. It holds out hope for a better future, a more harmonious society in which everyone, whatever their background, can feel they belong. But the fact that younger people are, in general, less prejudiced, makes it all the more disturbing that, when it comes to Jews, the opposite seems to be the case.

The discrepancy in the trendlines is apparent from several different polls and surveys. While younger people are less racist than their parents' or grandparents' generations and less prone to bigotry overall, when it comes to Jews they appear to be consistently less accepting, more hostile and suspicious, and more susceptible to conspiracy theories and negative stereotypes. According to a 2019 poll analysed by academics from Kings College London, 18–24-year-olds are the least likely to say they are just as open to having Jewish friends as they are to having friends from other sections of British society, despite also, according to other polls, being the age group most likely to be comfortable with their children marrying people from other ethnicities (of course, it might be different people agreeing with these two statements; it is always risky to ascribe the views of a segment to the population as a whole). People aged 18–24 are the most likely age group to say that compared to other groups, Jews have too much power in the media; the most likely to agree that 'Jewish people talk about the Holocaust just to further their political agenda'; and the most likely to think that 'Jewish people consider themselves to be better than other British people.'[10]

We are only talking about a minority of young people who are involved. Just as in the population as a whole – and I can't stress this enough – antisemitism is currently a minority pursuit for teens and young adults. Most people in Britain of every age do not harbour conscious hostility towards Jewish people, and this is the same for younger as for older generations. In the Kings College London poll I quoted above, which shows younger people are the least likely to want Jewish friends, two-thirds of 18–24-year-olds still answered positively about Jewish people while only 12 per cent didn't like the idea of having Jewish friends. However, amongst the over-50s, the figures were very different: 89 per cent wanted Jewish friends and just 3 per cent didn't. The cause for worry is the direction of travel, rather than the overall numbers.

At its core, the difference between racism and antisemitism is the difference between a prejudice and a conspiracy theory: and while prejudice is out of fashion for today's youth, conspiracy theories are all the rage. Those same polls that show younger age groups are worryingly prone to believing in myths about Jewish power and influence also show that they are more likely to have swallowed other conspiracy tales, whether about Covid-19, vaccines or vaguer stuff about who is 'really in charge'. Thirty-one per cent of 25–34-year-olds think that 'Covid-19 has been intentionally released as part of a "depopulation plan" orchestrated by the UN or New World Order', and 29 per cent believe that 'a Covid-19 vaccine will be used maliciously to infect people with poison or insert microchips into people'. This was the age group most likely to believe in both of those Covid-19 conspiracy claims, with 18–24-year-olds not far behind, which might help to explain why vaccination rates remain stubbornly lower in those age cohorts.[11] If the polling is correct that 50 per cent of people aged twenty-five to thirty-four believe that 'regardless of who is officially in charge of governments and other organisations, there is a single group of people who secretly control events and rule the world together', then it is not such a great leap to conclude that this single group of people might be Jews; or at least, that that is one of the answers that the internet will offer them when they go looking.[12]

SCHOOLING PREJUDICE

When Sadiq Khan was standing for Mayor of London in 2016, he reflected on the fact that his two teenage daughters had never experienced the kind of racist abuse he had to put up with growing up in London a generation ago. He told the *Evening Standard*:

> When my parents came here there were signs saying, 'No blacks, no Irish, no dogs'. The next generation, I suffered abuse and got into fights and was called the P-word. My daughters live five minutes from the area I was brought up in and have never suffered racial

abuse. That's the progress we have made in thirty years. That's the joy of London.¹³

This is the story of progress we like to tell ourselves about Britain. I'm sure Khan would be the first to say that far too much anti-Muslim prejudice still exists, and a lot of anti-Muslim hate crime especially targets women. Khan himself has received so many death threats since becoming Mayor that he needs police protection whenever he goes out. Nonetheless, the picture he describes of a society that is becoming more at ease with its own diversity, in which the racism that minorities face recedes with each successive generation, is surely one that we would like to believe in.*

Sadiq Khan's comment stuck with me, because I am also the parent of teenagers growing up in London and both of my children have experienced antisemitism. In fact, ask pretty much any Jewish teenager growing up in Britain and they will almost certainly have stories to tell about anti-Jewish insults they have endured from classmates, social media 'friends' or random peers they encounter. Some will have worse experiences to relay, about threats and assaults just because they are Jewish. According to a 2018 poll looking at how antisemitism has affected Jewish people across Europe, 45 per cent of young Jewish Europeans had personally experienced antisemitism in the twelve months immediately prior to the poll date. This is a regular occurrence for young Jews, and it happens to them much more than to Jews in older age groups.¹⁴

This shouldn't be a competition. People of colour growing up in

---

* Khan made this comment in 2016, so it was presumably accurate at the time. I sincerely hope that his daughters have not experienced any racist or Islamophobic abuse since then, but it's certainly possible.

Britain are likely to face indirect discrimination in ways that won't affect most young Jews, and you might argue that in the grand scheme of things this is the more important and insidious form of racism, one that requires more fundamental change. But if we want to push racism out of society and permanently alter the thinking that lies behind it, then that must include tackling antisemitism. There were at least 1,000 incidents of anti-Jewish abuse recorded by secondary schools and further education colleges in England in the five years from 2017 to 2022, with a year-on-year increase of 173 per cent over the five-year period.[15*] I don't believe it is acceptable that my teenage children had to look at swastikas carved into the doors when using the toilets at their very normal, very liberal, London state secondary school. If you want to live in a country that doesn't tolerate racism, then you shouldn't tolerate this.

Most young people around the country have little daily interaction with Jews of their own age. Almost two-thirds of Jewish school-age children in Britain attend Jewish faith schools, leaving around 20,000 Jewish children studying in mainstream schools alongside children of other faiths and ethnicities.[†] There has been an explosion in Jewish schooling since the early 1990s, originally driven by a fear that younger generations of Jews were drifting away from the community through a lack of education and a weakening of cultural and religious ties.[16] This has been successful in one respect – the number of people identifying as Jewish in the UK has held steady over the past decade, after falling considerably for many

---

* This figure is taken from a Freedom of Information request sent to every secondary school and further education college in England. Only 39 per cent of schools replied, so the real total could be more than double.

† To put this into context, in 2021/22 there were just under 9 million children in primary or secondary education in the UK, and more than 24,000 schools.

years before that – but it has come at a cost. Across huge swathes of the country, especially outside London, Manchester and the other main centres of Jewish communal life, young people are unlikely to have any Jewish friends or classmates, because they are mostly going to different schools. Admittedly, the Jewish community is so small and geographically concentrated, that even if Jewish schools didn't exist and every Jewish child studied at a mainstream school, this problem would still exist: but not so acutely as it does today.

This is a shame, because there is compelling evidence that personal contact can overcome prejudice. One meta-study of over 500 research projects in thirty-eight countries looking at exactly this question found that 'intergroup contact typically reduces intergroup prejudice'. This did not only improve relations between the people who took part in the studies: 'Attitudes toward the entire outgroup, outgroup members in other situations, and even outgroups not involved in the contact' also benefited.[17] In other words, a positive experience with one Jewish person can enhance someone's attitude towards all Jews. There are too many children who never get this opportunity when they are growing up, because they don't have the kind of daily interaction with Jewish peers that would generate this kind of positive familiarity.

There is nothing intrinsically wrong with Jewish parents choosing to send their children to Jewish schools. Many are fine schools with excellent academic results, and they help to enrich a positive Jewish identity for young Jews growing up in Britain. Plus the more we hear about antisemitism in mainstream schools, the more likely Jewish parents are to prefer the sanctuary of an all-Jewish environment. My children have been educated in both Jewish and mainstream schools, so I'm hardly one to judge. But if there are millions of children up and down the country who don't have any Jewish friends because they are not going to the same schools, then this daily contact isn't going to happen. And while they might not meet many real Jews, some of them, sat in their bedrooms, chatting online or scrolling through apps on their phones, will encounter 'The Jew'. The one invented by antisemites that loves money, controls the media and delights in murdering Palestinian children. The one that Jack Reed thinks has set up a 'kike system' in Durham. A vessel for all the myths of the past and fears of the present, as real and vivid on a smartphone as they were in a medieval sermon.

Nor is this just a problem of young Nazis. The period when my teenage children experienced the most intense outbreak of antisemitism from their peers and classmates was during the war in Israel and Gaza in May 2021. Jokes about Jews in the classroom and posts comparing Israel to Nazi Germany on Instagram were the order of the day, and their school was far from unusual. Statistics from the Community Security Trust show that anti-Jewish hate incidents involving Jewish school students and teachers at mainstream schools (i.e. not at Jewish faith schools) increased by 600 per cent in 2021, most of which happened in the month of May.[18] I know of Jewish children, and even Jewish teachers, who had to move schools because of anti-Jewish bullying during that period. One Jewish girl in south London had already put up with a year of antisemitic abuse when the outbreak of conflict in Israel meant her situation 'became unendurable'. What had started with shouts of 'Free Palestine' led to Nazi salutes from fellow students, so she left her school and now traverses London every day so she can go to a Jewish school where she feels safe.[19] In general, over half of young Jewish Europeans (those aged sixteen to thirty-four) say that they have been blamed by other people for the alleged actions of the Israeli government because they are Jewish. This is a common way for anti-Israel sentiment to translate into anti-Jewish harassment and abuse, and, yet again, it happens to young Jews more often than to older ones.[20]

I mentioned earlier that young people of all backgrounds were the age group most likely to support the Black Lives Matter movement in 2020: 60 per cent of 18–24-year-olds did so, compared to 45 per cent of 25–34-year-olds and even lower levels in older age groups.[21] This is relevant because the Black Lives Matter movement affected how people perceived and understood racism in this country. It emphasised the role of colour in racism, and it highlighted the connection between Britain's history of empire and racism at home. These developments were not merely understandable following the murder of George Floyd; they are important and necessary aspects of the struggle against racism. However, this had a probably unintended, but significant, secondary impact on how Jews, Israel and antisemitism are all perceived. The conflict in Israel and Gaza in May 2021 came a year after the murder of George Floyd and the rise of Black Lives Matter. As we saw in the previous chapter, those events emphasised an alternative framing through which people could interpret the Israel–Palestine conflict: one that viewed it as a manifestation of Western colonialism and therefore of racism, rather than as a long-standing conflict of national movements. It is a way of fitting the Israel–Palestine conflict into a broader, but also simplistic, understanding of the world, one that makes sense for politically conscious teenagers and students who don't actually know anything about Israel and Palestine but who have absorbed the argument that the world is organised to protect and privilege systemic white supremacy.

Politically, in this context 'white' means privileged; powerful; incapable of suffering racism; and sharing in the collective guilt for the actual, real racism suffered by people of colour. If all oppressors are white, and Israel is the oppressor, then logically Israel must be white, and so must its supporters amongst diaspora Jewish communities. It encourages the assumption that all Jews are white, which not only erases the internal diversity of colour within the Jewish world but also ignores the fact that Jews were treated as alien – as not white – for a very long time in our history. This hits antisemitism in two ways: it subtly supports stereotypes about Jews being rich and powerful, while leaving little space for recognition of antisemitism as a form of racism at all. It's tragic, in a way. Black Lives Matter forced a much-needed and well-overdue examination of racism across society, and ideally a rising anti-racist tide would lift every boat. Sometimes though, when different understandings of racism and discrimination are in play they can end up obscuring rather than complementing each other as they should.

Conflicts involving Israel always trigger antisemitic reactions in the UK, but in May 2021 those reactions were especially extreme in schools and universities, more so than in previous years. This newly fashionable explanation of what was going on in Israel and Palestine may help to explain why. It encouraged the tendency some already had to view it not as an overseas conflict but as a manifestation of the same kind of racism that blights our own societies. In short, if you are under the impression that Israel is a settler colonial enterprise, then opposing racism means that today's anti-racist must treat Israel and its supporters with the same contempt you would treat racists.

The rise of Black Lives Matter followed five years of painful and very public rows over antisemitism in the Labour Party under

Jeremy Corbyn's leadership. It would be an enormous digression to explain how and why the Labour Party's antisemitism crisis happened,[*] but it put much of the Jewish community in direct conflict with a political leader who was supported by younger voters in far greater proportions than other age groups. It was easy, at the time, to find commentators and activists claiming that talk of antisemitism in Labour was a 'smear' designed by right-wingers 'who just cannot reconcile themselves to the idea of a socialist party that fights for socialism'.[22] Perhaps some of this left an impression on Corbyn's younger followers. It might explain why in September 2019, at the climax of Labour's antisemitism crisis, 24 per cent – almost a quarter – of 18–24-year-olds agreed that 'Israel and its supporters are a bad influence on our democracy' (again, more than any other age group). This was one of those questions that made me stumble when I read it. Who are Israel's supporters, who these young people think are so dangerous? What is it that they are supposedly doing to British democracy? The same poll found 22 per cent of 18–24-year-olds agreed that 'Israel can get away with anything because its supporters control the media', an old anti-Jewish conspiracy theory retooled in anti-Israel language.[23] It all stirs a deep fear that Jews are, once again, seen as subverters of the national interest, an obstacle to humanity's progress and a threat to others' way of life.

MEDIEVAL WINE IN DIGITAL BOTTLES

Social media is integral to the way that these ideas spread in today's world, so it is ironic that the social media platforms that hoover

---

[*] To do so would take a whole other book, and as luck would have it I've already written one on exactly this subject. It's called *The Left's Jewish Problem: Israel, Jeremy Corbyn and Antisemitism* and, although it fulfils every Jewish stereotype to use one book to plug another one, I can't help myself.

up most of the world's screentime seem like they come from their own conspiracy theory: giant global corporations, run by enigmatic leaders who supposedly use mysterious algorithms to manipulate and seduce whole populations into thinking, voting or buying against their own interests. This may be a caricature, but there is plenty of evidence that social media plays an essential role as a shop window for antisemitism. Research by the Community Security Trust, working with academics from the Woolf Institute at Cambridge University, found that antisemitism on Instagram often appears alongside general conspiracy content, even if the user isn't looking for it. A person searching for the hashtag #chemtrails – which, for those of you not in the know, is the theory that the long white lines of exhaust fumes left in the sky by passing jet planes are secretly spraying noxious chemicals into our lungs – might also get posts about #zionistagenda. Someone looking for information about alien landings (although why anyone would look for that on Instagram beats me) might end up reading about #zionazis. Worst of all, the research suggested that Instagram's algorithm pushes anti-Jewish posts proactively towards its users, concluding that 'such content is provided by the platform regardless of the users' intentions and chosen search terms. For antisemitic content, this would appear to represent supply rather than demand.'[24]

Most people don't go to Instagram for conspiracy theories, but they do go there for news. Instagram is the most popular source of news for 16–24-year-olds in Britain, 46 per cent of whom prefer it above the BBC, Sky News, ITV or any traditional media source to tell them what is going on in the world. This trend is only going to intensify as each age cohort matures: it will be no surprise to parents of teens that for 12–15-year-olds, Instagram (29 per cent),

TikTok (28 per cent) and YouTube (28 per cent) are the three most popular news sources.[25] For many, this is just another way to access content originating from those same traditional media, such as a story on the BBC news website or a clip from Channel 4 news. The difference is that as you scroll through the Sky News app you won't find conspiracy theories about 5G phone towers or #zionistagenda in between the regular news stories. Late in 2022, TikTok recommended a slideshow of eighteen neo-Nazi images to my son, each one more antisemitic than the last. He wasn't looking for it, just scrolling through videos of footballers and comedians, but TikTok's algorithm decided that hardcore Nazi Jew-hate was perfect 'For You' material. Perhaps for some this is the added value that social media offers. That same 2019 research by Kings College London also revealed that almost half – 47 per cent – of 18–24-year-olds agreed that 'by using social media (Facebook, YouTube, etc), we can get the news that major newspapers and TV channels want to keep secret'.[26]

Indeed, there is growing evidence of a correlation between youth, social media usage and belief in conspiracy theories. A different poll by Kings College London, published in October 2022, found that 14 per cent of people in Britain believe that 'people weren't really killed or injured' in the 2017 Manchester Arena bombing and that the casualties seen on TV news were '"crisis actors" who pretended to be injured or killed'. A total of twenty-two people were murdered when Salman Abedi detonated his bomb in the foyer of the arena in May 2017 and a further 160 people required hospital treatment for their injuries, but for some people, it was all a hoax. The proportion of people believing this conspiracy theory was 27 per cent amongst 18–24-year-olds and 25 per cent amongst 25–34-year-olds. And while people who rely on mainstream TV and radio to get their news were slightly less likely to believe in the 'crisis actors' conspiracy theory about the arena bombing (13 per cent did so), a whopping 44 per cent of people who rely on the messaging app Telegram for their news agreed with it, as did 33 per cent of people who rely on TikTok, 30 per cent of those who turn to podcasts for their news, 29 per cent of those who mainly use Instagram as a news source, and so on.[27]

This is why social media now plays such an elemental role in the way that antisemitism spreads. It amplifies and directs anti-Jewish myths and slanders, ensuring they get in front of thousands of new pairs of eyeballs that otherwise, in the days before smartphones, would have been far less likely to see them. For those people who think they aren't getting the truth, or who have unanswered questions about why there is a pandemic, or immigration, terrorism and war, or simply why they can't get a job or a girlfriend, social media will offer the same answer that some people have come up with for centuries: it's all down to the Jews. Social media did not invent hating Jews, but antisemitism, like everything else, has come to depend on it.

Social media has also been blamed for facilitating malicious interference in democracy itself. The question of how much, and to what effect, Russia has sought to influence election outcomes in the United States, Great Britain and other countries has been a subject of much contention ever since the double whammy in 2016 of Trump's election and the Brexit vote. I'm not going to claim any special insight into the ability of Russian automated Twitter accounts ('bots') to influence public debate or voting patterns, but there was one detail that left me with a wry smile. According to a *Times* investigation, the most prolific pro-Brexit bot account active on Twitter during the EU referendum campaign had the highly un-Brexity name 'Israel Bombs Babies'. This account tweeted a whopping 1.55 million times from September 2011 until it was closed down in November 2017. On the day of the referendum itself it tweeted 492 times about Brexit, with hashtags like #voteleave and all sorts of terrifying claims about the EU.[28] The account's timeline was also teeming with antisemitic tweets, such as 'Jews against free speech', 'Did the Holocaust Really Happen?', 'European Jews Should Get Out of Palestine' and 'Holocaust or Holohoax? 21 Amazing Facts'. Its profile picture was of a Palestinian flag with the slogan 'Free Palestine', and the account name 'Israel Bombs Babies' evoked the medieval blood libel that charges Jews with child-murder.[29]

Before anyone gets the wrong idea, I'm not suggesting that people who supported Brexit are disproportionately antisemitic or that anti-Jewish sentiment had anything to do with the referendum campaign. Nor do I know whether the Russian troll farm that created this account thought that people who hate Jews would also support Brexit or whether they were just multitasking. The account began tweeting about Israel in 2011, well before the EU referendum was a glint in David Cameron's eye. Russian disinformation campaigns try to exploit any kind of division in society without necessarily having a coherent political goal that links them together,* but the confluence of antisemitism and some extreme, divisive rhetoric over Brexit is a neat illustration of how antisemitism can be used as a tool to sow division within democratic societies.

---

* My favourite example of this was the suggestion that Russian bot accounts were responsible for much of the negative online reaction to the Star Wars film *The Last Jedi*. From what I can tell the scale of their involvement and probable impact has been overstated, but the idea that Russian bots would even try to exploit the divided fan reaction to the film shows that this is not about promoting a particular political line but about attacking the cohesiveness of society in general. For what it's worth I thought *The Last Jedi* was a bit meh, but I didn't go on Twitter to say so.

I also think it is unlikely that disinformation campaigns by Russia (or anyone else) are the reason why young people fall for antisemitic conspiracy theories more often than older people do. I haven't seen any evidence in that direction, and I'm wary of painting some grand conspiracy with Vladimir Putin at the centre of a giant web of Twitter bots and dodgy YouTube videos toying with the minds of British youths. On the contrary, I think the increase in interest in antisemitic conspiracy theories amongst younger people is genuine. We can speculate about why these old ideas might have renewed appeal. Perhaps it is because of a sense amongst young people they have been dealt an unfair hand, with the expectation that they will struggle to find affordable housing or get a job commensurate with their education and aspirations. The pandemic hit younger people especially hard in terms of the impact it had on their daily lives; unfairly so, given that the health risk to them from catching Covid-19 was relatively low. Even before then, the disproportionate support for Jeremy Corbyn amongst younger voters suggested that a lot of young people wanted radical change. Or maybe it is just that social media has made antisemitic ideas, in the form of conspiracy theories, easier to find, and they fit with a growing attitude towards power and politics that increasingly sees conspiracies as more plausible explanations than democratic ones for why things happen.

Whatever the reason, it is a reminder that progress is never guaranteed. Societies, political movements or whole nations can slip backwards into irrationality and barbarism as well as becoming more enlightened and free. I don't deny that there are many advances in human life to celebrate. I'm an optimist, after all. But we shouldn't forget that sometimes things get worse, not better. Populist politics fuelled by conspiracy theories about global elites, combined with an assault on liberal values and suspicion of outsiders, are a rising force in Europe and the United States. When I see the evidence for growing antisemitism amongst younger people in Britain, while at the same time there are powerful people and political movements around the world eating away at liberal democracy, I worry about what the future holds, for Jews and for wider society – and the two usually move in tandem.

In some ways, the complexity of the modern world, overflowing with information and a dizzying array of choices, makes the simple, self-sustaining 'truth' of antisemitism even more useful and appealing as a guide for the perplexed. Today's teenagers who think their understanding of society is enhanced by the idea that the Jews run the banks or that Israel's supporters control the media may not be aware of just how much they are parroting their ancestors, but there is nothing original in their speculations about hidden Jewish power and influence. This is medieval wine in digital bottles. 'Anti-Judaism should not be understood as some archaic or irrational closet in the vast edifices of Western thought', wrote historian David Nirenberg, but 'rather one of the basic tools with which that edifice was constructed'.[30] Despite so much human progress in so many other fields, we are not necessarily any less susceptible to the enticement of antisemitism, because those anti-Jewish myths were ingrained in the way the modern world was built. We may have done a good job of suppressing them in the decades since the Holocaust, but they always remained, buried less deeply than we like to think, ready to resurface whenever opportunity strikes. It's up to us to make sure they don't get the chance.

CONCLUSION

This is the part where I'm supposed to come up with a set of original and imaginative proposals that will completely solve the problem you have been reading about. It's a promise of resolution after the gloom, a programme of action that will lead us all to a brighter, happier future. I'd love to be able to oblige. Everybody loves a happy ending, right? Unfortunately, Jewish stories don't work that way. Not because there isn't any happiness in Jewish history: that would be to fall into the same old trap of assuming antisemitism is the beginning and end of all Jewish life. Rather, it is that the Jewish experience demands a certain humility in the face of reality, born 'from the knowledge that one cannot be true to the human experience while pretending to make sense of the world'.[1] In other words, antisemitism has been around for too long, and is too ingrained within the bedrock of our civilisation, for us to hope that we can remove it simply by tweeting the right hashtags on Holocaust Memorial Day. This thing has been with us for ever, and who are we to believe we can make for ever end here?

However, that does not let us off the hook. Just as the Jewish tradition warns against Panglossian optimism, so it also does not permit us to give up on trying to improve our world. There is a well-known Jewish saying in *Ethics of the Fathers*, a collection of Jewish aphorisms that dates as far back as 200 BCE, that reads: 'It is not your duty to complete the task, but neither are you free to desist from it.' It has always struck me as a fitting description of what it means to fight antisemitism. There may not be a silver bullet that can slay this most persistent of beasts, but sitting on our hands and assuming all is lost is not an option. Even if it is unrealistic to imagine that we can erase antisemitism entirely from our world, there are things we can do that will, with sustained and collective effort, push it back to the margins and significantly reduce its deleterious impact. In that spirit, here are some suggestions for how we can start to dismantle the legacy of antisemitism that is woven into our world. They may not complete the job on their own, but as I've said, it is not up to you to end antisemitism; just to do your bit.

You now know that antisemitism is not only a prejudice, but a fantasy about imaginary, diabolic Jews built from centuries of myths, legends and stereotypes. It is a conspiracy theory and a way of explaining our flawed world. Antisemitism is not limited to one type of politics, ideology or religion; nor is it the sole preserve of extremists, although it is essential to their world view. It is built on some core ideas: that Jews are unusually bloodthirsty, cruel, manipulative and cunning. That they love money more than is healthy and lack basic human values. It can be traced back to the origin stories of the crucifixion of Jesus Christ, but it is transmitted today via the most modern technology. We are not dealing with a foreign virus that infects an otherwise healthy body politic, but a familiar

CONCLUSION

and distinct weave that can be found in the fabric of our society, in our greatest literature and culture, available for people to pull on whenever it suits. This anti-Jewish worldview is expressed via dramatic texts like *The Protocols of the Elders of Zion*, throwaway comments that Jewish people hear and read from ordinary people, every day. At its most extreme, antisemitism still causes Jews to face hate crimes and murder, even today. You also now know that Britain, and England before it, has contributed more to this history than we would like to admit.

We can be reassured that most people are not consciously hostile to Jews, while remaining aware that many of those same people have absorbed antisemitic beliefs along the way. It sucks in magnates like Henry Ford and teenagers plotting from their bedrooms. The history of antisemitism lives in the here and now, constantly regenerating to remain relevant in times of war, pandemic, economic struggle and social division. Jews have been persecuted as a race and as a religion at different times, reflecting the politics and society of their age, and always as the antithesis of what society deems healthy, moral and good. Much of today's antisemitism harks back to medieval myths like the blood libel and well-poisonings, but it keeps up with the times: the two transformational events for Jews in the past century were the Holocaust and the creation of the State of Israel, and the language and obsessions of 21st-century antisemites reflect this in ways that their nineteenth-century counterparts could not have done. And if you know all of that, then you also know that your first responsibility is to not ignore it. Speak up when you witness it rather than turning the other way. Share the knowledge and don't leave it to others.

INCLUDING ANTISEMITISM

My first suggestion, and the one that underpins all others, is to ensure that our basic understanding of racism, and all the anti-racist campaigns, initiatives and education that flow from it, includes antisemitism. This might sound obvious, but the two have become tragically separated and need to be reconnected. It was not always thus. As long as anti-racism and anti-Fascism overlapped, the need for anti-racists to combat antisemitism went unquestioned. When my grandpa and 100,000 others prevented Oswald Mosley's black-shirted fascists from marching through the East End of London in 1936, Jews, Communists, dockers and other local residents all fought side by side. In the decades following The Second World War, as the politics of anti-racism began to take shape in Britain, antisemitism and racism were treated as part of the same problem. The legislation that was introduced to prevent racial discrimination was written with Jews in mind just as much as other more recent immigrants. It couldn't be any other way, given that the same far-right gangs who were trying to burn down synagogues were also assaulting black communities.

Somewhere along the way this connection between antisemitism and racism has been lost. A friend told me recently about a meeting of senior managers at their workplace, a major national institution, that was discussing that institution's commitment to anti-racism. In the meeting, my friend pointed out that there had been high-profile incidents of antisemitism in their industry, so they should not limit their work to addressing only racism against people of colour in case they miss any potential antisemitism at their institution, with all the reputational damage that would bring. The meeting chair – the most senior person in the room – refused to even consider it,

CONCLUSION

to the surprise of many around the table, Jewish and not. This is just one example, born of ignorance rather than malice. The person involved later conceded that they simply (and mistakenly) didn't understand antisemitism as a form of racism, but the episode illustrates the problem I am talking about.

I remember exactly when I realised that the need to fight antisemitism had become detached from the outlook of Britain's anti-racist left: September 2000, the start of a new millennium, and the outbreak of a new round of violence in Israel and the occupied territories. The Second Intifada, as it was known, was a dirty, depressing and frightening period of bloodshed in the Middle East. It coincided with the 9/11 terrorist attacks in the United States and the 2003 war in Iraq, and taken together, they generated a cauldron of anger that poured over Jewish communities around the world. There were over 250 'violent antisemitic incidents against Jewish sites worldwide' in the weeks following the outbreak of the Second Intifada. The United Kingdom saw a fourfold increase in antisemitic incidents (both violent and non-violent) in October 2000 compared to October 1999. In Britain and France, six synagogues were burned down and arson attempts occurred at a further twenty-four synagogues and Jewish schools in just three weeks.[2] In London, an Orthodox Jewish man called David Myers was stabbed twenty times in the head and neck by an Algerian assailant on the top deck of a bus, almost killing him; when the perpetrator was arrested he told police: 'Israel are the murderers. They kill women and children, so I stabbed him.'[3]

This pattern continued. In 2002 there were 311 serious violent incidents worldwide, and whereas in previous years physical attacks were directed primarily at synagogues and Jewish cemeteries, now it was Jewish people who were being targeted.[4] Most of this anti-Jewish violence came in western Europe, but the deadliest attack was in Tunisia where an al-Qaeda suicide bomber murdered nineteen people at the historic El Ghriba synagogue on the island of Djerba. The following year, twenty-three were killed in a double suicide bombing at the Neve Shalom and Beth Israel Synagogues in Istanbul.

The response from the pillars of Britain's anti-racist establishment to this wave of anti-Jewish violence and hatred was, largely, silence. This was a period when much of the political left forgot its own tradition of opposing antisemitism, and even at times stoked the fire. The *New Statesman* published a notorious front cover that showed a golden Star of David piercing a prostrate Union flag, under the headline 'A kosher conspiracy?' Left-wing newspapers published opinion columns with headlines like 'Israel simply has no right to exist', and others comparing Israel to Nazi Germany.[5] Pro-Palestinian rallies replete with antisemitic placards and blood-curdling chants would be addressed by Labour MPs and trade unionists. Evidence emerging from organisations in Jewish communities that monitor anti-Jewish hate crimes (including the one I work for, the Community Security Trust) indicated that the surge in anti-Jewish violence was increasingly coming from within Europe's Muslim minority, fired up by hatred of Israel, but this was too inconvenient or discomforting for some to accept. It is 'an absurd slur' to suggest that hatred of Israel is fuelling antisemitism, wrote Seumas Milne in the *Guardian*, who went on to erroneously claim that 'all the evidence is that it is the far right, the traditional fount of anti-semitic poison, which has been overwhelmingly responsible' for anti-Jewish attacks in Europe.[6] This ostrich-like denial occurred at institutional level too: when the European Union commissioned two reports into the rising antisemitism affecting its member states, it was so disturbed by the findings that it 'sought to bury the first report, delay publication of the second, and then publish both with a press release at variance with the assessments made by the reports' authors'.[7]

I expect it didn't help that many of the people and organisations involved in anti-racist campaigns were themselves strongly opposed to Israel and didn't want to be told that they might be part of the problem. They could only face one way and chose to turn their collective face away from the Jews. Whatever the reason, the outcome was that Jewish communities across Europe felt abandoned. This was a time when Jews were under attack – literally, as jihadist terrorism left a trail of death at Jewish schools, synagogues, shops and museums – yet too many people who were convinced anti-racists could not identify this as antisemitism. Instead, it was rationalised away as a misguided, but perhaps understandable, expression of anger over Israel. The film director Ken Loach has said that any rise in antisemitism in reaction to conflict in Israel 'is perfectly understandable because Israel feeds feelings of anti-Semitism'.[8] Veteran leftist Tariq Ali voiced the same idea: 'Every time they bomb Gaza, every time they attack Jerusalem – that is what creates antisemitism. Stop the occupation, stop the bombing and casual antisemitism will soon disappear.'[9] It is as if antisemitism didn't exist before Israel; as if the entire universe of anti-Jewish ideas, motifs and motivations is a figment of the Jewish imagination, and if only Israel would behave itself, Jews could sleep more easily.

A lot of ink has been spilt trying to explain why tackling antisemitism no longer appears to be a priority issue for much of the progressive left, and this summary barely scratches the surface.

For now, I'll only add this: the widespread abandonment of the Jewish community by much of the anti-racist movement needs to be reversed. Those organisations, campaigns and educators who are doing valuable and necessary work tackling racism need to ensure that they incorporate antisemitism into their campaigns and their programmes. Some do already, and it is encouraging that more do now than just a few years ago. I think the years of turmoil during Jeremy Corbyn's leadership of the Labour Party woke a few people up. We need more to follow.

Crucially, anti-racist education and campaigning must use a model of antisemitism that is fit for purpose. It needs to be able to account for the Holocaust, pogroms and historic discrimination, as well as conspiracy theory videos on TikTok. It must be able to explain why more than a dozen French Jews have been murdered in the past two decades, all because they are Jewish, and none by neo-Nazis; how David Icke's show about 'Rothschild Zionists' can fill venues across the UK;[10] why there are teenagers in this country who have never met a Jew but still want to kill them. Perhaps most difficult to achieve, but so essential to strive for, is a common understanding of how different reactions to the conflict in Israel and Palestine influence hostility towards Jews in Britain. Most of all – and I will keep repeating this – once you have this knowledge, you have to use it. Don't turn the other way or stay silent the next time you encounter antisemitism; if you are responsible for promoting equality, diversity and inclusion, don't forget about Jews.

KNOWING WHAT TO MEASURE

Greater advances require a more strategic shift, and one way to encourage the change of mindset we need would be to formally

CONCLUSION

include Jews in ethnicity-based monitoring of exclusion and disadvantage. It's a step that would be both practical and symbolic, and it is well overdue. The fact that Jews are usually not included is an anomaly, given that they are already recognised as an ethnicity in law and a significant proportion of Jewish people self-identify that way. Currently Jews are treated solely as a religious group on the census and are largely ignored by most ethnic minority monitoring, whether by the public or private sector, which means that efforts to track the impact of antisemitism are divorced from the much more substantial research into wider discrimination. If you don't measure something you can't know whether it is getting better or worse or even if it is happening at all; if you are measuring racism, you should be including antisemitism within that work.* One organisation that did try to assess discrimination against Jews was the European Union Agency for Fundamental Rights, which found in 2018 that 17 per cent of British Jews felt they had been discriminated against on the grounds of their religion over the previous twelve months, and 9 per cent felt they had been discriminated against on the ground of their ethnicity during the same period.[11] Nobody in Britain is measuring this on a regular basis, which leaves a substantial gap in our understanding.

However, this raises the next challenge, which is the question of what we measure when we measure discrimination. The Commission on Race and Ethnic Disparities, set up in 2020 and concluded

---

* Even some of the things you'd expect to be measured and tracked by the relevant authorities aren't counted. At the time of writing, nobody knows how many prosecutions for antisemitic hate crimes take place each year in the United Kingdom. Nobody knows whether the number goes up or down each year, where in the country most of them happen or anything else about how antisemitism is prosecuted through the courts, because the Crown Prosecution Service cannot produce this data from within its own computer system. So when I say 'nobody knows', I don't mean that I don't know the number; nobody *inside* the Crown Prosecution Service knows either.

in 2021, was typical in seeking to measure inequality through outcomes in poverty, education, employment, health and the criminal justice system. These are standard markers for racial exclusion and discrimination and used by a wide range of bodies. They have developed over time as the metrics used to assess racism, because they measure the types of inequality that predominantly affect people of colour, and this is the kind of discrimination that we know people of colour experience. It's a circular loop from which Jews are excluded twice over. First, because almost all monitoring for ethnicity-based inequality does not include Jews as a relevant group to monitor, and second, because the forms of discrimination that are monitored are not always the ones that most affect the Jewish community.

This is far from uniform, but on the whole the Jewish community is not as likely to experience disadvantage through, for example, employment, education or housing. Generally speaking, British Jews are rarely kept out of the best universities or the most powerful boardrooms because they are Jewish. It hasn't always been this way. There were certain law firms and city banks that were known for a long time as places not to bother applying. There are several golf clubs dotted around the country known locally as 'Jewish' golf clubs, that were set up because Jews were unofficially barred from joining older, established clubs. Dunham Forest in Cheshire is one example, Lee Park in Liverpool is another, and there are plenty of others. These 'Jewish' golf clubs weren't created because Jews prefer to play golf with each other but because other people didn't want to play golf with Jews. Discrimination of this sort does happen from time to time, but not as often or as systematically as it can affect other minorities. Poverty, low educational attainment and poor

CONCLUSION

housing are problems in parts of the Jewish community, but less so than in wider society.

Instead, antisemitism comes in the form of conspiracy theories, myths and stereotypes, which feed a different kind of exclusion that never gets measured or counted. That same 2018 EU survey found that 38 per cent of Jews across the twelve EU countries will sometimes avoid going to places in their local neighbourhood because they do not feel safe there as a Jew. Twenty-seven per cent of British Jews even sometimes choose not to go to a Jewish event or site because they would not feel safe, either at the event or on the way to and from it. Those Jewish events, like all synagogues, Jewish schools and communal buildings, need to have security because nobody wants to be the unlucky one who is in the building on the day that a terrorist turns up to kill Jews, as has happened in Pittsburgh, Poway, Halle, Toulouse, Colleyville, Brussels, Paris and Copenhagen in the past decade. All that security absorbs huge amounts of Jewish community time, money and human resources that small communities would much rather be spending on more positive activities. The police count the number of hate crimes against Jews and others keep track of terrorist attacks targeting synagogues or other Jewish community locations, but what gets missed is the way that antisemitism affects daily Jewish life.

There is anecdotal evidence that in some industries Jewish people are more likely to hide the fact they are Jewish because they have learned, either from their own experience or from that of others, that it can be an impediment to getting ahead.[12] Jews are sometimes told they benefit from white privilege in a way that is not available to other minorities. This may be true for many Jewish people,

253

although it ignores all those Jews who are black or Mizrahi, and it also ignores all the times when 'white' Jews are asked 'where are you from exactly?' – visibility is a fluid concept when it comes to Jews – but even for those Jews for whom this is true, it is hardly a privilege to have to hide your identity to be confident of getting equal treatment or to avoid being attacked or threatened in the street. It's a different kind of exclusion that would need to be measured in a different way, but no less real for that.

Even if you stick to the traditional ways of measuring inequality, the fact that Jews are not counted as an ethnic minority can lead to unequal treatment. During the Covid-19 pandemic, it quickly became apparent that people from ethnic minorities in Britain were experiencing disproportionately high levels of infection, hospitalisation and death. The same was the case for the Jewish community, but the two were rarely joined up because Jews were regularly excluded from the enormous body of research done into Covid-19 health outcomes for ethnic minorities. One of the few pieces of research to combine Covid-19 mortality in religious and ethnic groups found that, when adjusting for ethnicity, Jewish men were twice as likely as Christians to experience a death involving Covid-19.[13] Even when the data was adjusted for other factors such as age and geography, there remained 'a large and unexplained increased risk for Jewish males'.[14]

There are several research projects to investigate the impact of Long Covid by various different risk factors, including ethnicity, but it's hard to find one that includes religious affiliation as a factor – so again, the impact on Jews is missed. Instead, it is down to a Jewish think tank, the Institute for Jewish Policy Research, to survey the Jewish community in an effort to track Long Covid. They

CONCLUSION

are more than capable of doing the job, but really this should be done by a national body as part of the wider work to track Long Covid across all ethnic minorities. Elevated mortality from Covid-19 amongst Jews isn't necessarily caused by antisemitism, but then the elevated mortality experienced by other minorities isn't necessarily caused by racism. It's just an example of how Jews are omitted from so much official monitoring of exclusion and discrimination.* As well as recognising Jews as an ethnicity, we need to expand how we define discrimination and what counts as inequality.

WHOSE HISTORY IS THIS?

I sometimes think we have got the way we explain about antisemitism back to front, and this is where we come to the next challenge: education. There are dozens of Jewish museums in Europe and many others around the world. Visit any one of them and you are likely to find accounts of antisemitism and persecution suffered by the Jews in that city or country, alongside more positive exhibits about the life of that community. A 2016 survey of sixty-four Jewish museums in Europe found that a majority saw it as part of their mission to 'promote understanding and tolerance between Jews and non-Jews and to fight anti-Semitism.'[15] This is perfectly understandable. Antisemitism is part of the Jewish experience so it would be strange for a Jewish museum not to mention it. This is especially true in those parts of mainland Europe that were, in the past, home to substantial and important Jewish communities: someone has to explain where those Jews all went and why their synagogues are no

---

* Shortly after I wrote this chapter, the NHS Race & Health Observatory issued a tender document for a review of how the health service engages and communicates with the Jewish community, as a way of addressing health inequalities affecting the Jewish community. This is the first time such a research project has happened in the UK and is scheduled to conclude in 2024.

longer used for prayer but instead are now tourist sites competing for Tripadvisor reviews. There are Jewish museums who do this in a sensitive and nuanced way, balancing it well with stories of the Jewish life that was destroyed and I wouldn't want this to change. But sometimes, when I am walking round these museums in cities full of Jewish ghosts, I find myself asking: whose history is this and whose responsibility should it be to teach it?

Antisemitism, after all, is not a story of what Jews did. All these accounts of blood libels, expulsions, massacres, forced conversions and the rest are things that were done to us, and it sticks in the craw that this history is mainly relayed by Jewish museums to Jewish visitors, when it tells us much more about non-Jewish society than about who Jews are and how they lived. This was brought home to me when I visited Prague in July 2022. The old Jewish quarter of the Czech capital has a decent claim to holding Europe's most compelling array of Jewish museums and memorials. The story it tells is full of colour and life, and it has achieved what few Jewish museums manage in becoming a tourist magnet for everyone – not just for Jews. I can see why. The repurposed synagogues are magnificent, the exhibitions are engaging and the haunting old Jewish cemetery looks like a film set. You can visit the oldest surviving synagogue in Europe and learn about the legend of the Golem, a Frankenstein-style monster made of clay. Or you can stand in silent awe in the 500-year-old Pinkas synagogue, where the names of all 80,000 Jews from the Czech lands killed in the Shoah are inscribed on the whitewashed walls.

Prague's Jewish Museum brings the story of antisemitism up to date with an exhibit about the Slánský trial, a purge of Czech Communists in the early 1950s that was shot through with antisemitism.

CONCLUSION

Fourteen leaders of the Czech Communist Party were put on trial for treason, eleven of whom, including party secretary Rudolf Slánský, were Jewish. The charge was itself antisemitic, a fantastical allegation that these Communist leaders, who had proven their loyalty over decades, were in fact part of an international conspiracy led by the Israeli government and American Zionists. Even the non-Jewish defendants 'were being accused of "Jewishness"' in the trial. The men were held for over a year until, broken by relentless interrogation and torture, they 'confessed' to the spurious crimes. Their interrogators were viciously antisemitic, promising the defendants 'that Hitler was right about the Jews "and we will finish what he started"'.[16] In court, each defendant read out a lengthy confession entirely confected by their interrogators. In a sign of how far removed from reality the allegations were, Slánský even 'admitted' that *The Protocols of the Elders of Zion* were authentic.[17] All were found guilty; Slánský and ten others were hanged. The museum has archive footage of the trial running on a loop, projected onto the wall alongside secret surveillance photographs of Jewish community buildings and activists found in the Communist secret police archives. It is a dramatic exhibit that drives home the intolerable suppression of Jewish life under the Communist dictatorship.

Ten minutes' walk from the Jewish Museum is Prague's Museum of Communism, which also tells the story of the Slánský trial but, unlike the Jewish Museum, misses out the episode's most salient feature. These were just 'political trials', according to the Museum of Communism, from which 'even leading members of the Communist Party' were not exempt. There is no mention of the preponderance of Jewish defendants or that the charges were explicitly based on their Jewishness or the antisemitic behaviour of their interrogators.

In fact, there is an absence of any discussion of Czech Jews or antisemitism throughout this museum. A panel about 'persecuting the faithful' only mentions repression of Christianity. The one about the impact of the Second World War on the Czech population says, 'A hard-line racial policy of Germanisation was implemented, including the "final solution" [sic] in concentration camps.' If you only visited the Museum of Communism you would have no idea that Jews had even lived in Czechoslovakia, never mind that tens of thousands were deported and killed by the Nazis and that those who survived had to live through decades of repression under Communism. Visiting these two museums back-to-back is like inhabiting two completely different worlds, even though they are supposed to be educating you about exactly the same events.

It brings me back to the questions I asked earlier: whose history is this and who should teach it? Jewish museums have become adept at conveying how antisemitism has affected Jewish communities, mainly to Jewish visitors. But the story of antisemitism ought to be about antisemites, not Jews. It is a topic that belongs in national museums as part of the narrative that we tell ourselves and others about how our societies have developed, and the lives lived by different peoples in our countries. Instead of educating about antisemitism from the standpoint of, 'Learn about what happened to Jews,' as if antisemitism came out of nowhere and was some peculiar feature of Jewish existence, how about, 'Here is what we did to Jews, and this is what we might learn from it about ourselves.' British antisemitism is part of the story of Britain and how we came to be the country we are today. The history of Britain's minority communities reaches much further back than modern accounts of immigration and discrimination usually allow for and the medieval

CONCLUSION

Jewish experience should be integrated into our understanding of how this island nation has treated its minorities. It is encouraging that in recent years this is starting to happen, with the erection of public statues and plaques to draw attention to stories of Jewish settlement and persecution in British towns and cities where there are few Jews today. This is how it should be and we need more of it.

ONLINE SAFETY, OFFLINE HARMS

Education obviously begins in schools, which returns us to the challenge set by the previous chapter: what to do about the growth of antisemitic beliefs amongst younger people. Holocaust education is much more developed in the United Kingdom than in most countries and it does a fantastic job in its own right. However, learning about the Holocaust won't necessarily help people identify and understand the types of antisemitism faced by British Jews today. There is even a risk, if it is not taught well, of leaving the impression that anti-Jewish hatred is something limited to Germany, in what increasingly feels like the distant past, or that it only comes from the far right, so we don't need to worry about it too much in modern Britain. Introducing more education in schools specifically about antisemitism today, alongside other efforts to teach about racism and discrimination, would be an obvious place to start.

The appeal of antisemitic ideas is inseparable from the popularity of conspiracy theories, and it may be that increasing resistance to the latter would be the most effective way to inhibit the spread of the former. There is a growing body of advice for teachers about how to address conspiracy theories, both proactively and reactively, when they come up in the classroom. Research suggests that people are less likely to believe a conspiracy theory if they have been warned against it before hearing it for the first time – known as 'prebunking' – rather than trying to debunk the idea once they are familiar with it. A guide produced by academics at the Institute for Education, University College London, warns teachers against getting drawn into direct discussion of conspiracy theories, suggesting instead that they close down the conversation and then pick it up informally with the individual student later. There is general agreement that work needs to be done to improve media literacy so that children and adults are able to identify credible sources of information and spot the fakes. It has also been suggested that scientific and historical literacy are just as important, as so many conspiracy theories rely either on pseudo-science or on falsified versions of history.[18]

This research is still evolving and some of the suggestions seem rather optimistic. Prebunking as a strategy has obvious limitations when it comes to antisemitism, given how old some conspiratorial ideas about Jews are and how easily accessible they have become. One thing everyone seems to agree on is that it is almost impossible to persuade a committed conspiracy theorist out of their views: they just think that your efforts to change their mind are part of the conspiracy. Nevertheless, if the signs of growth of anti-Jewish attitudes amongst younger people are to be stunted before they sprout further, there needs to be much greater understanding of what works, and what doesn't, when it comes to building resilience against the false appeal of conspiracy theories. The British government published a Media Literacy Strategy in 2021 that was designed to plug some of the gaps in people's ability to critically evaluate online content, identify unverified stories or doctored images and recognise their potential harm. The following year the All-Party Parliamentary Group on Media Literacy followed up with its own recommendations, including adding media literacy to the national curriculum and ensuring that teachers, as much as their students, have the necessary skills. There is some evidence that this would help: research by the Reboot Foundation found that people who had been taught critical thinking in school were 26 per cent less likely to believe in conspiracy theories (interestingly, people who described themselves as 'critical thinkers' but had never been taught how to do it properly were 63 per cent *more* likely to believe in conspiracies).[19] This would bring much wider benefits than those felt by the Jewish community, but it is an essential step for tackling the type of antisemitism that spreads most easily today.

The other side of this coin is the need for social media companies to stop aiding the spread of conspiracy theories. Most mainstream platforms now have policies banning hate speech or incitement to violence (although their enforcement of these rules is often quite poor), but across the industry there is a reluctance to recognise conspiracy theories as harmful in and of themselves. This is a foolhardy and dangerous error of judgement, given the role of conspiracy theories in preparing the ground for the most heinous of crimes against Jews throughout the ages. This is not a question of free speech, because conspiracy theories are not just a bad opinion like any other. 'A deliberate lie is not an "idea",' wrote Judge Hadassa Ben-Itto in her history of legal attempts to debunk *The Protocols of the Learned Elders of Zion*. It is 'a dangerous weapon', and 'unlike some weapons, a lie like the Protocols is never used in self-defense'.[20] When it comes to antisemitism, conspiracy theories are the gateway to a whole set of anti-Jewish slanders that end, ultimately, with incitement to murder.

There has been extensive debate in the United Kingdom over

whether online content informally described as 'legal but harmful' should be subject to regulation. I can think of no better example of 'legal but harmful' material than the conspiracy theories about Jews, Zionists, Rothschilds and all the other codewords that swamp social media. I don't know whether the UK's proposed regulation will suffice, but experience shows that social media giants only move when they are forced to, either by the threat of legal action, government regulation or punitive financial loss. In an ideal world the people who own and work for social media companies would ask themselves whether teaching a new generation that Jews run the banks and control the media is what they get out of bed for every morning. Rather than wait for that day to come, there is an urgent need for this mechanism of hate to be brought under control and for antisemitic conspiracy theories to be more widely recognised and treated as a dangerous tool for inciting hatred against Jews.

As well as trying to limit the spread of negative ideas about Jews, we should do what we can to encourage the spread of positive ones, and this is where there is something for the Jewish community to do: we need to get out more. Most importantly, we need to find ways for our children to have more contact, in a positive and structured way, with their peers who are not Jewish. The research I cited in Chapter Eight showing that contact between people from different groups reduces prejudice also showed that the benefits are increased if the interactions occur through 'carefully structured contact situations'.[21] Schools, youth clubs and sports teams should all actively seek opportunities for Jewish and non-Jewish children to mix from an age before they start to become widely exposed to conspiracy theories or anti-Jewish stereotypes (which happens as soon as they are allowed to roam free on YouTube or TikTok).

CONCLUSION

I know this already happens, but we need more of it. Ideally the responsibility for reducing antisemitism shouldn't fall primarily onto Jews. This is a problem of wider society and it should be up to others to take the lead. Realistically, it is something we cannot afford to ignore and this is a practical suggestion for what we can do to help move things along.

This does not only apply to children. This work requires more interactions between Jewish and non-Jewish people, groups and communities, especially those who do not normally mix. Our challenge is to change how people think about Jews, but people do not only think with their brains. They think with their gut too, perhaps in a more forceful yet less self-aware way, and the human warmth and unspoken, lasting bonds that are only found through personal interaction have a better chance of influencing that way of thinking than anything I can explain in a book.

EVERYDAY HATE

It can be difficult to remain an optimist sometimes. England has contributed more than most to the mechanisms and language of antisemitism. The first European country to expel its Jews, the inventor of the blood libel, the birthplace of Shylock and Fagin. In the time since Jews were readmitted to England in 1656 it has been a relative haven for my people, sheltered from the ravages of continental antisemitism, but it has not always felt like a wholly welcoming one. It took a century from readmission until foreign-born Jews could be legally naturalised, and another century after that before a Jewish MP was able to take his seat in Parliament. Each advance was made in the teeth of vigorous opposition, and only after numerous setbacks. More recent times have seen antisemitism become a national story in Britain for the first time I can remember, with alarming headlines and debates in Parliament not for some artificial political purpose but because antisemitism is genuinely worsening. The rise in anti-Jewish hate crimes is real, as is the increase in self-made terrorists who want to kill us. Conspiracy theories are more popular than ever and the dangers of antisemitism in mainstream politics have been made clear in unprecedented, dramatic fashion.

Then I look around at the life we have now, in what every opinion poll assures me is one of the least antisemitic countries on earth. I think of all the people I have seen and heard standing up for their Jewish friends, family or workmates, calling out the abuse and harassment we face. The Jewish characters that grip the popular imagination in today's culture are more likely to be sympathetic or heroic – think of Alfie Solomons from *Peaky Blinders* or Martin from *Friday Night Dinner* – than the antisemitic caricatures of the past. Yotam Ottolenghi's cuisine has transformed middle-class kitchens and Israeli restaurants are the toast of London's food scene. And I am reassured that antisemitism remains a minority interest in Britain, an abhorrence that appals most people once they are brought to think about it. We face serious and growing problems and challenges, but I would rather confront them in today's Britain than almost anywhere else.

Progress is never guaranteed, but that doesn't mean it isn't within our gift. I opened this chapter with a saying from *Ethics of the Fathers* and I will close with another, one of the best-known of all Jewish quotations: 'If I am not for myself, who will be for me? And if I am only for myself, what am I? And if not now, when?' As a precept for action it is hard to beat, which is why you'll find it everywhere. It's been quoted in speeches by Presidents Reagan and Obama and

CONCLUSION

used by Jewish sages as diverse as Primo Levi and Ivanka Trump (although Trump misattributed it to Emma Watson rather than its true author, the first-century Talmudic scholar Rabbi Hillel). I've even seen it on a charity tote bag from Glastonbury Festival, with the extra line 'If not you, who?' added for effect and the logos of Oxfam, Greenpeace and Water Aid all sitting happily under this most ancient of Jewish proverbs.

The instruction is to seize the moment and act, for ourselves and for others. The task of dismantling antisemitism, removing it piece by piece from our society, is not only for Jews to do, nor is it only for the benefit of Jews. It is for all of us, together, to resist this poison, reduce its harm, and in the process build a less hateful world to replace the one constructed with superstitions and lies. It will take an extraordinary effort, but we have no choice if we are to erase this most enduring of everyday hatreds.

ACKNOWLEDGEMENTS

This book could not have happened without the assistance and support of many people. All the thoughts it contains are my own, the result of nearly thirty years of working in the field of researching and tackling antisemitism, but I am the first to admit that a great deal of my knowledge and thinking on the subject has been influenced by the work of others. This includes, of course, my colleagues past and present at the Community Security Trust (CST), some of whom I have worked alongside for decades and have become close friends as well as co-workers. I owe a similar debt to countless academics, writers, campaigners, investigators and activists who have contributed so much to our collective understanding of what antisemitism is, where, how and why it happens, and who is involved. There are far too many to list here, but if I've ever had a conversation or email exchange with you about antisemitism, read one of your articles or books or listened to you at a seminar or conference: thank you.

Some of the contemporary examples of antisemitism I have used in this book were originally unearthed by CST staff and volunteers in the course of their work, and I am grateful to be able to cite them here. Their research skills are, in my (admittedly biased) opinion, without parallel and the material they find every day continues to both shock and inspire. Mark Gardner was as encouraging as always throughout the writing of this book and his thoughts and suggestions have been particularly useful. Jonathan Freedland, Becky and Scott Matthewson, John Steele and Helen Hague, Clare Annamalai, Imran Ahmed and Jon Clements all offered invaluable observations. Jonathan Freedland also took the time – while publishing his own book and writing a play – to read and comment on the chapter that addresses the Holocaust, and his insights were as valuable as ever. A lifetime ago, Jonny (as he was then) was one of my leaders on a Habonim-Dror youth camp that spent two weeks learning about the Shoah. I hope I remembered my lessons from back then.

Jonny Geller and Viola Hayden at Curtis Brown were wonderfully supportive agents, always positive and full of helpful advice. It was a conversation with Jonny that pushed me to pursue this project from the beginning. I am especially grateful to Olivia Beattie, James Stephens, Ryan Norman and Suzanne Sangster at Biteback Publishing, who showed faith in my writing when other publishers did not see the value in a book about antisemitism. They were as enjoyable and easy to work with as I remember them being first time around. Simon Gallant was, as ever, both generous and judicious with his legal advice.

However, my debt to all those above is of nothing compared to the one I owe at home. Encouragement, suggestions, time and space to write, cups of tea, sleeping cats – as if that was not enough, Miriam was the first to read every word of this book and had limitless

ACKNOWLEDGEMENTS

patience for my constant conversations about it. Any flaws or errors in the text are my own, but everything good in it bears her influence. As for Esther and Jacob: six years ago they made me promise never to write another book, and they have graciously forgiven me for going back on my word. I am sorry to have broken that pledge, but on the other hand they also regularly ask me what I do at work each day. I hope this book answers their questions.

ABOUT THE AUTHOR

Dr Dave Rich is one of the UK's leading experts on antisemitism. He has worked for almost thirty years for the Community Security Trust, a Jewish charity that protects the UK Jewish community, and has advised the police, the Crown Prosecution Service, football clubs, political parties and many other organisations on how to tackle antisemitism. This is his second book, following *The Left's Jewish Problem: Jeremy Corbyn, Israel and Antisemitism* (Biteback, 2016 and 2018). You will regularly find him writing about antisemitism or extremism for national and international media or appearing on TV and radio broadcasts, including for the *Guardian*, *New York Times*, *New Statesman*, *Jewish Chronicle*, *Haaretz*, BBC News, ITV News, Sky News, Radio 5 Live, LBC, Panorama, Newsnight and others.

Dave is a Research Fellow at the London Centre for the Study of Contemporary Antisemitism and is on the editorial board of the *Journal of Contemporary Antisemitism*. His academic work includes chapters and articles about hate crime, conspiracy theories, the abuse of Holocaust memory, anti-Israel boycotts, campus antisemitism and the campaign for Soviet Jewry.

NOTES

INTRODUCTION
1. All details of antisemitic incidents are taken from direct reports made by victims, witnesses or other sources to the Community Security Trust.
2. All posts from BitChute and Gab. I have URLs and screenshots for each, but I won't include links here to extremist sites.
3. 'IS supporters launch campaign against "deviant" Muslim school of thought', BBC Monitoring (21 September 2022)
4. Cnaan Liphshiz, 'Antisemitism seen seeping into Russian media landscape as Ukraine invasion slows', *Times of Israel* (29 September 2022)
5. Berkeley LSJP [@berkeleylawforpalestine], infographic about pro-Palestinian bylaw, Instagram (21 August 2022), available at https://www.instagram.com/p/Chh_43tpLnm/
6. Lesley Stahl, 'Iran's President Ebrahim Raisi says he cannot trust Americans, calls sanctions "tyrannical"', CBS News (18 September 2022)
7. 'Qatar's envoy loses bid for human rights post, called Jews "enemies" & gays "disgusting"', UN Watch (19 September 2022)
8. UK Home Office, 'Official Statistics: Hate crime, England and Wales, 2021 to 2022', gov.uk (6 October 2022), available at https://www.gov.uk/government/statistics/hate-crime-england-and-wales-2021-to-2022/hate-crime-england-and-wales-2021-to-2022
   UK Home Office, 'Official Statistics: Hate crime, England and Wales, 2020 to 2021', gov.uk (12 October 2021), available at https://www.gov.uk/government/statistics/hate-crime-england-and-wales-2020-to-2021/hate-crime-england-and-wales-2020-to-2021
9. European Union Agency for Fundamental Rights, *Experiences and perceptions of antisemitism – Second survey on discrimination and hate crime against Jews in the EU* (Publications Office of the European Union, December 2018) p. 56
10. UK Home Office, 'Hate Crime, England and Wales, 2017/18', gov.uk (16 October 2018), available at https://assets.publishing.service.gov.uk/government/uploads/system/uploads/attachment_data/file/748598/hate-crime-1718-hosb2018.pdf
11. L. Daniel Staetsky, *Antisemitism in contemporary Great Britain: A study of attitudes towards Jews and Israel* (Institute for Jewish Policy Research, September 2017) pp. 16–26
12. Rosa Doherty, 'Fewer than half of British adults know what "antisemitism" means, poll reveals', *Jewish Chronicle* (14 March 2019)
13. Peter Pulzer, *The Rise of Political Anti-Semitism in Germany & Austria* (Peter Halban, 1988) p. 49
14. 'This week in Jewish history: Jewish–American journalist Daniel Pearl murdered by terrorists', *World Jewish Congress* (2 February 2022)

15 Laura E. Adkins, 'I listened to Kanye West slander Jews for three hours so that you don't have to', *Forward* (17 October 2022)
16 Khamenei.ir [@khamenei.ir], 'I openly state that the recent riots & unrest in Iran were schemes designed by the US; the usurping, fake…', Twitter (3 October 2022), available at https://twitter.com/khamenei_ir/status/1576886347151069184
17 Donald J. Trump [@realDonaldTrump], 'No President has done more for Israel than I have. Somewhat surprisingly, however, our wonderful Evangelicals are far more appreciative…' Truth Social (16 October 2022), available at https://truthsocial.com/@realDonaldTrump/posts/109177817932811190
18 Sergio DellaPergola & L. Daniel Staetsky, *Jews in Europe at the turn of the Millennium: Population trends and estimates* (Institute for Jewish Policy Research, October 2020) p. 30
19 European Union Agency for Fundamental Rights, *Experiences and perceptions of antisemitism – Second survey on discrimination and hate crime against Jews in the EU* (Publications Office of the European Union, December 2018) pp. 36–7
20 'New polling shows crisis of faith in democracy', Centre for Policy Studies (22 July 2018)
21 'Lack of trust in politics threatens democracy: New report and poll', Carnegie UK (20 January 2022)
22 'Revealed: Trust in politicians at lowest level on record', IPPR (5 December 2021)
23 Gabriel R. Sanchez, Keesha Middlemass & Aila Rodriguez, 'Misinformation is eroding the public's confidence in democracy', Brookings (26 July 2022)
24 Kim Hart, 'Exclusive poll: Only half of Americans have faith in democracy', Axios (5 November 2018)
25 Alex Woodward, '"Fake news": A guide to Trump's favourite phrase – and the dangers it obscures', *The Independent* (2 October 2020)
26 Barbara Goldberg, 'Anti-Semitic acts spiked since Trump election win, watchdog says', Reuters (24 April 2017); 'Pennsylvania AG: Trump called wave of anti-Semitic attacks "reprehensible", but says they're sometimes done in "the reverse"', Yahoo! News (28 February 2017)
27 Jose A. DelReal & Julie Zauzmer, 'Trump's vigorous defense of anti-Semitic image a "turning point" for many Jews', *Washington Post* (8 July 2016)
28 'Jeremy Corbyn first speech of the 2017 General Election campaign', Labour Party (20 April 2017), available at https://labour.org.uk/press/jeremy-corbyn-first-speech-of-the-2017-general/
29 Marc F. Plattner, 'Illiberal Democracy and the Struggle on the Right', *Journal of Democracy*, vol. 30, no. 1 (January 2019) pp. 5–19

CHAPTER ONE: JEWCRAFT
1 Daniel Jones, *Monty Python's Life of Brian*, Handmade Films, Python (Monty) Pictures (1979)
2 Daniel Sugarman, 'Association of British Scrabble Players updates definition of "Jew" after complaints', *Jewish Chronicle* (16 September 2019)
3 Rabbi Sacks, 'The Mutating Virus: Understanding Antisemitism', rabbisacks.org (27 September 2016)
4 Seth Stephens-Davidowitz, *Hidden Hate: What Google Searches tell us about Antisemitism Today* (Antisemitism Policy Trust & Community Security Trust, 2019), pp. 10–12
5 Ofcom Broadcast and On Demand Bulletin, Issue 446 (7 March 2022), p. 6
6 Trey Parker, 'Casa Bonita', *South Park*, Season 7, Episode 11, Braniff Productions (2003)
7 Trey Parker 'The Entity', *South Park*, Season 5, Episode 11, Braniff Productions (2001)
8 Trey Parker, 'The Passion of the Jew', *South Park*, Season 8, Episode 11, Braniff Productions (2004)
9 Trey Parker, 'Two Days Before the Day After Tomorrow', *South Park*, Season 9, Episode 8, Braniff Productions (2005)
10 Meagan Flynn, 'Trump accused of "dipping into a deep well of anti-Semitic tropes" during speech to Jewish voters', *Washington Post* (9 December 2019)
11 Martin Bright, 'Jews won't vote for me because they are rich, Ken Livingstone tells Labour activists', *Jewish Chronicle* (22 March 2012)
12 Alex Richards, 'Wigan owner Dave Whelan in anti-Semitic controversy after declaring "Jewish people chase money"', *Daily Mirror* (20 November 2014)

CHAPTER TWO: FILTHY RICH
1 William Shakespeare, *The Merchant of Venice*, Act 4 Scene 1
2 John Gross, *Shylock* (Chatto & Windus, 1992), p. 17
3 William Shakespeare, *The Merchant of Venice*, Act 3 Scene 1
4 Dominic Green, *The Double Life of Doctor Lopez* (Century, 2003), pp. 88–9
5 Emily Banks, 'Man who called developer "Shylock" convicted of anti-semitic abuse', *Ham & High* (17 November 2016)

NOTES

6. Barak Ravid, 'Argentina's Jews Riled by President Kirchner's "Merchant of Venice" Comments', *Haaretz* (8 July 2015)
7. Jeremy Warner, 'Creditors must brace for a tsunami of losses in a world awash with debt', *Daily Telegraph* (9 February 2016). Original version and changes discussed available at https://cst.org.uk/news/blog/2016/02/18/daily-telegraph-removes-shylock-references-from-article-about-jewish-hedge-fund-manager
8. Tom Banner, 'Blue Plaque in Copenhagen Street honouring Jewish community', *Worcester News* (24 July 2022)
9. 'The Jews in London', *Graphic* (16 November 1889)
10. Jonathan Boyd, *Child Poverty and Deprivation in the British Jewish Community* (Institute for Jewish Policy Research, March 2011); Jonathan Boyd, Carli Lessof & David Graham, *Acute Disadvantage: Where are the needs greatest?* (Institute for Jewish Policy Research, October 2020)
11. *A Portrait of Jewish Americans* (Pew Research Center, October 2013), Chapter 2
12. *Supporting Older People*, World Jewish Relief, available at https://www.worldjewishrelief.org/how-we-help/supporting-older-people
13. David Graham & Jonathan Boyd, *Charitable giving among Britain's Jews: Looking to the future* (Institute for Jewish Policy Research, March 2016)
14. Eric Hananoki, 'Marjorie Taylor Greene penned conspiracy theory that a laser beam from space started deadly 2018 California wildfire', Media Matters for America (28 January 2021)
15. 'The Football Association v Tom Pope', Report of the Football Association Regulatory Commission (22 July 2020)
16. Seth Stephens-Davidowitz, *Hidden Hate: What Google Searches tell us about Antisemitism Today* (Antisemitism Policy Trust & Community Security Trust, 2019), p. 14
17. 'Top 50 Banks in the World', LexisNexis, available at https://risk.lexisnexis.com/insights-resources/article/bank-rankings-top-banks-in-the-world
18. Charles de Montesquieu, *The Persian Letters*, trans. George R. Healy (Aegitas, 2017), p. 114 Kindle edition
19. Charles de Montesquieu, *The Spirit of the Laws*, trans. Thomas Nugent (Digireads.com, 2011), pp. 295–6 Kindle edition
20. Edmund Burke, *Reflections on the Revolution in France* (Digireads.com, 2004), p. 52 Kindle edition
21. David Nirenberg, *Anti-Judaism: The History of a Way of Thinking* (Head of Zeus, 2013), pp. 376–83
22. Karl Marx, 'On The Jewish Question' (1843), trans. Marxists Internet Archive, available at https://www.marxists.org/archive/marx/works/1844/jewish-question/
23. David Nirenberg, *Anti-Judaism: The History of a Way of Thinking* (Head of Zeus, 2013), p. 439
24. H. W. Charles, *The Money Code: Become a Millionaire With the Ancient Jewish Code* (Universal Power Publishing, 2012), available at https://www.amazon.co.uk/Money-Code-Become-Millionaire-Ancient/dp/0991690311; H. W. Charles, *The Investing Code: Ancient Jewish Wisdom for the Wise Investor* (CreateSpace Independent Publishing Platform, 2016), available at https://www.amazon.co.uk/H-W-Charles/e/B00A50MGU2?ref=dbs_a_def_rwt_hsch_vu00_tkin_p1_i0
25. Colin Holmes, *Anti-Semitism in British Society, 1876–1939* (Routledge, 2016), p. 178
26. United States Holocaust Memorial Museum, 'Page from the anti-Semitic German children's book, "Der Giftpilz" (The Poisonous Mushroom)' (1935), available at https://collections.ushmm.org/search/catalog/pa1069730
27. Lev Korneyev, *Israel: The Reality Behind the Myths* (Novosti Press Agency Publishing House, 1980), p. 7
28. Daniel Finkelstein, 'Corbyn's praise for deeply antisemitic book', *The Times* (30 April 2019)
29. J. A. Hobson, *God and Mammon: The Relations of Religion and Economics* (Watts & Co., 1931), pp. 10, 40–41

CHAPTER THREE: BLOOD AND FIRE

1. 'Tahra Ahmed convicted of stirring up racial hatred for antisemitic posts', CST Blog (14 January 2022)
2. Dominic Kennedy, 'Grenfell conspiracy theorist guilty of race hate', *The Times* (14 January 2022); 'Grenfell charity volunteer on trial after referring to blaze as a "Jewish sacrifice"', *Jewish Chronicle* (6 January 2022); 'Prominent Grenfell Tower volunteer aid worker Tahra Ahmed found guilty of publishing written material in order to stir up racial hatred, after being reported to police by CAA', Campaign Against Antisemitism (14 January 2022)
3. John 8: 44
4. Matthew 27: 1–25
5. Tom Holland, *Dominion: The Making of the Western Mind* (Abacus, 2019) p. 102
6. John Chrysostom, quoted in Simon Schama, *The Story of the Jews: Finding the Words 1000 BCE – 1492 CE* (Vintage, 2014) p. 214
7. David Nirenberg, *Anti-Judaism: The History of a Way of Thinking* (Head of Zeus, 2013). Chapters Two and Three set out this argument in more detail

8   Pope Paul VI, 'Declaration on the Relation of the Church to Non-Christian Religions' (The Vatican, 28 October 1965), available at https://www.vatican.va/archive/hist_councils/ii_vatican_council/documents/vat-ii_decl_19651028_nostra-aetate_en.html
9   Lee Harpin, '"Jews are Christ killers" banner at anti-Israel protest', *Jewish News* (22 May 2021)
10 David Nirenberg, *Anti-Judaism: The History of a Way of Thinking* (Head of Zeus, 2013) p. 459
11 Darren O'Brien, *The Pinnacle of Hatred: The Blood Libel and the Jews* (Hebrew University Magnes Press, 2011) pp. 314–16
12 Alex Kaplan, 'Here are the QAnon supporters running for Congress in 2022', Media Matters for America (2 June 2021)
13 David Lawrence & Gregory Davis, *QAnon in the UK: The Growth of a Movement* (Hope Not Hate Charitable Trust, October 2020) p. 29; *State of Hate 2022: On the March Again* (Hope Not Hate, 2022) p. 53
14 John Carlin, '"Some Jews are bloodsuckers", says man who plans to lead black rally', *The Independent* (14 October 1995); David D. Kirkpatrick, 'Morsi's Slurs Against Jews Stir Concern', *New York Times* (14 January 2013)
15 'West wants to make Iranians disappointed by system, Islam – Supreme Leader', Voice of the Islamic Republic of Iran (16 February 2012) translated by BBC Monitoring
16 Jacob Jefferson [@jojefferson99], 'Placard at today's Palestinian protest at Warwick University. Difficult to justify how that's not anti-Semitic.', Twitter (21 May 2021), available at https://twitter.com/jojefferson99/status/1395742974064136193
17 Carlos Latuff, 'Gaza in Blood and Fire' (2006), available at https://commons.wikimedia.org/wiki/File:Latuff4.jpg
18 'Missing Algerian children had their organs removed', *alMarada* (6 September 2009), translation from Political Theatrics website
19 'New Jewish organ theft gang busted', Press TV (9 September 2009)
20 Anthony Julius, *Trials of the Diaspora: A History of Anti-Semitism in England* (Oxford University Press, 2010) p. 90
21 Cecil Roth, ed., *The Ritual Murder Libel and the Jew* (Woburn Press, 1934) pp. 101–2
22 Monty Noam Penkower, 'The Kishinev Pogrom of 1903: A Turning Point in Jewish History', *Modern Judaism*, vol. 24, no. 3 (October 2004) pp. 187–225
23 Raed Salah Mahajna v The Secretary of State for the Home Department (2012), Upper Tribunal (Immigration and Asylum Chamber) Appeal Number: IA/21631/2011, paras 49–59
24 George Orwell, 'Antisemitism in Britain', *Contemporary Jewish Record*, vol. 8, no. 2 (April 1945) pp. 163–71
25 Geoffrey Chaucer, *The Canterbury Tales* (Guild Publishing, 1986) pp. 109–13
26 Simon Schama, *The Story of the Jews: Finding the Words 1000 BCE – 1492 CE* (Vintage, 2014) p. 325
27 'Fourth Lateran Council: 1215', Papal Encyclicals Online, available at https://www.papalencyclicals.net/councils/ecum12-2.htm
28 'De Montfort University students call for "anti-Semitic" name to go', BBC News (19 November 2020)

CHAPTER FOUR: CARS, CONSPIRACIES AND COVID

1   Henry Ford, *The International Jew – The World's Foremost Problem: Aspects of Jewish Power in the United States* (CreateSpace Publishing, 2016), available at https://www.barnesandnoble.com/w/the-international-jew-the-worlds-foremost-problem-henry-ford/1123708867?ean=9781532850271
2   Henry Ford, *The International Jew: The World's Foremost Problem* (Manuscript Wisdom Resources, 2008), p. 541
3   Ibid.
4   'Deadly Shooting at Pittsburgh Synagogue', Anti-Defamation League (27 October 2018); Lois Beckett, 'Pittsburgh shooting: suspect railed against Jews and Muslims on site used by "alt-right"', *The Guardian* (27 October 2018); Criminal Complaint, United States of America v Robert Bowers (27 October 2018)
5   Jean-Paul Sartre, *Anti-Semite and Jew*, trans. George J. Becker (Schocken Books, 1976), p. 28
6   *From #CoronaVirusCoverUp to #NukeChina: An analysis of conspiracy theories, hate speech and incitements to violence across Twitter related to Covid-19* (Moonshot, April 2020), p. 5
7   *From anti-vaxxers to antisemitism: Conspiracy theory in the COVID-19 pandemic* (The Office of HM Government's Independent Adviser on Antisemitism, Oct 2020), pp. 5–7
8   *The Rise of Antisemitism Online During the Pandemic: A Study of French and German Content* (Institute for Strategic Dialogue, June 2021), p. 8
9   Emma Yeomans, Anna Lombardi, Ali Mitib, 'Kill health workers, antivax campaigners demand in Telegram chats', *The Times* (10 January 2022)
10 *Antisemitic Incidents Report 2021* (Community Security Trust, 2021)
11 Nico Voigtländer & Hans-Joachim Voth, 'Persecution Perpetuated: The Medieval Origins of Anti-Semitic Violence in Nazi Germany', *The Quarterly Journal of Economics*, vol. 127, no. 3 (August 2012), pp. 1339–92

NOTES

12. Norman Cohn, *Warrant for Genocide: The myth of the Jewish world conspiracy and the Protocols of the Elders of Zion* (Eyre & Spottiswoode, 1967), p. 17
13. Norman Cohn, *Warrant for Genocide: The myth of the Jewish world conspiracy and the Protocols of the Elders of Zion* (Serif, 1996), p. 134
14. Ibid., p. 149
15. Ibid., p. 168
16. Tony Kushner, *The Persistence of Prejudice: Antisemitism in British society during the Second World War* (Manchester University Press, 1989), pp. 112–13
17. Adolf Hitler, *Mein Kampf*, trans. James Murphy (Hurst and Blackett, 1942), p. 174
18. Norman Cohn, *Warrant for Genocide* (Serif, 1996), p. 151
19. Randall L. Bytwerk, 'Believing in "Inner Truth": The Protocols of the Elders of Zion in Nazi Propaganda, 1933–1945', *Holocaust and Genocide Studies*, vol. 29, no. 2, 212–29
20. 'The Great Reset', World Economic Forum, available at https://www.weforum.org/great-reset/
21. Jamie Bartlett & Carl Miller, *The Power of Unreason: Conspiracy Theories, Extremism and Counter-Terrorism* (Demos, August 2010), p. 21
22. Dr Ghulam Farid Bhatti, *Zionism and Internal Security* (Islamic Publications Ltd, 1984)
23. David Icke, *The Robots' Rebellion: The Story of the Spiritual Renaissance* (Gateway Books, 1994), p. 138
24. Mark Dankof, 'Empire continues to sweat over Press TV', Press TV (25 May 2011)
25. Hamas Covenant 1988, 'The Covenant of the Islamic Resistance Movement', Yale Law School: Lillian Goldman Law Library (18 August 1988), available at https://avalon.law.yale.edu/20th_century/hamas.asp
26. Vasily Grossman, *Life and Fate* (Vintage Classics, 2006), p. 468
27. Elisabeth Zerofsky, 'Viktor Orbán's far-right vision for Europe', *New Yorker* (7 January 2019)
28. András Tóth-Czifra (@NoYardstick), 'So you're shocked and appalled by Viktor Orban's speech today, in which he talked about Hungarians not being "mixed-race"', Twitter (23 July 2022), available at https://twitter.com/NoYardstick/status/1550965162911449090. See the whole thread for the multiple times Orbán has expressed this idea.
29. 'Hungary passes anti-immigrant "Stop Soros" laws', *The Guardian* (20 June 2018)
30. Robert Tait & Flora Garamvolgyi, 'Viktor Orbán wins fourth consecutive term as Hungary's prime minister', *The Guardian* (3 April 2022)
31. 'PM Orbán: Hungarians Can Only Survive as Christians, Each New Church "Bastion in Nation's Struggle for Freedom and Greatness"', *Hungary Today* (27 September 2021); original text of speech available at https://miniszterelnok.hu/orban-viktor-beszede-az-osszetartozas-templomanak-szentelesen/
32. David Smith, 'Orbán urges Christian nationalists in Europe and US to "unite forces" at CPAC', *The Guardian* (4 August 2022)
33. Hannes Grassegger, 'The Unbelievable Story Of The Plot Against George Soros', Buzzfeed News (20 January 2019)
34. David Lawrence, 'Inside David Icke's Watford Talk', Hope Not Hate (26 November 2018)
35. Peter Walker, 'Farage criticised for using antisemitic themes to criticise Soros', *The Guardian* (12 May 2019); OrionPrime, 'Nigel Farage & Katie Hopkins: George Soros/Tommy Robinson on Tucker Carlson Tonight', YouTube (31 May 2018), available at https://youtu.be/ON8fnPgsdno?t=85
36. Leave.EU (@LeaveEUOfficial), 'WATCH | @Nigel_Farage at @CPAC on George Soros: "He is attempting to intervene in every single election and cause across the Western…"', Twitter (23 February 2018), available at https://twitter.com/LeaveEUOfficial/status/967158112707858432
37. Leave.EU (@LeaveEUOfficial), 'READ | Globalist billionaire George Soros pledges another £100,000 of his foreign money to overturn Brexit – and still we get silence…', Twitter (12 February 2018), available at https://twitter.com/LeaveEUOfficial/status/962991143389671426
38. Leave.EU (@LeaveEUOfficial), 'The face of the People's Vote campaign. Support us at http://leave.eu/get-involved', Twitter (12 October 2018), available at https://twitter.com/LeaveEUOfficial/status/1050687525218643968
39. 'Jews, Zionism and Islamophobia', *Antisemitic Discourse in Britain in 2011* (Community Security Trust, 2012), pp. 26–8
40. Jamie Doward, Toby Helm & Jonah Ramchandan, 'Second MP investigated in row over Labour's antisemitism code', *The Observer* (28 July 2018)
41. The Golem (@TheGolem_), 'EXCLUSIVE – In January 2012 @JeremyCorbyn gave an interview in Parliament to an antisemitic conspiracy theorist in which he agreed that…', Twitter (31 January 2019), available at https://twitter.com/TheGolem_/status/1090995532603027456?s=20
42. Khamenei.ir (@khamenei_ir), 'Today, #Zionism is an obvious plague for the world of #Islam. The Zionists have always been a plague, even before…', Twitter (8 June 2022), available at https://twitter.com/khamenei_ir/status/1534481981681111041

43 Khamenei.ir (@khamenei_ir), 'The Western powers are a mafia. The reality of this power is a mafia. At the top of this mafia...', Twitter (27 July 2022), available at https://twitter.com/khamenei_ir/status/1552262175674322949
44 Palestine Declassified (@PDeclassified), 'Special report on Bradford Literature Festival's disturbing funding sources (Part 1)', Twitter (23 June 2022), available at https://twitter.com/PDeclassified/status/1536210506532458496
45 Palestine Declassified (@PDeclassified), 'Academic @Tracking_Power says Twitter takes advice from the groups that are "apologist for Zionist crimes"', Twitter (22 July 2022), available at https://twitter.com/PDeclassified/status/1550384566996803584
46 Palestine Declassified (@PDeclassified), 'Academic @Tracking_Power touches on how the Zionist movement controls the music industry.', Twitter (21 March 2022), available at https://twitter.com/PDeclassified/status/1505850312623538178
47 Harry's Place, 'Prof David Miller from Bristol University "The enemy we face here is Zionism"', YouTube (15 February 2021), available at https://www.youtube.com/watch?v=zrAlJl73NCQ; Ben Bloch (on annual leave) (@realBenBloch), 'I just received this disgusting statement from David Miller, a lecturer at @BristolUni. @TheTab could not publish it in full...', Twitter (18 February 2021), available at https://twitter.com/realBenBloch/status/1362432493593505796
48 IHRCtv, 'Islamophobia Conference 2021 – Day 1 – 11.12.21', YouTube (11 December 2021), available at https://youtu.be/EUiAfMAXxlQ
49 Paul McKeigue, David Miller & Piers Robinson, *Assessment by the engineering sub-team of the OPCW Fact-Finding Mission investigating the alleged chemical attack in Douma in April 2018* (Working Group on Syria, Propaganda and Media, 13 May 2019)
50 Paul McKeigue, David Miller & Piers Robinson, 'Briefing Note: Update on the Salisbury poisonings', Working Group on Syria, Propaganda and Media (10 May 2018)
51 Harry's Place (@hurryupharry), 'Miller: "The theatre, which appears to also have been a false flag attack, something that was dreamt up by Azov."...', Twitter (31 March 2022), available at https://twitter.com/hurryupharry/status/1509526257226039299
52 All letters available at https://supportmiller.org/
53 Colin Shindler, *Israel and the European Left: Between Solidarity and Delegitimization* (Continuum, 2012), p. 33
54 Avi Shlaim, 'Anti-Zionism and anti-Semitism in British politics', *Al Jazeera* (12 January 2017)
55 'About Us', Free Speech on Israel (8 January 2017); 'Free Speech on Israel Submission to the Chakrabarti Inquiry', Free Speech on Israel (8 June 2016)
56 Jonathan Rosenhead, 'Building an alternative voice', *Labour Briefing* (24 April 2018); Daniel Sugarman, 'JVL activist blames 'Zionists' for Shoah deaths', *Jewish Chronicle* (2 May 2018)
57 Mike Cushman, 'Al Jazeera lifts the lid on the swamp of Israeli subversion', Free Speech on Israel (17 January 2017)
58 *Investigation into antisemitism in the Labour Party*, Equality and Human Rights Commission (October 2020), p. 8
59 Martin Forde QC, *The Forde Report* (Labour Party National Executive Committee, 19 July 2022), pp. 37, 50
60 *The work of the Labour Party's Governance and Legal Unit in relation to antisemitism, 2014–2019*, The Labour Party (March 2020), p. 11
61 Peter Beaumont, 'Netanyahu's son Yair draws fire after posting "antisemitic cartoon"', *The Guardian* (13 September 2017)
62 Jean-Paul Sartre, *Anti-Semite and Jew* (Schocken Books, 1976), pp. 92–4
63 Claire Hirshfield, 'The Anglo-Boer War and the Issue of Jewish Culpability', *Journal of Contemporary History*, vol. 15, no. 4 (October 1980), pp. 619–31
64 The Nation of Islam, *The Secret Relationship Between Blacks and Jews vol. 1* (The Nation of Islam, 1991), p. vii; for the response from the American Historical Association see AHA Staff, 'AHA Council issues policy resolution about Jews and the slave trade', *Perspectives On History* (1 March 1995)
65 'Full text: bin Laden's "Letter to America"', *The Observer* (24 November 2002)
66 Paul Foot, 'Worse than Thatcher', *The Guardian* (14 May 2003)
67 The National Archives: Public Record Office, Kew (TNA: PRO) FCO/17/1763, FCO/51/297
68 Victor E. Marsden trans., *The Protocols of the Meetings of the Learned Elders of Zion* (Bloomfield Books, undated) pp. 41–2

CHAPTER FIVE: ALIENS AND THEIR FAMILIES

1 Julia Llewellyn Smith, 'Michael Bond: "I was worried that I'd let Paddington down..."', *Sunday Telegraph* (23 November 2014)
2 Paul King, *Paddington*, Heyday Films, StudioCanal, TF1 Films Production (2014)

NOTES

3 Louise London, *Whitehall and the Jews 1933-1948: British Immigration Policy, Jewish Refugees and the Holocaust* (Cambridge University Press, 2000), pp. 118–21
4 Tony Kushner, *The Holocaust and the Liberal Imagination: A Social and Cultural History* (Blackwell, 1994), pp. 61–2
5 Tony Kushner, *The Persistence of Prejudice: Antisemitism in British society during the Second World War* (Manchester University Press, 1989), pp. 143–51
6 Simon Parkin, '"I remember the feeling of insult": when Britain imprisoned its wartime refugees', *The Guardian* (1 February 2022)
7 TNA:PRO HO/405/50818
8 Daniel Sonabend, *We Fight Fascists: The 43 Group and Their Forgotten Battle for Post-war Britain* (Verso, 2019), p. 99
9 TNA:PRO/KV/25 & KV/26
10 Sam Coates, 'Official denied that alien image posted by Labour activist Kayla Bibby was antisemitic', *The Times* (October 2019)
11 *Royal Commission on Alien Immigration. Minutes of Evidence Taken Before the Royal Commission on Alien Immigration*, Command Paper 1742, Vol. II, 1903, pp. 19, 22
12 Ibid., p. 66
13 Ibid., p. 128
14 'Alien Immigration Commission', *The Times*, 7 May 1903
15 Winston Churchill, 'Zionism versus Bolshevism', *Illustrated Sunday Herald* (8 February 1920); Museum of Tolerance, 'Hitler Letter (Original in German)', available at https://www.museumoftolerance.com/assets/documents/hitler-letter-handout-1.pdf
16 Hansard, 'Mr. Jacob's Report on the Trade in Corn, and on the Agriculture of Northern Europe', 20 April 1826, Second Series, vol. 15, col. 397
17 Nicholas Fondacaro (@NickFondacaro), 'Sparks fly as The View panel confronts Whoopi after she says "the Holocaust isn't about race. No. It's not about…"', Twitter (31 January 2022), available at https://twitter.com/NickFondacaro/status/1488191258598199301; Dan O'Donnell (@DanODonnellShow), 'Stephen Colbert: The Nazis would say it's a racial issue. Whoopi: This is what's interesting to me because the Nazis lied…', Twitter (1 February 2022), available at https://twitter.com/DanODonnellShow/status/1488508181605228546
18 Anthony S. Wohl, '"Dizzi-Ben-Dizzi": Disraeli as Alien', *Journal of British Studies*, vol. 34, no. 3 (July 1995), pp. 375–411; Phyllis Goldstein, *A Convenient Hatred: The History of Antisemitism* (Facing History and Ourselves, 2012), pp. 29–220
19 'Past Prime Ministers: Benjamin Disraeli, the Earl of Beaconsfield', gov.uk, available at https://www.gov.uk/government/history/past-prime-ministers/benjamin-disraeli-the-earl-of-beaconsfield
20 Rebecca Lees, *Who Were the First MPs from Ethnic Minority Backgrounds?* (House of Commons Library, 28 October 2020); Elise Uberoi & Matthew Burton, *Ethnic Diversity in Politics and Public Life* (House of Commons Library, 30 September 2022)
21 'Britain's most ethnically diverse Cabinet ever', Diversity UK (25 July 2019); see also 'About Us', Diversity UK, available at https://diversityuk.org/about-us/
22 'List of ethnic groups', gov.uk, available at https://www.ethnicity-facts-figures.service.gov.uk/style-guide/ethnic-groups
23 Hansard, HC, 3 May 1965, vol. 711, col. 933; Didi Herman, *An Unfortunate Coincidence: Jews, Jewishness, and English Law* (Oxford University Press, 2011). Chapter Six has a fuller exploration of these debates.
24 Sergio DellaPergola & L. Daniel Staetsky, *The Jewish identities of European Jews: What, why and how* (Institute for Jewish Policy Research, 2021), pp. 21–2
25 Martin Bright, 'Jewish envoy not loyal to UK, says Labour MP', *Jewish Chronicle* (1 December 2011)
26 Oliver Miles, 'The key question: is Blair a war criminal?' *The Independent* (22 November 2009)
27 Richard Ingrams, 'Will Zionists' links to Iraq invasion be brushed aside?', *The Independent* (28 November 2009)
28 Richard Ingrams, 'I'm still on the train', *The Observer* (13 July 2003)
29 Jenni Frazer, '"Suits and good English" help Israelis on TV', *Jewish Chronicle* (25 June 2004)
30 Sir James Craig, *Shemlan: A History of the Middle East Centre for Arab Studies* (Palgrave Macmillan, 1998), pp. 116–21
31 Jake Wallis Simons, 'EXCLUSIVE: Jeremy Corbyn said British "Zionists" have "no sense of English irony despite having lived here all their lives" and "need a lesson", while giving speech alongside Islamic extremists at a conference publicised by Hamas' military wing', Mail Online (23 August 2018)

CHAPTER SIX: NEVER AGAIN

1 Antony Beevor ed. *A Writer At War: Vasily Grossman with the Red Army 1941–1945*, trans. Luba Vinogradova (Pimlico, 2006), p. 301

2   Theodor W. Adorno, *Negative Dialectics* (Routledge & Kegan Paul, 1973), p. 365
3   Jacqueline Borin, 'Embers of the Soul: The Destruction of Jewish Books and Libraries in Poland during World War II', *Libraries & Culture*, vol. 28, no. 4, pp. 445–60 (p. 457)
4   'Extract from the Speech by Adolf Hitler, January 30, 1939', Yad Vashem, available at https://www.yadvashem.org/docs/extract-from-hitler-speech.html
5   David Nirenberg, *Anti-Judaism: The History of a Way of Thinking* (Head of Zeus, 2013), p. 458
6   Amos Elon, *The Pity of It All: A Portrait of the German-Jewish Epoch, 1743–1933* (Picador, 2003), p. 119
7   Yahad in Unim, available at https://yiu.ngo/en
8   Christopher R. Browning, *Ordinary Men: Reserve Police Battalion 101 and the Final Solution in Poland* (Penguin Books, 2001), p. 164
9   Ibid., p. 170
10 Ibid., p. 184
11 Theodor W. Adorno, *Minima Moralia: Reflections from Damaged Life* (Verso, 2020), p. 248
12 Primo Levi, *The Drowned and the Saved* (Abacus, 1988), ch. 2
13 Laurence Rees, *The Holocaust: A New History* (Penguin, 2017), p. 351
14 Trần Thị Thanh Huyền, 'Story of Nicholas Winton BBC That's life – Short version', YouTube (23 November 2017), available at https://www.youtube.com/watch?v=PKkgO06bAZk
15 'Address by the President of the Russian Federation', Website of the President of Russia (24 February 2022)
16 Ofer Aderet, 'Et Tu, Lavrov? The Bountiful Conspiracies About Hitler's Jewish Blood', *Haaretz* (2 May 2022)
17 Brendan McGeever, 'Putin's War and Jewish History', Verso (25 March 2022)
18 *Zionism: Instrument of Imperialist Reaction* (Novosti Press Agency, 1970), p. 49
19 Ibid., p. 67
20 Dmitry Medvedev, 'Why contacts with the current Ukrainian leadership are pointless', *Kommersant* (11 October 2021)
21 Howard J. Ehrlich, 'The Swastika Epidemic of 1959–1960: Anti-Semitism and Community Characteristics', *Social Problems*, vol. 9, no. 3, pp. 264–72
22 'Vandalism in many cities', *Jewish Chronicle* (8 January 1960)
23 'Nazi infection persists', *Jewish Chronicle* (1 January 1960)
24 Thomas Rid, *Active Measures: The Secret History of Disinformation and Political Warfare* (Profile Books, 2021), ch. 9
25 ALASTAIR CAMPBELL (@campbellclaret), 'Der Sturmer', Twitter (4 August 2018), available at https://twitter.com/campbellclaret/status/1025831362576695299; ALASTAIR CAMPBELL (@campbellclaret), 'Der Sturmer. Look it up.', Twitter (28 September 2019), available at https://twitter.com/campbellclaret/status/1178068976221528065; ALASTAIR CAMPBELL (@campbellclaret), 'Popped out to buy some milk. Spotted Daily Mail front page, desperately, so desperately, trying to keep equating @Keir_Starmer having...', Twitter (30 April 2022), available at https://twitter.com/campbellclaret/status/1520307466403303424
26 'Joey Barton apologises for comparing Bristol Rovers displays to Holocaust', *The Guardian* (28 October 2021)
27 oGeMmAo, 'The Young Ones – Summer Holiday – Part 3', YouTube (11 April 2009), available at https://youtu.be/K0OD6RCb1II?t=311
28 Philippe Sands, *East West Street* (Weidenfeld & Nicolson, 2016), p. 111
29 For more details on this phenomenon, see Philip Spencer, 'Imperialism, Anti-Imperialism and the Problem of Genocide, Past and Present', *History*, vol. 98, no. 4 (October 2013), pp. 606–22; also Ben Cohen and Eve Garrard eds., *The Norman Geras Reader: 'What's there is there'* (Manchester University Press, 2017), ch. 9
30 Alvin H. Rosenfeld, *The End of the Holocaust* (Indiana University Press, 2011), p. 96
31 aleXsandro Palombo (@alexsandropalombo), image of Anne Frank burning a Russian military flag in Ukrainian colours, Instagram (24 March 2022), available at https://www.instagram.com/p/CbfduvGMmFQ/
32 Gidon Ben-Zvi, 'Dutch BDS Twitter Account Using Image of Anne Frank in Keffiyeh', *The Algemeiner* (2 January 2014)
33 Frank Csongos, 'World: "Anne Frank of Sarajevo" Presents Voices of War', Radio Free Europe Radio Liberty (26 January 2007)
34 L. R. Knost (@lrknost), screenshot of a tweet about the conditions at a border, Instagram (15 July 2019), available at https://www.instagram.com/p/Bz7HdueH4j7/c/18056847259093568/
35 Angelica Stabile, 'Mark Levin: how many Anne Franks are in Afghanistan tonight?' Fox News (2 September 2021)
36 Marni Dixit, 'Gym owner's Anne Frank comparison sparks fury online', Yahoo! Lifestyle (9 November 2020)

NOTES

37 'Robert F Kennedy Jr apologizes for Anne Frank comparison in anti-vax speech', *The Guardian* (25 January 2022)
38 Emily Goddard, 'Newspaper deletes article comparing Covid lockdown to Anne Frank's hiding from Nazis', *The Independent* (6 March 2021)
39 'North-east Pupils past and present share their stories', Aberdeenshire Council (6 August 2021)
40 Nathan Englander, *What We Talk About When We Talk About Anne Frank* (Weidenfeld & Nicolson, 2012) Kindle edition
41 Laurence Rees, *The Holocaust: A New History* (Penguin, 2017), pp. 129–36; 'Teaching Resources', facinghistory.org, available at https://www.facinghistory.org/resource-library/text/statements-representatives-evian-conference-july-1938
42 Sergio DellaPergola & L. Daniel Staetsky, *The Jewish identities of European Jews: What, why and how* (Institute for Jewish Policy Research, December 2021), p. 26
43 Howard Jacobson, *Kalooki Nights* (Vintage, 2007), p. 49
44 'Abba Kovner', Holocaust Encyclopedia, available at https://encyclopedia.ushmm.org/content/en/article/abba-kovner
45 Steven Spielberg, *Schindler's List*, Amblin Entertainment, Universal Pictures (1993)

CHAPTER SEVEN: JERUSALEM

1 David Aukin, Poppy Burton-Morgan, Leo Butler et al., 'Dismay at Globe invitation to Israeli theatre', *The Guardian* (29 March 2012)
2 Jennifer Lipman, 'Theatre ban "like Nazi book burning" say West End stars', *Jewish Chronicle* (4 April 2012)
3 Shakespeare's Globe, 'Dear Boycott from Within, Thank you for your open letter on the subject of the Hebrew-language Merchant of Venice...', Facebook (6 January 2012), available at https://www.facebook.com/ShakespearesGlobe/posts/10150584097455774
4 Louis Chilton, 'Sally Rooney confirms she turned down Israeli publisher in solidarity with Palestinians', *The Independent* (12 October 2021)
5 'Thousands march on Israeli embassy in London in "free Palestine" protest as marches of solidarity held worldwide', ITV News (16 May 2021)
6 Nicola Slawson, 'Thousands gather in London for Palestine solidarity march', *The Guardian* (22 May 2021)
7 'Nine officers hurt during Gaza violence protests in London', BBC News (16 May 2021)
8 The Zionist (@The_Zionist1), 'At the #FreePalestine demonstration in London today cries of: "Khayber Khayber Ya Yehud jaish Mohammad Sauf Ya'ud" (Khaybar Khaybar...', Twitter (15 May 2021), available at https://twitter.com/The_Zionist1/status/1393559694023725056
9 Self Declared Zionists (@SussexFriends), 'UNBELIEVABLE! "F**k the Jews" "F**k their daughters" "F**k their mothers" "Rape their daughters" "Free Palestine" Finchley Road, London, this afternoon!', Twitter (16 May 2021), available at https://twitter.com/SussexFriends/status/1393925736851984385
10 'Yemen: Why is the war there getting more violent?', BBC News (22 March 2022)
11 Data from Metropolitan Police hate crime dashboard, available at https://public.tableau.com/app/profile/metropolitan.police.service/viz/MonthlyCrimeDataNewCats/Coversheet
12 Association of Chief Police Officers, 'ACPO: Total of recorded hate crime in England, Wales and Northern Ireland by police force area, 2013/14', report-it.org, available at https://www.report-it.org.uk/files/acpo_recorded_hate_crime_201314_as_posted.pdf; The National Police Chiefs Council, 'Hate Crime Data NPCC 2014-15', report-it.org, available at https://www.report-it.org.uk/files/hate_crime_data_npcc_2014-15.pdf
13 'Jailed and Wanted Journalists in Turkey – Updated List', Stockholm Center for Freedom, accessed 9 July 2022, available at https://stockholmcf.org/updated-list/
14 Harriet Sherwood, 'Mahmoud Abbas accused of being traitor over rejection of Israel boycott', *The Guardian* (21 December 2013)
15 Mehdi Hasan, 'We Single Israel Out Because We in the West Are Shamefully Complicit in Its Crimes', *Huffington Post* (16 July 2014)
16 L. Daniel Staetsky, *Antisemitism in contemporary Great Britain: A study of attitudes towards Jews and Israel* (Institute for Jewish Policy Research, September 2017), pp. 5, 37
17 David Graham & Jonathan Boyd, *The apartheid contention and calls for a boycott: Examining hostility towards Israel in Great Britain* (Institute for Jewish Policy Research, 2019), p. 12
18 Jonathan Fox & Lev Topor, *Why Do People Discriminate against Jews?* (Oxford University Press, 2021), p. 184
19 'Aims, Constitution and Code of Conduct', Stop the War Coalition, available at https://www.stopwar.org.uk/aims-constitution-code-of-conduct/
20 '2nd Cairo Declaration: With the Palestinian and Iraqi Resistance – Against Capitalist Globalization

and US Hegemony', Stop the War Coalition (14 December 2003), available at http://web.archive.org/web/20040603223147/https://www.stopwar.org.uk/article.asp?id=141203
21 Brian Eno, 'In a world of horrors, why I single out the war crimes of Israel', Stop the War Coalition (5 August 2014)
22 Richard Kuper, 'Singling Out Israel', *Red Pepper* (January 2006)
23 Norman Cohn, *The Pursuit of the Millennium* (Pimlico, 1993), p. 64
24 Simon Sebag Montefiore, *Jerusalem: The Biography* (Phoenix, 2012), p. xxv
25 Early Day Motions 3, *Violence perpetrated by Israeli authorities against Palestinian civilians in Sheikh Jarrah* (11 May 2021)
26 'Head Office Circular NP/153/21: National Day of Action for Palestine – Saturday 15th May', RMT (13 May 2021)
27 Avi Bell & Eugene Kontorovich, 'Almost Nothing You've Heard About Evictions in Jerusalem Is True', *Wall Street Journal* (14 May 2021); Tareq Baconi, 'Sheikh Jarrah and after', *London Review of Books* (14 May 2021)
28 Tom Holland, *Dominion: The Making of the Western Mind* (Abacus, 2019), p. 356
29 Simon Schama, *Belonging: The Story of the Jews 1492–1900* (Bodley Head, 2017), pp. 393–4
30 Martin Woollacott, 'Now Europeans see Israel as a threat to their existence', *The Guardian* (7 November 2003)
31 Daphna Baram, *Disenchantment: The Guardian and Israel* (Guardian Books, 2004), p. 235
32 David Aaronovitch, 'A debate of the deaf poisoning young minds', *The Times* (21 November 2006)
33 Ben Cohen, '"We Haven't Shown Enough Outrage:" French PM Issues Blistering Denunciation of Antisemitism', *The Algemeiner* (14 January 2015)
34 Alexandra Pollard, 'Maxine Peake: "People who couldn't vote Labour because of Corbyn? They voted Tory as far as I'm concerned"', *The Independent* (25 June 2020)
35 'A Letter Against Apartheid', Against Apartheid, available at https://www.againstapartheid.com/
36 Jonas Fossli Gjersø, 'Israel – the last of the settler colonies', Open Democracy (10 September 2014)
37 Asa Winstanley, 'Why Israel is a settler-colony', *Middle East Monitor* (23 January 2021)
38 Elior Levy, 'PA President Abbas: "Israel a colonial project, has nothing to do with Jews"', *Ynet News* (14 January 2018)
39 Zeev Sternhell, 'In Defence of Liberal Zionism', *New Left Review*, no. 62 (Mar/Apr 2010)
40 'The Farhud', Holocaust Encyclopedia, available at https://encyclopedia.ushmm.org/content/en/article/the-farhud
41 Caryl Churchill, 'Read Caryl Churchill's Seven Jewish Children', *The Guardian* (26 February 2009)
42 Caryl Churchill, 'My play is not anti-Semitic', *The Independent* (21 February 2009)
43 Bernard Harrison, *The Resurgence of Anti-Semitism: Jews, Israel and Liberal Opinion* (Rowman & Littlefield, 2006), p. 155
44 'Hamas in 2017: The document in full', *Middle East Eye* (2 May 2017)
45 Amir Vahdat & Jon Gambrell, 'Iran leader says Israel a "cancerous tumor" to be destroyed', AP News (22 May 2020)
46 Rusi Jaspal, 'Antisemitism and anti-Zionism in the British Pakistani Muslim community', in Jonathan G. Campbell & Lesley D. Klaff eds. *Unity and Diversity in Contemporary Antisemitism: The Bristol–Sheffield Hallam Colloquium on Contemporary Antisemitism* (Academic Studies Press, 2019), pp. 156–84
47 Bernard Lewis, *Semites & Anti-Semites* (Weidenfeld & Nicolson, 1997), p. 121
48 'Chapter 3. Views of Religious Groups', Pew Research Center (4 February 2010), available at https://www.pewresearch.org/global/2010/02/04/chapter-3-views-of-religious-groups/
49 L. Daniel Staetsky, *Antisemitism in contemporary Great Britain: A study of attitudes towards Jews and Israel* (Institute for Jewish Policy Research, September 2017), p. 64
50 The Anti-Defamation League, 'The ADL Global 100' (2019), available at https://global100.adl.org/country/united-kingdom/2019
51 L. Daniel Staetsky, *Antisemitism in contemporary Great Britain: A study of attitudes towards Jews and Israel* (Institute for Jewish Policy Research, September 2017), p. 60
52 Rusi Jaspal, *Antisemitism and Anti-Zionism: Representation, Cognition and Everyday Talk* (Routledge, 2014), p. 166
53 Ibid., p. 241, emphasis in the original
54 Ibid., p. 168
55 Hna Fi Hna, 'Journalist Seumas Milne | The Guardian, "Palestinians have every right to defend themselves."', YouTube (24 November 2012), available at https://youtu.be/1EBjlQ-PI7g?t=188
56 Inminds, 'Gaza Flotilla Massacre: London Demo – Jeremy Corbyn [inminds]', YouTube (3 June 2010), available at https://youtu.be/vQLYXJUH2uY?t=295

NOTES

57 Jean-Paul Sartre, *Anti-Semite and Jew*, trans. George J. Becker (Schocken Books, 1976), p. 10, emphasis in the original

CHAPTER EIGHT: THINGS CAN'T ONLY GET BETTER

1 Lizzie Dearden, 'One of UK's youngest terror plotters named after losing anonymity battle', *The Independent* (11 January 2021)
2 '"Terror threat" boy spared custody over synagogue bomb Twitter post', BBC News (27 April 2022)
3 I have several examples of this slogan being used on 4chan, Gab and Telegram, but I'm not going to include links to extremist content here.
4 'National statistics: Operation of police powers under the Terrorism Act 2000 and subsequent legislation: Arrests, outcomes, and stop and search, Great Britain, quarterly update to March 2022', gov.uk (9 June 2022), available at https://www.gov.uk/government/statistics/operation-of-police-powers-under-the-terrorism-act-2000-quarterly-update-to-march-2022/operation-of-police-powers-under-the-terrorism-act-2000-and-subsequent-legislation-arrests-outcomes-and-stop-and-search-great-britain-quarterly-u
5 David Lawrence & Gregory Davis, *QAnon in the UK: The Growth of a Movement* (Hope Not Hate Charitable Trust, October 2020), p. 29
6 *Fear and Hope 2022: A Realignment Of Identity Politics* (Hope Not Hate Charitable Trust, 16 August 2022), pp. 38–9
7 NatCen Social Research, '30 Years of British Social Attitudes self-reported racial prejudice data', available at https://www.bsa.natcen.ac.uk/media/38110/selfreported-racial-prejudice-datafinal.pdf
8 Attitudes to race and inequality in Great Britain, Ipsos (15 June 2020)
9 Sunder Katwala, *Race and opportunity in Britain: Finding common ground* (British Future, March 2021), p. 22 & *Fear and Hope 2022: A Realignment Of Identity Politics* (Hope Not Hate Charitable Trust, August 2022), p. 37
10 'YouGov / KCL Survey Results', YouGov (2019), available at https://d25d2506sfb94s.cloudfront.net/cumulus_uploads/document/6lybmr9kty/KCL_Antisemitism_190925%20%28002%29.pdf
11 David Lawrence & Gregory Davis, *QAnon in the UK: The Growth of a Movement* (Hope Not Hate Charitable Trust, October 2020), p. 30
12 *Fear and Hope 2022: A Realignment Of Identity Politics* (Hope Not Hate Charitable Trust, July 2022), p. 38
13 Sarah Sands & Joe Murphy, 'Sadiq Khan: My two daughters have rights here – and they can wear what they like', *Evening Standard* (14 April 2016)
14 *Young Jewish Europeans: perceptions and experiences of antisemitism* (European Union Agency for Fundamental Rights, 2019), p. 26
15 Charlotte Littlewood, *Antisemitism in Schools* (Henry Jackson Society, 2022), p. 12
16 L. Daniel Staetsky & Jonathan Boyd, *The rise and rise of Jewish schools in the United Kingdom: Numbers, trends and policy issues* (Institute for Jewish Policy Research, 2016), pp. 6–7
17 Thomas F. Pettigrew & Linda R. Tropp, 'A meta-analytic test of intergroup contact theory', *Journal of Personality and Social Psychology*, vol. 90, no. 5 (May 2006), pp. 751–83 (p. 766)
18 Antisemitic Incidents Report 2021 (Community Security Trust, 2022), p. 32
19 David Rose, '"My daughter was driven out of her school by antisemitic bullying"', *Jewish Chronicle* (14 July 2022)
20 *Young Jewish Europeans: perceptions and experiences of antisemitism* (European Union Agency for Fundamental Rights, July 2019), p. 19
21 Sunder Katwala, *Race and opportunity in Britain: Finding common ground* (British Future, March 2021), p. 22
22 Paul Mason, 'How Labour can fight back against the British establishment's attempt to destroy it', *New Statesman* (4 April 2018)
23 'YouGov / KCL Survey Results', YouGov (2019), available at https://d25d2506sfb94s.cloudfront.net/cumulus_uploads/document/6lybmr9kty/KCL_Antisemitism_190925%20%28002%29.pdf
24 *Instagram: Bad Influence* (Community Security Trust & Antisemitism Policy Trust, 2021), p. 5
25 *News Consumption in the UK: 2022* (Ofcom, 21 July 2022), pp. 7, 10
26 'YouGov / KCL Survey Results', YouGov (2019), available at https://d25d2506sfb94s.cloudfront.net/cumulus_uploads/document/6lybmr9kty/KCL_Antisemitism_190925%20%28002%29.pdf
27 'King's College London/BBC Panorama – Disaster Deniers Survey 2022', Savanta ComRes (31 October 2022), available at https://savanta.com/wp-content/uploads/2022/11/Omni_KCL-BBC_W1-and-W2_v3.xlsx
28 Katie Gibbons, 'Pro-Brexit "Twitter bot" suspended', *The Times* (23 November 2017)
29 *Antisemitic Discourse in Britain 2017* (Community Security Trust, 2018), p. 36
30 David Nirenberg, *Anti-Judaism: The History of a Way of Thinking* (Head of Zeus, 2013), p. 6

EVERYDAY HATE

CONCLUSION

1. Dara Horn, *People Love Dead Jews: Reports from a Haunted Present* (W. W. Norton, 2021), p. 79. Horn makes an intriguing argument that there is a fundamental difference between Christian-inspired storytelling, which demands a neat ending in which the protagonists reach either salvation or epiphany, and Jewish literature, which is more about 'endurance and resilience'.
2. *Antisemitism Worldwide 2000/1* (The Stephen Roth Institute for the Study of Contemporary Antisemitism and Racism, Tel Aviv University, 2002) p. 65
3. 'Muslim who stabbed Jew to be detained in hospital', *The Guardian* (19 September 2002)
4. *Antisemitism Worldwide 2002/3* (The Stephen Roth Institute for the Study of Contemporary Antisemitism and Racism, Tel Aviv University, 2004) p. 99
5. Faisal Bodi, 'Israel simply has no right to exist', *The Guardian* (3 January 2001); Paul Oestreicher, 'Israel's policies are feeding the cancer of anti-semitism', *The Guardian* (20 February 2006); Paul Oestreicher, 'The legacy of Kristallnacht', *The Guardian* (4 November 2008); John Prescott, 'Israel's bombardment of Gaza is a war crime – and it must end', *Daily Mirror* (1 August 2014)
6. Seumas Milne, 'This slur of anti-semitism is used to defend repression', *The Guardian* (9 May 2002)
7. Michael Whine, 'Two Steps Forward, One Step Back: Diplomatic Progress in Combating Antisemitism', *Israel Journal of Foreign Affairs*, vol. 4, no. 3 (2010), p. 95
8. Jonny Paul, 'British film director: Rise in anti-Semitism understandable', *Jerusalem Post* (17 March 2009)
9. Lee Harpin, '"Jews are Christ killers" banner at anti-Israel protest', *Jewish News* (22 May 2021)
10. David Lawrence, 'Inside David Icke's Watford Talk', Hope Not Hate (26 November 2018)
11. European Union Agency for Fundamental Rights, *Experiences and perceptions of antisemitism: Second survey on discrimination and hate crime against Jews in the EU* (Publications Office of the European Union, 2018), p. 60
12. Jenni Frazer, 'EXCLUSIVE: Equity row as Jewish actors fear being "blacklisted"', *Jewish Chronicle* (27 May 2021)
13. 'Coronavirus (COVID-19) related deaths by religious group, England and Wales: 2 March to 15 May 2020', Office for National Statistics (19 June 2020)
14. C. H. Gaughan, D. Ayoubkhani, V. Nafilyan et al., 'Religious affiliation and COVID-19-related mortality: a retrospective cohort study of prelockdown and postlockdown risks in England and Wales', *Journal of Epidemiology & Community Health*, vol. 75, no. 6 (January 2021), pp. 509–14
15. Brigitte Sion, *A Survey of Jewish Museums in Europe* (The Rothschild Foundation (Hanadiv) Europe, 2016), p. 25
16. Colin Shindler, *Israel and the European Left: Between Solidarity and Delegitimization* (Continuum, 2012), pp. 142–5
17. Arnold Krammer, 'Prisoners in Prague: Israelis in the Slansky Trial', in Robert S. Wistrich ed., *The Left Against Zion: Communism, Israel and the Middle East* (Vallentine Mitchell, 1979), p. 82
18. For examples of guidance about tackling conspiracy theories, see Jeremy Hayward & Gemma Gronland, *Conspiracy Theories in the Classroom: Guidance for teachers* (Institute of Education, UCL, 2021); Stephan Lewandowsky & John Cook, *The Conspiracy Theory Handbook* (Skeptical Science, 2020); *Guide to Conspiracy Theories* (COMPACT Education Group, 2020); Andrew Jones, 'How to handle conspiracy theories in the classroom', *SecEd* (15 June 2022); Alex Phoenix, 'Combatting Extremism and Conspiracy Theories in the Classroom', *Shout Out UK* (15 June 2022)
19. *Science Fictions: Low Science Knowledge and Poor Critical Thinking are Linked to Conspiracy Beliefs* (Reboot Foundation, September 2022)
20. Hadassa Ben-Itto, *The Lie That Will Not Die: The Protocols of the Elders of Zion* (Vallentine Mitchell, 2020), p. xxvii
21. Thomas F. Pettigrew & Linda R. Tropp, 'A meta-analytic test of intergroup contact theory', *Journal of Personality and Social Psychology*, vol. 90, no. 5 (May 2006), pp. 751–83 (p. 766)

INDEX

9/11 attacks (2001) 11, 28, 40, 99, 102
43 Group 114, 170
62 Group 170

Aaron of Lincoln 21
Abbas, Mahmoud 183, 200
academia, double standards and 178
Ahmed, Tahra 39–41, 42, 47
Aktion (definition) 136
Algeria 53
Ali, Tariq 249
Alice of Battenberg, Princess 154
'aliens' 109–11, 115–18, 127, 128, 133
Aliens Act (1905) 117–18
Amini, Mahsa xxiii
'antisemitism' (etymology) xvii, xviii
antisemitism, including 246–50
Arab Nationalist Movement 209
Argentina 19
Arthur (informant) 222–3
Assad, Bashar al- 90
Association of Jewish Ex-Servicemen and Women (AJEX) 114
Auschwitz 137, 144, 146, 147, 150, 170
   see also Holocaust
Austria 29–30, 109, 166, 167

Baghdad 201
Balfour Declaration (1917) 199

Balliet, Stephan 70
Bandera, Stepan 158
Barton, Joey 162
Bauer, Bruno 32
BDS (Boycott, Divestment and Sanctions) movement 185
Beautiful World, Where Are You (Rooney) 177–8
Bedane, Albert 156
Beilis, Mendel 54
Belarus 25
Ben & Jerry's 186
Bible stories 43–4, 45, 169, 202
Biden, Joe 163
Bier, David 109, 110
Bier family 110–11, 126
Bier, Louis 24, 110
billionaires 34–5
Birnbaum, George 85
Black Death persecutions 73–5
Black Lives Matter 199, 226, 233–4
Blair, Tony 87, 100, 208
Blake, William, *Jerusalem* 190, 191
'blood libel' ritual 40, 43–4, 48–58
Board of Deputies of British Jews 160–61
Bolshevik Revolution (1917) 77
Bond, Michael 106–7
books, burning of 141
Borat Subsequent Moviefilm 51

Bowers, Robert 69–70
Breivik, Anders 89
Brexit xxvii, 86–7, 238–9
British Empire 199–200, 233
British National Party (BNP) xxi, xxii, 222
Brooks, Mel, 'Jews in Space' 116
Browning, Christopher, *Ordinary Men* 149
Burke, Edmund 31
Bury St Edmunds 49
Bush, George W. 100
business advice 33–4
Butterworth, Jez, *Jerusalem* 190, 191

cabal (definition) 100
Cabinet, UK 122
Callow, Simon 176
Cameron, David 190
Campbell, Alastair 161
Canada 166
Canterbury Tales, The (Chaucer) 57–9
cartoons 10–11, 52–3, 86–7, 98
Catholic Church 46, 50, 61
censuses 123, 126, 220, 251
Chamberlain, Neville 166
Channel Islands 155–6
Chanukah 59
charities and foundations 25, 26
Charles III, King 23
Charles, Howard Ward 33–4
Chaucer, Geoffrey, *The Canterbury Tales* 57–9
China 29, 34, 72
'Chosen People' 37, 211
Christian Europe xviii, 30
Christianity 20, 32, 45–7, 50, 54
  conversion to 16, 78, 121, 140, 143
Churchill, Caryl, *Seven Jewish Children: A Play for Gaza* 210–12
Churchill, Winston 118, 119
citizenship 111–12, 115
Clinton, Hillary xxv, 51
coin-clipping 22
Combat 18 xxii
comments, incidental 13–14
Communism 36, 112–14, 257–8
Communist Party 112–14
Community Security Trust (CST) xx, 56, 150, 222, 232, 236
Complete International Jew: The World's Foremost Problem, The (Ford) 66–9, 81, 99
Conservative Party 86
conspiracy theories/movements xxv–xxvii, 27–30, 51–3, 65–83, 86, 89–102, 224–5, 228–35, 259–62
Copeland, David 222, 223
Copin 48
Corbyn, Jeremy 36, 56, 90, 217
  Labour leader xxvi, 45, 96–7, 131, 240, 250
Corbyn, Piers 161
Covid-19 72–3, 80, 102, 161, 164, 240, 254–5
Craig, Sir James 130
cricket 190, 191
Cromwell, Oliver 58, 63, 195
Crown, the 21–2, 30
Crown Prosecution Service 251
Crusades xviii, 60, 191
Cursor Mundi (poem) 17
Cushman, Mike 96–7
Czech Republic 256–7

Daily Telegraph 19
Dalyell, Tam 100
David, Larry, *Curb Your Enthusiasm* 4
De Montfort University 62
Dearborn Independent 66–7
death camps 136–73
democracy, crisis of faith in xxiv
Demos (think tank) 80–81
'de-Nazification' 156–7, 161
Denmark 154
Deputies of British Jews, Board of 97
Der Stürmer (newspaper) 54
Diary of Anne Frank, The 163–5
Dickens, Charles, *Oliver Twist* 10
discrimination, measuring 250–55
Disraeli, Benjamin 120–22
Diversity UK 122
Dracula 50
Dreyfus, Capt. Alfred 131–2
Dubno, Ukraine 135–7, 147

education 228–35, 259–63
Edward I, King 62, 195
Eichmann, Adolf 145
El Ghriba bombing (2002) 248
Elliott Management (hedge fund) 19
emigration 55, 69
Englander, Nathan, 'What We Talk About When We Talk About Anne Frank' 164
Eno, Brian 187–8, 189
Equality Act (2010) 122–3
Equality and Human Rights Commission 97
Ethics of the Fathers 244, 264–5
European Union (EU) 84, 239, 249, 253

INDEX

European Union Agency for Fundamental Rights 251
Évian-les-Bains, France 166
executions 22, 48, 49, 148
expulsions, from Europe 16, 23, 30, 58, 62, 263

Facebook 7, 27, 39–41, 72, 98, 116
fake news xxv, 75–83
Farage, Nigel 86–7
Farrakhan, Louis 52, 99
far-right politics 10, 23, 70, 94–5, 113–14, 222
Fascism 35, 36
feminism 70
Fiddler on the Roof (musical) 105–6
Filipović, Zlata 163
Final Solution (genocide plan) 140, 145, 150, 258
Finkelstein, Arthur 85
First World War 77, 167
Floyd, George 198–9, 233
Flynn, Paul 127–8
Foley, Frank 154
Foot, Paul 100
football 12, 103, 190
Football Association (FA) 28
Forbes magazine 34
Ford, Henry, *The Complete International Jew:* … 65–9, 75, 81, 92, 99
Forde Report (2020) 97
Foreign and Commonwealth Office (FCO) 100–101, 129–30
France xxiii, xxvii, 49, 74, 131–2, 195–7, 250
Frank, Anne, *The Diary of Anne Frank* 163–5
Franklin, Benjamin 99–100
Free Speech On Israel 96
Freedman, Sir Lawrence 128
French Revolution 31, 78

Galloway, George 90
Gaza 180, 182, 187, 194, 204, 209–10, 232–3, 249
Gaza War (2008–2009) 179
genocides 138, 139–40
    see also Holocaust
George VI, King 112
Georgia 25
Germany 49, 74–5, 101, 120, 160, 166, 167
ghettos 58, 78, 150–51, 153, 171
Gibson, Mel, *Passion of the Christ* 8, 10
Gilbert, Sir Martin 128
Glastonbury Festival 192
Godwin's Law (internet) 162
Goldberg, Whoopi 119–20
golf clubs 252

Google 5–6, 29
Gospels, the 44
Gould, Matthew 127
Graebe, Hermann Friedrich 147, 151–2
graffiti 73, 159–60, 230
Graphic (newspaper) 25
Great Replacement Theory 69, 221
Great Reset, The (WEF) 80
Greek Empire 46
Greene, Marjorie Taylor 27–8
Grenfell Tower fire (2017) 39–41, 42
Griffin, Nick 90
Grossman, Vasily 138
Groysman, Volodymyr 157
Guardian, The 56, 100, 176–7, 248
Guilds 20, 22

Habima Theatre, Tel Aviv 96, 176–7, 212
Habonim-Dror (Jewish youth movement) xxi, 171
Habsburg family 30
Haiti 53
Hamas 82, 213
Hampshire, HMS 110
Hardie, Keir 98–9
Hasan, Mehdi 184–5
hate crimes, religious xiv, 19, 180, 219–21, 248
Hawking, Prof. Stephen 178
Hebrew Immigrant Aid Society (HIAS) 69–70
Heine, Heinrich 146–7
Henry III, King 48
hiding identity xxiii–xxiv
Hillel, Rabbi 265
history, brief xviii–xxviii
Hitler, Adolf, *Mein Kampf* 41, 66, 69, 79, 119, 142–3, 157
Hizb ut-Tahrir xxii
Hobson, John, *Imperialism: A Study* 36–7
holidays, Jewish 133, 207
Holocaust 40, 53, 61, 119–20, 133, 136–73, 259
    lessons from 144–51, 211
Holocaust Education Trust 144
Holocaust Memorial Day 144, 170
Holocaust Memorial and Learning Centre, UK 63, 144, 146
Holocaust Remembrance Center, Yad Vashem 153, 155, 156
Hope Not Hate 52, 225
Hugh of Lincoln, Little Saint 48–9, 58
human rights abuses 177–8, 183–4, 197–8
Hungary 83–4
Husseini, Hajj Amin Al- 209

Icke, David 82, 85, 250
immigration 24, 67, 69–70, 87, 108, 117–18
incomes, family 25
Ingrams, Richard 128–9
Instagram 164, 186, 232, 236
insults, 'Jew' 3–9, 24, 33, 116, 219, 229, 232
Interfaith For Palestine 45
internment camps 109, 110
investment banks 24, 27
Iran xiii–xiv, 52, 82, 91
Islamic State xiii, 90
Israel xxi, 52–3, 88–90, 92–3, 175–90, 193–218, 232–5, 247–50
   independence 167–8
   Kovner and 172
   Palestinians and 163
   Pravda on 159
   race and 125
   support for xiii
Israel–Palestine conflict 175–87, 192–4, 199–202, 212–14, 233
Israeli Defense Forces (IDF) 172–3
Israeli embassy, London 179
Istanbul 248

Jacobson, Howard, *Kalooki Nights* 170
Jaspal, Rusi 213–14, 216
jazz music 68
Jerusalem 190–95
Jerusalem (Butterworth) 190, 191
Jerusalem (hymn) 190–92
Jerusalem: The Biography (Montefiore) 192
Jew (definitions) 1–5
Jewish Policy Research, Institute for 254–5
'Jewish Question' (JQ) 32, 195, 221–2
'Jewish race' (etymology) 119
Jews vs Jews 94–104
jihadism 90
John, King 22
journalists 56, 114, 182
Judaism 26, 32, 45–7, 124

Kalooki Nights (Jacobson) 170
Kennedy, Robert F. Jr 164
KGB 159–60, 161
Khamenei, Ayatollah xxiii, 52, 91, 213
Khan, Sadiq 228–9
Khmelnytsky, Bohdan 136, 158
Kindertransport 107, 109, 154–5, 166
King, William Lyon Mackenzie 166
kings, English 21–2, 23
Kirchner, Cristina Fernández de 19

Knost, L. R. 163
Kovner, Abba 171–2
Kurds 181–2, 213

Labour Party xv, xxvi, 96–7, 116, 209, 235–6
bin Laden, Osama 99
Latuff, Carlos 52–3
Lavrov, Sergey 157
Lawrence, Stephen 223
Le Pen, Marine xxvii
Leech, Thomas 221
Left's Jewish Problem: Israel, Jeremy Corbyn and Antisemitism, The (Rich) 235
Leicester 61–2
Levi, Primo 152, 265
Levin, Mark 163
Levy, Michael, Lord 100
Licoricia of Winchester 23
Life of Brian, The (film) 3
Lipke, Jan and Johana 154
Lithuania 74, 168, 171
Livingstone, Ken 12, 209
Llewellyn, Tim 129
Loach, Ken 249
Lopez, Roderigo 16–17
Ludendorff, Gen Erich 77
Lynch, Mick 192–3

Mackay, Malky 12
mafia 91
Manchester 24, 110, 231
Mandelson, Peter 100
Marr, Wilhelm xvii
Martinez, Herminio 19
Marx, Karl, 'On The Jewish Question' 32
massacres, Jewish 49, 55, 60–61, 70, 136, 215, 248
matzo/matzah 49–50, 169
Max (maternal grandpa) 111–13, 115–16
May, Theresa 55–6
media literacy 260–61
medieval England 20–24, 57–62, 95
Medvedev, Dmitry 159
Mein Kampf (Hitler) 41, 66, 69, 79
Merchant of Venice, The (Shakespeare) 15–19, 31, 175–6
Merkel, Angela 86
Metsola, Roberta 197
MI5 111–12, 114–15
Middle Ages 20–24, 57–62, 95
Middle East Centre for Arab Studies (MECAS) 130

INDEX

Miles, Oliver 128
Miller, David 91–4
Milne, Seumas 217, 248
minorities, treatment of 23–4, 42, 122–3, 254
Mizrahi Jews 201, 254
Moldova 25, 55
money, in society 31–8
money, Jews and 2, 7, 9, 10, 11–13
money talks 24–30
moneylenders
    charging interest 20, 22, 31
    in fiction 15–19, 36
    medieval England 21–3
    Napoleon and 132
Montefiore, Simon Sebag, *Jerusalem: The Biography* 192
Montesquieu, *Persian Letters* 31
Montfort, Simon de, Earl of Leicester 61–2
Moonshot (think tank) 72
Morsi, Mohamed 52
Mosley, Oswald 35, 112
Mossad 40
'Mountain Jews', Soviet Union 140
murders xxiii, 42–3, 48–9, 196
    attempted 247
museums, Jewish 255, 258
Muslim communities 213–17
Muslim-majority countries xix, 81, 214–15
Muslim rule, Holy Land xviii
Muslims, 'moderate' xiii
Myers, David 247

naming, noticing and 127–33
Nation of Islam 52, 99
National Holocaust Centre and Museum 144
NATO 181
Nazism 35–6, 54, 61, 74–5, 100, 109, 120, 136–73, 208–12
Netanyahu, Benjamin 52
Netanyahu, Yair 97–8
New Statesman 248
New World Order (NWO) 80
newspapers 41, 78–9
Nicholas II, Tsar 77
noticing, and naming 127–33
Nuremberg Race Laws (1935) 120

Obama, Barack xxv, 86, 264
Ofcom 8, 82
Oliver Twist (Dickens) 10
'On The Jewish Question' (Marx) 32
Oppenheimer, Samuel 30

Orbán, Viktor xxvii, 83–5
Ordinary Men (Browning) 149
organ theft 53
Orwell, George 57
Ottoman Empire 195, 202, 204, 214

Paddington Bear 106
Palestine 115, 163, 166, 167, 204–6, 217
Palestine Declassified (TV series) 91–2
Palestinian National Authority 183
Palombo, aleXsandro 163
Passover 169
Peake, Maxine 198–9
Pearl, Daniel xxii
Pelley, William D. 100
Persian Letters (Montesquieu) 31
Petliura, Semyon 158
Phillips, Horace 130
philosemitism 195–6
pogroms 55, 74, 168, 201, 215
Poland 74, 141, 168
politics 8, 35–6, 51, 53, 83–7
Pope, Tom 28–9
Portugal 16
poverty 24–5
Prague 256
profiteering 37, 67
protests 47, 52, 160, 178–9, 199, 209–10, 212
Protocols of the Elders of Zion, The xx, 75–83, 88, 99, 102–3, 257
Putin, Vladimir 156, 161

al-Qaeda 40, 99, 248
QAnon movement 51–2, 102
Qatar xiv

Race and Ethnic Disparities, Commission on 251–2
Race & Health Observatory, NHS 255
Race Relations Act (1965) 123
Race Relations and Immigration, Select Committee on 108
racist abuse x–xii, 19, 228–30
Rafiq, Azeem 7
Raisi, Ebrahim xiii
Reagan, Ronald 264
Reboot Foundation 261
Red Pepper magazine 188
Reed, Jack 219–21
refugees 85, 106, 107, 109, 154–5, 166, 180
Rich family 24
Richard I, King 60, 63

riots, anti-Jew 167
Roman Empire 46, 203
Romania 168
Rooney, Sally, *Beautiful World, Where Are You* 177–8
Rosenhead, Jonathan 96
Ross, Dennis 129
Rothschild family 27–9, 37
Russia xiii, 54–5, 75–83, 77, 86, 93, 141, 156–9, 161, 163, 180, 212, 238–9
Rylance, Mark 176, 193

Sacks, Chief Rabbi Jonathan 5
Salah, Sheikh Ra'ed 55–7
Sartre, Jean-Paul 71, 218
Saudi Arabia 130, 180, 185, 188, 212–13
Schindler, Oskar 152, 172
Schindler's List (film) 152, 172
Scottish National Party 86
screen and stage depictions 105, 264
Searchlight 222
Second Intifada (2000–2005) 247
Second World War 79–80, 106–7, 109, 168, 201, 258
settlements, Jewish 21, 74
Seven Jewish Children: A Play for Gaza (C. Churchill) 210–12
Shabbat dinner 105, 110
Shakespeare, William, *The Merchant of Venice* 15–19, 31, 175–6
Shakespeare's Globe theatre 175–7, 193, 212
shame, displacing 195–208
Sheikh Jarrah, East Jerusalem 192–3
Shlaim, Avi 96
Short, Clare 196
Siege of the Church of the Nativity, Bethlehem 194
Singer, Paul 19
Slánský trial (1952) 256–7
Socha, Leopold 153–4
social media
    abusive posts xii–xiii, xiv, xxii–xxiii, 39–41
    conspiracy theories and 72–3, 224, 235–41, 261–2
    fringe 70
    insults 7, 24, 116
Soros, George 83–7, 98
Soskice, Sir Frank 123–4
South Park (TV series) 8–10
Spain 16, 214–15
SS *Einsatzgruppen* 148–9
Star of David 116, 209, 248

Statutes of Jewry (1275) 22
Stone, Matt 9
Stop The War Coalition 187, 214
Straw, Jack 100
strikes 112
Students' Unions xxi–xxii
surveys 25–6, 144–5, 169, 206, 213–16, 225–8, 253–5
swastikas 159–60, 185, 209–10, 230
Sweden 53
Switzerland 73, 74, 88
synagogues 30, 70, 141, 160, 214, 219–21, 247, 248
Syria 90, 93

Talmud, the 34
Telegram 72, 73, 82, 238
Temple of Jerusalem 202–3
terrorism 82, 89–90, 115, 219–23, 248–9, 253, 264
    9/11 attacks 11, 28, 40, 102
That's Life (BBC) 154–5
Theobald of Cambridge 95
Thomas of Monmouth 43, 95
TikTok 237, 238, 250, 262
Times, The 119, 238
Tonge, Jenny 53
Torah (Old Testament) scrolls 141
Tower of London 23
trade unions 112–13, 118, 178
Trocmé, André 154
Trump, Donald xxiii, xxv, xxvi, 11–12, 238
Trump, Ivanka 265
Tunisia 248
Turkey 181–2, 194–5, 213
Twitter 27–8, 45, 91–2, 238–9

Ukraine xiii, 25–6, 80, 93, 135–7, 156–9, 163, 168, 258
UN General Assembly 186
United States xiii, xxv, 25, 69–70, 100–101, 116, 160, 200
University and College Union (UCU) 178
Upholsterers, Amalgamated Union of 112–13
usury 19–20, 31, 33, 37, 99

Valls, Manuel 196–7

Warsaw Ghetto 150–51, 171
Watson, Emma 186, 265
Weber, Dorothea 156
wells, poisoning 73–5

INDEX

Wesker, Sir Arnold 176
West Bank 88, 182, 183, 186, 194, 204–6
West, Kanye xxii–xxiii
Whelan, Dave 12
Wilhelm II, Kaiser 77
William III, King 30
William the Conqueror 21
William of Norwich 42–3, 95
Williamson, Chris 91–2
Winton, Nicholas 154–5
Woollacott, Martin 196
World Economic Forum (WEF) 80
World Jewish Relief 25, 26
World Trade Center (WTC) 102
Wróblewski, Stefan 153–4

yellow stars 61, 161
Yemen 179, 185, 213
Yevsektsiya 95–6
Yom HaShoah (Holocaust Remembrance Day) 171, 172
York 60–61
Young Ones, The (BBC) 162
youth, antisemitism and 219–24, 228–35, 250, 262
YouTube 237, 262

Zelenskyy, Volodymyr 157, 158, 159
Zionism xi, 82, 88–94, 95–7, 126, 159, 200, 203–5, 213–14
Zionist Occupied Government (ZOG) 80–81